A Sister of Marie Antoinette; the Life-story of Maria Carolina, Queen of Naples

A SISTER OF MARIE ANTOINETTE

BY THE SAME AUTHOR

Fully Illustrated. Large crown 8vo, cloth, **10/6** *each.*

A LEADER OF SOCIETY AT NAPOLEON'S COURT (LAURA PERMON).

A QUEEN OF NAPOLEON'S COURT: THE LIFE-STORY OF DÉSIRÉE BERNADOTTE.

PICTURES OF THE OLD FRENCH COURT.

LIVES AND TIMES OF THE EARLY VALOIS QUEENS.

Fully Illustrated. Large crown 8vo, cloth, **10/6** *net.*

HEROINES OF FRENCH SOCIETY IN THE COURT, THE REVOLUTION, THE EMPIRE AND THE RESTORATION.

LONDON: T. FISHER UNWIN

MARIA CAROLINA CHARLOTTE,
WIFE OF FERDINANDO IV., QUEEN OF THE TWO SICILIES.
From the painting by Mme. Vigée Le Brun at Versailles.

Frontispiece.

A SISTER OF MARIE ANTOINETTE

THE LIFE-STORY OF MARIA CAROLINA, QUEEN OF NAPLES

By
Mrs. Bearne

Author of "Heroines of French Society," "A Leader of Society at Napoleon's Court," &c., &c.

WITH THIRTY-TWO ILLUSTRATIONS

LONDON
T. FISHER UNWIN
ADELPHI TERRACE
MCMVII

(All rights reserved.)

PREFACE

ALTHOUGH the tragic history of the life and death of Marie Antoinette, Archduchess of Austria and Queen of France, is so familiar to the most casual of readers, many people appear to know nothing whatever about any of her sisters, of whom seven grew up into girlhood and womanhood and several survived her.

Most of these daughters of the Empress-Queen Maria Theresia were pretty and attractive, some were highly gifted and beautiful, but with one exception they were all overshadowed by a fatality which doomed them either to an early death, a disappointed life, or else to sorrows, dangers, and calamities which, as well as the grandeur of their birth, separated them from ordinary women.

That fortunate exception was not Maria Carolina, whose brilliant and eventful career is the subject of this book—the sister who, nearest in age and rank to Marie Antoinette, resembled her in beauty but far surpassed her in talent; while the magnificent prosperity of the earlier part of her life and the perils and misfortunes which clouded her later years were only exceeded by the still more lofty position and more terrible fate of the favourite sister whom she strained all her energy to save, and whose murder changed and embittered the rest of her days.

In writing this life of a woman once so widely celebrated, so flattered and worshipped by many, so cruelly slandered by others, I do not pretend by research or discovery to throw any fresh light upon what is already known and recorded concerning her by students and historians. But it appears to me that amongst general readers of the present day, at any rate in England, very little is known about this once famous Queen. Many have no idea who she was at all; others confuse her in a hazy manner with the upstart interloper who usurped her throne, to whom no woman could be more different in every respect. Even the name of Caroline did not in fact belong to the sister of Buonaparte and wife of Murat, whose baptismal name was Annunziata, and who, besides her utter want of dignity, refinement and good-breeding, was really guilty of the immoralities unjustly attributed to the Queen she had supplanted.

If I had attempted to write a biography claiming to refute the accusations brought against this Queen by those who from political reasons were her bitterest enemies, an entirely different sort of work would have been necessary. It would have required not only careful comparison of the various writers upon the subject, but the examination of numbers of documents in Vienna and elsewhere, with accurate references to and descriptions of them, besides explanations and information as to the character, motives, and credibility of their authors.

All this is to be found in the deeply interesting and instructive works of the compatriot of the Queen, Freiherr von Helfert, from whose important details and circumstantial accounts I have drawn a great part of the information contained in this book, and by which he proves not only the improbability but the impossibility of many of the charges brought against Maria Carolina.

In reading Mr. Jeaffreson's "Queen of Naples and Lord Nelson" I have also benefited by the valuable information derived by the author from his study of the Morrison MSS., corroborating so exactly all that is said by Freiherr von Helfert. Besides these two authors I have consulted the works of General Colletta, MM. Bonnefonds, de Trognon, de Seriéys, Swinburne, Miss Cornelia Knight, and other writers. For the part of the book relating to the early life of Maria Carolina and of her parents at the court of Vienna I am chiefly indebted to the Comte de Villermont, M. de Berman, von Vehse, and above all to the splendid and voluminous works of Alfred, Ritter von Arneth, upon the reign of the Empress-Queen, Maria Theresia.

I have to thank Mr. A. M. Broadley for the letters of Ferdinando and Maria Carolina, King and Queen of Naples (pp. 83, 201, 313, 406, 407), for the most interesting picture of the whole of the Austrian court on the occasion of the reception of Ferdinando and Maria Carolina at Vienna, and for the photographs of the portraits of the King and Queen of

Naples and Lord Nelson, the originals of which portraits are in the possession of Mr. Hardy Manfield, by whose kind permission I make use of them.

From the above mentioned materials I have written a life of Maria Carolina, Archduchess of Austria and Queen of Naples, which I hope may interest those who are not acquainted with the fuller histories of her life and that of her still more illustrious mother given by the distinguished German authors I have quoted.

In the opening chapters I have described the court of her parents, the Emperor and Empress, the home life and surroundings of the imperial family at Vienna, and the scenes and habits which were so vividly impressed upon the Archduchess during her childhood and early youth, helped to form her character, and always retained the strongest influence over her during the vicissitudes of her brilliant, stormy career.

Of the revolutionary war and important political events in the Two Sicilies it was of course impossible in a book of this kind to give anything but a sketch, the personal history and adventures of the Queen of Naples being the subject which concerned me, and which I have tried to place before my readers.

CONTENTS

	PAGE
PREFACE	V

PART I

MARIA THERESIA AND HER CHILDREN

CHAPTER I

The Archduchess Maria Theresia—François de Lorraine—The court of Carl VI.—The French Ambassador—Death of Carl VI.—The war—Flight of Maria Theresia—Rising of Hungary—The monarchy saved—Coronation of the Emperor—The imperial family—An adventure in a vineyard 3

CHAPTER II

The court of Maria Theresia—Kaunitz—The imperial children—Christine and Carl—The Archduchess Marianne—Love-affair of the Archduchess Christine and Albrecht of Saxe-Teschen—Their marriage—The Archduchess Elisabeth—An unwilling Abbess—The Archduke Joseph—Character of the Empress—Her despotic rule—The amusements of the Emperor—His love-affairs and *liaisons* . . . 14

CHAPTER III

The Empress and her children—Betrothal of the Archduchess Johanna to the King of Naples—Joseph, Carl, and Leopold —Death of Carl—Isabella of Parma—Strange romance of her history—Her marriage with the Crown Prince—Her friendship with Christine—Gloomy presentiments—Death of Johanna—"It is the summons"—Death of Isabella— Unhappy second marriage of the Crown Prince—Marriage of the Archduke Leopold—Death of the Emperor . 27

CHAPTER IV

Grief of the Empress—She resumes the government—The Archduchess Josepha — Marriage of the Archduchess Christine—Her favourite daughter—The small-pox again —Death of the Empress Joseph — Recovery of the Empress-mother—Splendid preparations for the wedding of Josepha—In the Capucine church—A terrible calamity —Death of Josepha—Recovery of Elisabeth—The presentiment fulfilled 40

PART II

MARIA CAROLINA

CHAPTER V

Carolina and Antoinette—"You are fifteen years old"—Mother and daughter—Carolina or Amalie?—The choice of the King of Naples—Unwillingness of Carolina—The Empress insists—Amalie and the Duke of Parma—The Countess von Lerchenfeld—"Love your husband" . . 53

CHAPTER VI

Marriage of Carolina to the King of Naples—Her journey—The Grand-duke of Tuscany—Arrival at Naples—Unhappiness of Carolina—Letters of Leopold to his mother—Of Carolina to her governess—Becomes reconciled to her lot—Her influence over the King—"My wife knows everything"—*Fête* at Naples—Visit of the Emperor Joseph—The King of Naples and the Duke of Parma . 66

CHAPTER VII

Popularity of the Queen—Tanucci—The dictation of Spain—Correspondence with the Empress—Birth of an heir—The Queen enters the Council—The *lazzaroni*—Amusements of the King—His love-affairs—Ambition of the Queen—Her life at Naples—Caserta—The King and the peasant woman—The court of Naples—A court intrigue—The Marchesa di San Marco—The Abbé Galiani—Second-sight—Guarini—Birth of Prince Francesco—Death of the Prince Royal 83

CHAPTER VIII

The Queen's Government—Acton—Death of the Empress Maria Theresia—Scandalous reports—Jealousy of the King—Violent scene—Reconciliation—Visit of the Archduchess Christine—Scenes in an earthquake—On board the fleet—Death of the King of Spain—Of two children of the Queen—The eve of the French Revolution—Mme. Le Brun—Journey to Vienna—Death of the Emperor Joseph—Marriages of two daughters of the Queen—Coronation of the Emperor Leopold—Stay in Austria—Rome—Marie Antoinette—Varennes—Escape of the Comte and Comtesse de Provence—The Archduchess Christine 100

CHAPTER IX

Return to Naples—Leopold and Maria Carolina—State of Tuscany—Of Naples—The Queen's society—Awakening—Change of policy—The secret police—Warlike preparations—The French Ambassadors at Naples and Venice—Mme Le Brun—Slanders against the Queen—San Gennaro—Lady Hamilton . . . 138

CHAPTER X

Early career of Emma Hart—Arrives at Naples—Her life there—Marries Sir William Hamilton—Prosperous and splendid career of the Queen—The turn of the tide—Death of the Emperor Leopold and of the King of Sweden—Danger to Naples—Disputes with France—The French Ambassador—Evil news from Paris—On the brink of war—A patched-up peace—The Ambassador of the Republic—Threatened bombardment of Naples—Life at Naples—News of the murder of Louis XVI—Outrageous conduct of the French Ambassador—His reception at a *fête* at court—He is recalled—Attempt to save the Queen and Madame Elisabeth . . . 152

CHAPTER XI

The Queen's popularity declines—Her proceedings give offence—The Neapolitans—Faults and virtues of Maria Carolina—Violence and calumnies of her enemies . 172

CHAPTER XII

Return of the French fleet—Treachery of La Touche and Mackau—The Jacobin supper—Conspiracies—Disguised as porters—The secret police—A secret treaty—Capture of Toulon—Alliance with England—Nelson—Splendid reception at Naples—The Queen and Captain Nelson—

Departure of the *Agamemnon* — The Queen and her daughters—The Princess Amélie—The murder of Marie Antoinette—The Office for the Dead—The Marchesa Solari—Vows of vengeance 184

CHAPTER XIII

Dark days—Gallant efforts of the Queen—Society at Naples—"Let us eat and drink, for to-morrow we die"—Earthquake and fearful eruption—Trial of the conspirators—Execution of the leaders—Attacks on the Queen—Friendship with Lady Hamilton 205

CHAPTER XIV

Another conspiracy—Terrible tragedies—State of society in Naples— Prince Caramanico — Attempts to obtain the release of Louis XVII. and Madame Royale—Death of Louis XVII.—Distress of the Queen—The King pays homage to Louis XVIII.—Hunting at Carditello—The fish-market—Shrove Tuesday at San Carlo . . 220

CHAPTER XV

The Queen's justice—An Ambassador of the Republic—Marriage of the Duke of Calabria—A patched-up peace—The battle of the Nile—The English fleet at Naples—Declaration of war—Exciting times—Ferdinando enters Rome—Disasters and defeats—Approach of the enemy—Horrors and dangers—Preparations for flight . . 235

CHAPTER XVI

Alarming state of things—Escape of the royal family—Terrible storm—Death of Prince Carlo Alberto—Arrival at Palermo—Adventures of Lady Knight and her daughter—Perils and hardships—Palermo—Lovely scenery—Loyal Sicily—Death of the Archduchess Christine—The Parthenopeian Republic—Departure of Caracciolo—The King's warning . 253

CHAPTER XVII

Preparations for the reconquest of Naples—Ruffo—Calabria—A fearful war—State of Sicily—Travellers in the olden times—The brigands of Sicily—An escort   267

CHAPTER XVIII

The King's country house—End of the Parthenopeian Republic—Recovery of Naples—The treaty annulled—Attitude of the Queen—The King returns to Naples—Miss Knight and Lady Hamilton—Capture of the *Généreux*   286

CHAPTER XIX

Triumphant return of the King—Honours to the Hamiltons—Pardons obtained by the Queen—Her generosity and charities—Depression of the Queen—Sir William Hamilton recalled—Scene with the King—Visits Naples—Leaves Palermo with Nelson—Perilous voyage to Livorno—The battle of Marengo—Dangerous journey to Vienna—Anxiety of the King   308

CHAPTER XX

Arrival at Vienna—Departure of Lord Nelson and the Hamiltons—The two surviving daughters of Maria Theresia—The imperial family circle—Life at Vienna and Schonbrunn—The Prime Minister Thugut—The war—Flight of the Grand-duke and Grand-duchess of Tuscany—Treaty of Luneville—Naples threatened—Paul, Emperor of Russia—Naples saved by the Queen—A dramatic concert—The Archduke Anton and Princess Amélie—The Spanish proposals—Terror of Amélie—The Prince of the Asturias chooses Antoinette—A melancholy parting   323

CHAPTER XXI

Return to Naples—Death of Clementine, Princess Royal—Renewal of influence with the King—Death of the Grand-duchess of Tuscany—More conspiracies—Two Spanish marriages—Isabel, Princess Royal—Threatened dangers—Nelson—The ninety dogs of the King—Unhappy fate of Antoinette, Princess of the Asturias—The King of Spain and the violinist—The Queen of Naples and her daughter-in-law—A dangerous breakfast—Lady Hamilton—Her extravagance and greed for money—Infatuation of Lord Nelson 334

CHAPTER XXII

Threatened dangers—The court of Naples—A fearful earthquake—*Le Roi s'amuse*—The allied fleet—Surrender of Mack—Trafalgar—Departure of the French Ambassador—Austerlitz—Alarm and perplexity at Naples—Flight of Ferdinando—The Queen and royal family prepare to escape—Farewell to Naples—A perilous voyage—Arrival at Palermo 362

CHAPTER XXIII

At Palermo again—Discomforts and hardships—Acton—The Princess of the Asturias—Terrible tragedy—Suspicions of poison—The war in Calabria—Fra Diavolo—Agostino Mosca, the brigand—Conspiracies at Naples—An infernal machine—Admiral Collingwood—The Sicilian farm of the Prince Royal—The Princess Royal—Domestic life of the Queen and her children 378

CHAPTER XXIV

The Princess Christine and the Duke of Genoa—Their marriage—Death of the Empress of Germany—Despair of the Queen—Sicily threatened—The Queen's letters—The son of Égalité—The love-affairs of Princess Amélie—The King refuses consent—The Princess threatens to take the veil—Her marriage to the Duke of Orléans . . . 395

CHAPTER XXV

"My grandmother the Queen of Sicily"—Obstinacy of Maria Carolina—The Duke and Duchess of Orléans—Illness of the Queen—Troubles and difficulties — Lord William Bentinck—Renewed troubles—The Queen leaves Palermo—The King agrees to the regency of the Prince Royal and retires to the country—A last attempt—Return of the King—Failure—Farewell to Sicily 408

CHAPTER XXVI

Departure from Palermo—The Queen's journey with Prince Leopold — The Marchesa Solari — Sad recollections—Arrival in Austria—The castle of Hetzenberg—Fall of the Emperor Napoleon—Arrival of the Empress Marie Louise—Her affection for her grandmother, the Queen of Naples—The King of Rome—The Queen's love for him—King Ferdinando orders the *Minerva* to fetch back the Queen and Prince Leopold—Death of the Queen . . . 421

LIST OF ILLUSTRATIONS

Maria Carolina Charlotte, Wife of Ferdinando IV., Queen of the Two Sicilies. (*Mme. Vigée Le Brun*) . . . *Frontispiece*

Maria Theresia, Empress of Germany, Queen of Hungary, Bohemia, &c. (*Marten*) *To face page* 4

Friederich the Great, King of Prussia (*Wolf*) . ,, ,, 9

Wenzel Anton, Prinz von Kaunitz (*Steiner*) . ,, ,, 17

François (Etienne), Duke of Lorraine, Emperor of Germany . . ,, ,, 25

Group of Cavaliers, including the Emperor Joseph II., the Archduke Maximilien, and Albrecht, Duke of Saxe-Teschen. (*Brano*) . . ,, ,, 42

Carlos III., King of Spain. (*Mengs*) . ,, ,, 58

JOSEPH II, EMPEROR OF GERMANY, AND
   LEOPOLD, GRAND-DUKE OF TUSCANY,
   AFTERWARDS EMPEROR, 1782 .   *To face page* 66

AUTOGRAPH LETTER OF MARIA CAROLINA,
   QUEEN OF THE TWO SICILIES. (*From
   the Collection of MSS. of Mr. A. M.
   Broadley*)   .   .   .   .   ,,   ,, 83

FERDINANDO IV. AND MARIA CAROLINA,
   KING AND QUEEN OF NAPLES, AND
   THEIR FAMILY   .   .   .   ,,   ,, 99

MARIE ANTOINETTE, QUEEN OF FRANCE,
   WIFE OF LOUIS XVI. ("*Faisant un
   bouquet.*" *Mme. Vigée Le Brun, Versailles*)   .   .   .   .   ,,   ,, 115

RECEPTION OF FERDINANDO IV. AND
   MARIA CAROLINA, KING AND QUEEN
   OF NAPLES, AT THE AUSTRIAN COURT.
   (*From a print in the Collection of Mr.
   A. M. Broadley*)   .   .   .   ,,   ,, 122

PIUS VI.   .   .   .   .   .   ,,   ,, 126

LA COMTESSE DE PROVENCE, WIFE OF
   MONSIEUR, AFTERWARDS LOUIS XVIII.   ,,   ,, 128

BOUILLÉ   .   .   .   .   .   ,,   ,, 136

LADY HAMILTON AS "NATURE" (*Romney*)   ,,   ,, 153

Louis XVI.	To face page	167
Lord Nelson. (*Abbott*)	,, ,,	194
Madame Elisabeth, Sister of Louis XVI.	,, ,,	225
Louis XVII.	,, ,,	227
Madame Royale	,, ,,	228
Battle of the Nile	,, ,,	244
Maria Carolina, Queen of Naples. (*From a print in the possession of Mr. Hardy Manfield. Picture given by Queen to Lady Hamilton*)	,, ,,	264
Lord Nelson. (*Italian Portrait painted at Naples and given by Queen Maria Carolina to Sir Thomas Hardy. From the original now in the possession of Mr. Hardy Manfield, of Portesham*)	,, ,,	287
Autograph Letter of Ferdinando IV., King of Naples. (*From Mr. A. M. Broadley's Collection of MSS.*)	,, ,,	313
Francis I., Emperor of Austria (*Kupelwieser*)	,, ,,	324
Princess Amélie, Wife of Louis Philippe, King of France	,, ,,	332

PRINCE ROYAL OF NAPLES . *To face page* 355

NAPOLEON BUONAPARTE, FIRST CONSUL.
(*Ingres*) . . . ,, ,, 369

LOUIS PHILIPPE, DUC D'ORLÉANS, KING
OF FRANCE. (*Gérard*) . . ,, ,, 404

FERDINANDO IV, KING OF THE TWO
SICILIES. (*From an original watercolour
given by Queen Maria Carolina to Sir
Thomas Hardy, now in the possession
of Mr. Hardy Manfield*) . ,, ,, 417

VIENNA . . . . . ,, ,, 424

PART I

MARIA THERESIA AND HER
CHILDREN

CHAPTER I

The Archduchess Maria Theresia—François de Lorraine—The court of Carl VI.—The French Ambassador—Death of Carl VI.—The war—Flight of Maria Theresia—Rising of Hungary—The monarchy saved—Coronation of the Emperor—The imperial family—An adventure in a vineyard.

MARIA CAROLINA CHARLOTTE was the thirteenth of the sixteen children born to the Empress Maria Theresia, Queen of Hungary, Bohemia, and the Netherlands, Archduchess of Austria, and the Emperor Franz, or François, of Lorraine,[1] Grand-duke of Tuscany; this latter province having been given him instead of his own Lorraine, which he had been compelled to cede to France.

The marriage of François de Lorraine with the Austrian Archduchess had been an affair of European importance, and for years the centre and object of intrigues and negotiations. For she was the eldest daughter of the Emperor Carl VI., her only brother had died in infancy, and her father,

---

[1] Though Lorraine was then an integral part of the German Empire, François, who was also Duc de Bar, was in tastes, habits, and characteristics a Frenchman. He never spoke German correctly, and during his reign French was as much used as German at the court of Vienna

finding that he was not likely to have any more sons, turned all his hopes and ambition and directed all his energy towards securing to his eldest daughter the whole of the vast succession of the house of Habsburg.

This he at length effected by means of an agreement known as the Pragmatic Sanction, which guaranteed that magnificent inheritance to Maria Theresia. The Milanese, the Low Countries, the kingdoms of Hungary and Bohemia, and all the great Austrian provinces were to pass under her sway; but it was stipulated that, in order to preserve the balance of power in Europe, the Archduchess should not be married either to any reigning sovereign or to any prince of a powerful governing house.

Under these circumstances it was impossible to find a more absolutely suitable husband for her than François de Lorraine.

Although not sufficiently powerful to cause any uneasiness, there was no family more illustrious than that of Lorraine; François was of the same religion as the Archduchess, was only a few years her senior, had an excellent disposition, was extremely handsome, accomplished, and attractive, and he and Maria Theresia were passionately in love with each other.

However, notwithstanding these considerations, his promises to the powers, and his love for his favourite child, the Emperor, weak and vacillating, listened first to one, then to another, and every now and then tormented his daughter by proposing to break off her engagement with François and marry her to someone else.

MARIA THERESIA, EMPRESS OF GERMANY,
QUEEN OF HUNGARY, BOHEMIA, ETC.
After a portrait by Marten.

At one time it was Friederich the Great of Prussia, though he was a Protestant, more than half an atheist, and the Archduchess could not bear him; but fortunately various opportune disclosures respecting his private life and habits put an end to this project.

Another time it was Don Carlos of Spain, and from him Maria Theresia was saved by her mother, the Empress Elisabeth, who interfered at her entreaty, declared that the happiness of her child should not be sacrificed, and used her powerful influence to such good effect that the marriage of the Archduchess and the Grand-duke of Tuscany was at last celebrated with all the pomp and splendour befitting an event of such world-wide importance (1736).

As it has already been said, François de Lorraine was remarkably handsome and fascinating, while Maria Theresia inherited to a great extent the beauty of her mother, the lovely Elisabeth of Würtemberg, whom she greatly resembled. At the time of their marriage she was nineteen and her bridegroom twenty-eight years old; they had known each other ever since she was four and he thirteen, when he had been brought to Vienna to be educated.

During the four remaining years of the life of Carl VI., François and Maria Theresia lived at the court of Vienna, which at that time was a remarkably dull one, as may be seen from the following letter from the Duc de Richelieu, French Ambassador at Vienna, to Cardinal Polignac, French Ambassador at Rome:

"J'ai mené ici à Vienne pendant tout le carême une existence étonnemment pieuse, qui ne m'a pas laissé un quart d'heure de liberté. Je l'avoue franchement, si j'avais prévu la vie qu'un ambassadeur s'amuse à mener à Vienne, rien au monde n'aurait pu me décider à accepter cette mission, où, sous couleur d'invitations et de cérémonies aux chapelles, les ambassadeurs sont obligés de suivre la cour comme des valets de chambre. Il n'y a pas de capucin, si forte que soit sa santé, qui puisse résister à une pareille existence pendant le carême. Pour en donner une idée à Votre Eminence, je suis resté en tout depuis le dimanche des Rameaux jusqu'au mercredi après Pâques, cent heures à l'église, à la suite de l'Empereur. Le Comte de Luc, qui a passé dix-huit mois à Vienne, dont neuf ou dix avant de se faire présenter à la cour, et qui s'est fait dire ensuite malade, nous avait caché ce trésor de piété, dont j'ai dû faire la découverte à mes dépens. Je dois l'avouer, je m'imagine que le respect pour la Divinité pourrait comporter un peu plus de liberté, et que l'ennui forcé dont on nous fait ici gracieusement largesse et qu'on ne rencontre à ce point dans aucune autre cour, m'est tellement insupportable que je ne puis m'empêcher de dire à Votre Eminence combien j'en suis excédé."

To which the Cardinal replied :

"En ce qui touche le tableau que vous me faites de la façon dont vous avez rempli votre devoir de chrétien pendant le carême et la semaine sainte, je ne puis que vous féliciter d'être sorti intact de ce pénible passage ; peut-être n'avez-vous jamais tant fait dans votre vie. .Pensez donc que c'est exactement la même chose pour un cardinal à Rome. Mais vous me direz sans doute que nous sommes payés pour cela." [1]

Such a personality as Richelieu must indeed have found himself out of place in a court thus described, a singular contrast to that of Louis XV.; and in the answer of the Cardinal one cannot but remark the scarcely concealed amusement with which he had received these lamentations.

[1] "I have passed here in Vienna, during the whole of Lent, an extraordinarily pious existence, which has not allowed me a quarter of an hour's freedom. I frankly acknowledge that if I had foreseen the life an ambassador at Vienna must amuse himself by leading, nothing on earth would have induced me to accept that position, in which, under pretext - of invitations and ceremonies in the chapels, the ambassadors are obliged to follow the court like *valets de chambre*. There is not a Capucin, however strong he may be, whose health could stand such a life during the whole of Lent. To give your Eminence an idea of it, I spent a hundred hours in church, in the suite of the Emperor, between Palm Sunday and the Wednesday after Easter. The Comte de Luc, who spent eighteen months at Vienna, was not presented at court during the first nine or ten months, and afterwards got himself declared to be ill, concealed from us this treasure of piety which I have had to discover at my own expense. I must say that I think respect for the Divinity might admit of a little more liberty, and the enforced *ennui* which they so graciously bestow upon us here, and which one does not meet with to this extent at any other court, is so insupportable to me, that I cannot help telling your Eminence how I am annoyed by it."

To which the Cardinal replied : "With regard to the picture you give me of the manner in which you fulfilled your duty as a Christian during Lent, I can only congratulate you on having come intact out of that painful passage (experience) , perhaps you have never done so much before in your life. Consider, then, that it is exactly the same thing for a cardinal at Rome. But you will doubtless say that we are paid for that."—" Marie Thérèse " (Comte de Villermont).

The death of Carl VI. (1740), which placed at the head of the court and country two young, handsome, high-spirited sovereigns, mitigated the asceticism of this *régime;* but the troubles and dangers which then arose were for a considerable time so serious as to obliterate all such comparatively unimportant considerations.

Friederich of Prussia claimed Silesia and the Elector of Bavaria the kingdom of Bohemia; the guarantees of the Pragmatic Sanction were thrown to the winds; George II. of England deserted Maria Theresia and signed a treaty of neutrality, while France joined with Prussia, Bavaria, and the other powers in their attempt to dismember the inheritance of the Habsburg.

The treasury was nearly exhausted, the army weakened and diminished; the people, overtaxed and poverty-stricken, were breaking into riots in different parts of the country; the Prussian troops poured into Silesia, Prague fell into the hands of the Bavarians, and Maria Theresia, with her husband, mother, and infant children, fled to Hungary. She appeared at the Diet in Presburg wearing the Hungarian costume, with the sword and crown of St. Stephen, and pointing to her infant son in the arms of his nurse, claimed the protection of the chivalrous nobles of Hungary in an eloquent speech, ending in a passion of tears, which called forth an outburst of enthusiastic loyalty.

All Hungary rose: a hundred thousand men flocked to her standard; the Hungarian army saved Maria Theresia, Vienna, and the monarchy.[1]

[1] "Memoirs of the Court and Aristocracy of Austria" (E. Vehse).

Wolf del.

FREDERICK THE GREAT, KING OF PRUSSIA.

She never forgot it; then and during her whole life her love and gratitude never failed her beloved Hungary, which had stood by her in her hour of need. Upon her dying bed the name of Hungary was one of the last words she spoke.

In 1745 François de Lorraine was elected Emperor and crowned at Frankfort, in spite of which supreme dignity he always played a secondary part to the Empress, who, absolute sovereign over her own vast dominions, held the reins with a firm hand, allowing no one, however near and dear, to interfere with her government or share her power.

With her great minister, Kaunitz, she governed wisely though despotically the many and various states and nations under her sway; but as this is the history, not of the Empress, but of one of her daughters, it is necessary to turn from these matters to describe the conditions and circumstances which surrounded and influenced the childhood and youth of the Archduchess Maria Carolina and her brothers and sisters.

The Empress was a devoted mother. She spent with her children all the time she could spare from the affairs of the state; she regulated and superintended every detail of their daily life and studies; she was intensely anxious for their religious principles and conduct; and if she were ready to sacrifice any of them to political reasons, it was because in her the Empress and Queen outweighed the mother, and the welfare of the state was her first consideration, to which everything, even the happiness of her children, must give way.

Meanwhile, the numerous young Archdukes and

Archduchesses led a happy life at Vienna, or at the delightful country palaces and castles of their parents, both of whom, their mother especially, were devoted to country life.

The only sister of the Empress had been married to Prince Carl, a younger son of the house of Lorraine, and died in childbirth a year afterwards; but for many years the imperial family circle included the Empress Dowager, who was adored by her daughter, son-in-law, and grandchildren, and the Princess Charlotte of Lorraine, only surviving sister of the Emperor, a kind-hearted, eccentric person, who hated Vienna, never ceased to regret Lorraine, which she had passionately loved, and finally, when her pretty nieces grew up, and she was still unmarried, declared she looked and felt absurd amongst them, especially as they had to take precedence of her, and persuaded the Emperor and Empress to allow her to retire from court. Maria Theresia made her Superior of the great Abbey of Mons, where she lived as the representative of the Empress, who, as sovereign of the Netherlands, was head of that noble order.

The little Archduchess Elisabeth, eldest child of the Empress, died at three years old, to the great grief of her parents; but after her came Marianne, Joseph, Christine, Carl, Leopold, Elisabeth, Johanna, Amalie, Josepha, Maria Carolina, Ferdinand, Maximilien, and Marie Antoinette, besides three babies that did not live.

There could scarcely be a greater contrast than that between the court in which these children were brought up and those over which some of them were afterwards called upon to reign. With all the state and ceremony of court functions mingled the simplicity and domestic life of Germany.

Maria Theresia cared little for dress, and thought nothing of her beauty except for the sake of her husband, for whom her love always remained unchanged. Her toilet in daily life was very simple; she rose at four or five o'clock in summer, and at six in winter, went to Mass, breakfasted hastily, heard a second Mass, then saw her children, and spent the morning in transacting business; dined at one o'clock, often alone, after which she allowed herself two hours' recreation before returning to work or to give audiences until six o'clock, when she attended vespers. The business of the day was then supposed to be over; the card-tables were arranged, and at eight o'clock was supper. Very often the Empress went to bed at ten, or even earlier.

From early spring till late autumn, she remained in the country at one or other of the imperial palaces, her favourites being Laxenburg and above all Schönbrunn, both near Vienna. At Schönbrunn she inhabited eight rooms on the ground-floor near the orangery, which were painted in what was called Indian fashion, with palms and tropical foliage, flowers, fruit, and birds, and furnished, some in white and gold, others grey and gold; her bedroom was painted ash-grey, and the bed hung with brocade curtains of the same colour. A glass door from these rooms opened into an avenue leading to a secluded arbour, where she used to go, carrying a tray full of letters and documents slung round her neck, with which she occupied herself hour after hour, while a sentinel stood outside to keep off intruders.

The young princes and princesses were taught the Magyar language, and the Archduke Joseph as a child wore the Hungarian dress and had for his governor one of the great Hungarian family of Batthiany.

The castle of Schönbrunn, on the banks of the river Wien, and surrounded by beautiful gardens, was added to and embellished by the Empress; Laxenburg was very near, and the court or some of the royal family were often there, or at other and more distant castles, such as Hofberg and Mannensdorf.

It was from the latter that, one hot afternoon in October, Franz and Maria Theresia went out for a walk unattended a little beyond the village. As they wandered amongst the vineyards, now glowing with autumn colour and loaded with ripe fruit, Maria Theresia, tired and thirsty, gathered a large bunch of grapes, and had begun to eat them when suddenly rough, angry voices were heard, and four *gardes-vignes* appeared, furiously demanding who had given them leave to gather the grapes.

"Yes, I gathered a bunch of grapes," said the Emperor, "and what then?"

"What then? What then?" cried the guards. "Why, you will pay five florins fine."

But they had neither of them any money, and the guards, refusing to listen to any explanations, hurried them to the house of the chief official of the village, pouring forth reproaches and threats all the way.

The *juge de la commune*, who was out in the fields,

was sent for, arrived in his shirt sleeves very angry, and asked, " Can you pay the five florins ? "

" No."

" Well, then, you will be imprisoned for twenty-four hours in the bacon-room," and pushing them in, he continued, " You will stay there till to-morrow, and I shall bring you some bread, which is all you will want."

So saying, he shut the door and departed, while his royal prisoners at first burst into fits of laughter, but after a time, becoming tired of the bacon-room, begged the guard who brought them some bread and water to go to the *administrateur* of the *château* and say that M. François Etienne asked for the loan of five florins to pay his fine.

The guard was very unwilling to go, saying that he would not be listened to or attended to, and would perhaps be reprimanded for coming; but after much persuasion and the promise of a large reward he consented, and reluctantly presented himself at the castle. Just as he expected, the officer in question, who was disturbed during his *siesta*, received him with displeasure and suspicion; but directly he heard the message, to the utter astonishment of the guard, that respectable personage sprang up and rushed out of the house without his hat, shouting to the guard to fetch the *juge de la commune* at once. That individual hastened to appear, and on hearing the truth, flung open the door and threw himself upon his knees before his illustrious prisoners, who only laughed, paid the fine, gave money to the guard, and exempted the vineyard from the *dîme*.

CHAPTER II

The court of Maria Theresia—Kaunitz—The imperial children—Christine and Carl—The Archduchess Marianne—Love-affair of the Archduchess Christine and Albrecht of Saxe-Teschen—Their marriage—The Archduchess Elisabeth—An unwilling Abbess—The Archduke Joseph—Character of the Empress—Her despotic rule—The amusements of the Emperor—His love-affairs and *liaisons*

THE Emperor François de Lorraine had soon introduced into the society of Vienna, with the use of the French language, much of the refinement and ease which had hitherto been wanting in the manners, customs, and amusements of the Austrian court. Gradually the old Spanish stiffness and German awkwardness were yielding to the grace and vivacity of France; far away seemed the days when Carl VI. would not even allow coffee to be drunk, and the Archduchess, after her marriage, was obliged to get her coffee berries smuggled in her bag of devotional books or the holsters of her husband's pistols. Splendid *fêtes* and balls were given—the Empress herself was extremely fond of dancing; the great nobles, enormously rich and powerful, vied with each other in splendour; the imperial household was exceedingly costly: there were two thousand two hundred horses in the stables; the furniture of the "Gilt Hall of Mirrors," where the Empress dined in public, cost 90,000 florins; the gold embroidered canopy under which the table stood, 30,000; the dinner service of massive gold, 1,300,000 florins. All of these were ordered by the Emperor. He passionately loved pleasure and magnificence, and, although not a Richelieu or Louis XV., was an enthusiastic admirer of beauty, very fond of the society of women, and much inclined to the sort of adventures and *liaisons* which were most displeasing to the Empress, from whom they had to be carefully concealed.

For there could be no question of introducing into the court of Maria Theresia the tone and the morals of that of Louis XV.; the Empress regarded the proceedings of the Emperor with a jealous eye, put an end to his flirtations whenever she discovered them, and visited their objects with her condign displeasure. She discouraged as far as possible all affairs of gallantry and love intrigues, and, in fact, carried her strictness and propriety to such an extreme that they became at times intolerable. She would not allow young women to walk about the streets by themselves unless they were going to church, and every now and then some harmless girl going to her work was arrested by one of the prying, meddlesome officers of a ridiculous society she had instituted for the preservation of morality, and called the "Society" or "Commission" of purity or chastity, whose agents patrolled the streets night and day.[1]

[1] E. Vehse.

Riding, music, masked balls, theatrical performances, and religious ceremonies were her favourite relaxations; she especially liked attending the profession of any one she knew who was entering a convent.[1]

The term *corps diplomatique* was first used under Maria Theresia, and of all the diplomatists of the imperial court comprehended in that convenient name, none could be compared in genius, power, and fame with the great Kaunitz; the Richelieu of Austria, though without the sanguinary disposition of the great Frenchman.

So powerful and so widespread was his influence that he was called "*le cocher de l'Europe*," and so supreme was his ascendancy over the Empress that she found herself obliged to condone the licence of his private morals in a manner most unusual and vexatious to herself.

For she could not do without Kaunitz, and during all the earlier portion of his career his intrigues and *liaisons* were so open and so notorious that he would take his mistresses in the carriage with him to the gates of the imperial palace, leave them there to wait for him during his audience with the Empress, and return to them when it was over.

It can be well understood how this irritated Maria Theresia, but when on one occasion she signified her displeasure, he replied coolly:

"*Madame, je suis venu ici pour parler des affaires de Votre Majesté, non des miennes.*"[2]

[1] "Geschichte Maria Theresia's" (Alfred Ritter von Arneth).
[2] "Madame, I came here to talk of your Majesty's affairs, not of mine" (Vehse).

WENZEL ANTON, PRINCE OF KAUNITZ.
After a painting by Steiner.

Wenceslaus Anton, Prince von Kaunitz, was born of an ancient Slavonic family in Moravia (1711). He followed the usual diplomatic career, but rose so rapidly that while he was still a young man the Minister Uhlefeld laid one of his despatches on the table of the Empress with the remark:

"Here is your Majesty's Prime Minister."

Tall and good looking, he was in manners, tastes, and habits so entirely French that he affected to speak German imperfectly, to the indignation of the old Austrian party, but he had certain German characteristics which contributed greatly to the success of his astonishing career.

He built two splendid country palaces at Mariahilf and Laxenburg, and kept open house in Vienna, his magnificent establishment being presided over first by his wife, Marie Ernestine, Countess of Starhemberg, whose morals, according to Swinburne, very much resembled his own; and, after her death (1749), by his sister, Countess von Questenberg, very much disliked in society; when she died her place was supplied by the Dowager Countess Clary, who was extremely popular, and was known as "*la petite veuve.*" She had married at fifteen a man of seventy-five, who soon died, and she had never re-married. During his later life Prince von Kaunitz took inordinate care of his health, and made an absurd fuss and difficulty about his food, which in those days was not usual.[1]

It is curious that a son of his, by a Belgian

[1] Vehse.

mistress, was a furious Jacobin in the French Revolution.

Notwithstanding the excessive strictness of the Empress, the lives of her children were by no means dull. Maria Theresia, whose early education had been much neglected, was very anxious about the studies of her sons; her daughters had shorter hours of lessons and more religious exercises. There was much freedom and relaxation of etiquette in their country homes: the park and gardens at Schönbrunn were open to the public, who walked freely about the grounds. The Empress would often say to the nobles and officials whom she met:

"Will you come and see my children act and dance?"

For there were plenty of children's balls, at which the little Archduchesses danced till they were tired out, and private theatricals were amongst their favourite amusements. Count von Kevenhüller mentions a play called "Saturnales" which was being performed in Vienna, and which the imperial children also acted. The Archduke Joseph took the part of Cæsar, Carl of Cinna; Leopold and the Archduchesses Marianne, Elisabeth, and Amalie also played in it. Kevenhüller was invited to see it, and thought the dialogue too long and too serious for actors of that age. Unfortunately he said so, and his remark was overheard by the Empress, who was not at all pleased.[1]

The Archduke Joseph, though possessing some

[1] Von Arneth.

valuable qualities, was by no means so attractive as some of his brothers, for he was selfish, priggish, and full of crotchets, and his progress in his studies was much slower than that of his next brothers, Carl and Leopold.

Carl and Christine, their second son and daughter, were the favourites of the Emperor and Empress. They were the most brilliant and gifted of all the children, both of them being extremely handsome, attractive, and talented. Christine was very like the Empress, not only in appearance but in character, and probably for this reason there was between Maria Theresia and this daughter a fuller sympathy and more perfect understanding than with the rest. And she was the only one of the daughters of Maria Theresia whose life was a thoroughly happy and prosperous one; for of all the thirteen merry children who danced and acted in the splendid *salons* of Vienna, or played in the shady gardens of Schönbrunn and Laxenburg, scarcely a single one had a fortunate lot. Either an early death, a disappointed and unsatisfied life, or else one filled with storms and trials, was the fate reserved for nearly every one of the handsome boys and pretty, fair girls upon whom the Emperor and Empress looked with such pride and affection and about whose future Maria Theresia was so occupied.

With all the simplicity of her daily life, the Empress every now and then gave magnificent *fêtes*. At one which took place at Schlosshof, although the *château* was very large, a temporary building four hundred feet long was erected in front of it and lighted with a hundred thousand lamps. Six thousand people were at the ball, and there were beds, doctors, and even midwives in attendance in case of accidents.

At a grand masquerade witnessed by Dr. Moore at Schönbrunn, for which four thousand tickets were issued, a company of dragoons kept order upon the road to Vienna. In three large halls on the ground floor tables were laid with a profusion of refreshments, fruits, and costly wines. There was a splendid ballet of twenty-four persons, including some of the Archdukes and Archduchesses, all wearing fancy dresses of white silk, trimmed with pink and blazing with diamonds. The court was enormously expensive, and Maria Theresia was most generous in her charities. Often when driving out she would fill her pocket with gold, to throw out of the window to poor people.

Her eldest daughter, the Archduchess Marianne,[1] had always delicate health, and the Empress made her after a time Abbess of Prague. She was clever, intellectual, and even learned, deeply interested in geological and mineralogical studies; she was a pupil of the celebrated Professor Born. With her peaceful, stately, religious life and intellectual pursuits in the sheltered splendour of her Austrian home, it is probable that her lot was much happier than those of her sisters, who were sent to distant homes in foreign countries with uncongenial husbands. For the remembrance of her own youth and

[1] The Archduchess Marianne was plain and slightly deformed; there could be no question of her marriage.

the romance of her love for François de Lorraine did not influence the Empress in her dealings with her daughters; only in one instance did she allow a marriage to be decided by inclination instead of policy.

Albrecht von Saxe-Teschen was a distinguished young officer in the Austrian service. He was a younger son of Augustus the Strong, King of Poland, and was related to the imperial family, but he had neither lands nor money, and when he fell in love with the Archduchess Christine and she returned his passion, it could not be supposed that the Empress, with her views concerning her daughters' marriages, would consent to entertain the idea of any such alliance. However, Maria Theresia was fortunately very fond of Albrecht and touched by their devotion to each other; therefore she yielded to the entreaties of her favourite daughter, allowed the marriage to take place (1766), and proceeded to provide magnificently for her daughter and son-in-law. Christine had a large dowry, and Albrecht was made Duke of Teschen, Commander-in-chief of the army, and Field-Marshal. The Empress gave him the order of the Golden Fleece, made him and her daughter Governors of Hungary, and they took up their abode at Presburg, where they held a splendid court, and where she frequently visited them. After the death of Charles of Lorraine she made Christine Governess of the Low Countries. The love of Albrecht and Christine never changed, and after she died in 1798 he ever remained faithful to her memory. He lived to be 84 (1822).

Much less fortunate was the third daughter, Elisabeth, by some considered the prettiest of all the Archduchesses. Several marriages proposed for her came to nothing; one project of marrying her to the King of Poland was stopped by the Empress Catherine of Russia; another suitor who pleased Maria Theresia was a son of the King of Sardinia, but he had no money, and so much had been spent upon Marianne and Christine that enough could not be spared for Elisabeth, which seems hard upon her. Then there was an idea of marrying her to Louis XV., after the death of Queen Marie Leczinska, daughter of Stanislaus of Poland; but meanwhile the small-pox, that fearful scourge to the imperial family, had destroyed the beauty of Elisabeth, and the King of France declared he would marry her only if she were good-looking, the fact being that he did not want to marry at all. The Empress therefore made her Abbess of Innsbruck, but, if her sister Marianne was satisfied with such a lot, Elisabeth was not. Lively, amusing, and high-spirited, she did not want to be an abbess at all, but to marry, and she complained bitterly of the dulness of her life when she had outgrown the diversions and pleasures of early youth without obtaining the freedom of later years.

For the despotic rule of the Empress continued as long as she lived over all the sons and daughters who remained with her, even the Crown Prince himself. Much as she loved the Emperor Franz, she would never allow even him in any way to interfere with her government, while from her sons and daughters and all around her she exacted the most implicit obedience.

When the Archduchess Elisabeth was forty years old, the English Ambassador, Sir Robert Keith, went to pay her a visit of condolence on being laid up with an abscess in her cheek, but the Archduchess laughed and said:

"Believe me, for an archduchess of forty years old who is not married, a hole in the cheek is an amusement!"

She proceeded to explain that she was thankful for *anything* that broke the dulness and *ennui* of her life, and to complain bitterly of the repression and tyranny of Maria Theresia, which she declared to be outrageous over daughters of that age, whom she kept under preposterous restraint.

But to return to the earlier and happier years of the Austrian imperial family, before any of these marriages or religious professions had been arranged, or the large circle of brothers and sisters had been broken into.

Carl was always the idol of his parents. Handsome, talented, and lively, though he had much more capacity than his elder brother, his tutor complained that he was so volatile that a fly or a grain of sand would attract his attention from his lessons.[1]

The Emperor, debarred from taking any active share in the government, was unjustly described afterwards by his son Joseph as "an idler surrounded by flatterers."

But Joseph was one of the sort of people fond of

[1] Arneth.

saying disagreeable things, to whom contradiction and opposition are a real pleasure. And the excessive strictness of the Empress had caused in him a strong reaction against the ideas she insisted on carrying out. It is constantly remarked that the children of overstrict parents, who are not allowed to do anything, and are brought up to think everything wrong, as they grow up seem to arrive at the conclusion that nothing is wrong, or, at any rate, certainly not the things they have been taught to consider so; and Joseph hated whatever his parents liked, and liked whatever they hated. The Emperor had become exceedingly anxious to preserve friendly relations with France—he was thoroughly French in taste and sympathies, and from his childhood had spoken no other language with ease. The Crown Prince could not bear France, or any person, thing, or custom connected with that country. His father was a good Catholic, and his mother an extremely strict one, whereas he was inclined to be lax in religious matters, opposed the clergy, and was a friend and admirer of Rousseau and the encyclopedists. He was full of good intentions, which he tried to carry out—generally with very little success—and was by no means popular.

The Empress Maria Theresia was not only a great sovereign, but a woman of noble and lofty character, strong alike in courage, intellect, principles and affections; but her proud, despotic temper threw its shadow over the otherwise happy family life in which she so delighted.

With all their love for each other, and the sunny, light-hearted disposition of the Emperor, the way in

FRANÇOIS ETIENNE, DUKE OF LORRAINE.
EMPEROR OF GERMANY.

which she excluded him from all share in the government vexed him and slightly roused his temper. On one occasion, when he was complaining of the money she threw away upon various hypocritical persons who by great pretence of religion and virtue insinuated themselves into her favour, she replied significantly, "The ducats are all Kremnitzers"; thereby reminding him that the gold mines of Hungary and their produce did not belong either to a German Emperor or a Grand-duke of Tuscany.

François, however, did many useful things for the state, especially for the administration of finance, which had been frightfully mismanaged. He discovered and exposed the gross frauds practised in the army, the imperial household, and elsewhere. His own financial matters he conducted with great success: his duchy of Tuscany yielded him a large revenue, and he bought great estates in Austria and Hungary, all of which were equally well managed.

Both he and the Empress were perfect riders, and he was also good at all outdoor sports. He hunted, shot, played billiards, collected pictures, coins, and antiquities, patronised painters, musicians, and actors,[1] and was extremely fond of society.

In spite of the vigilance of the Empress he contrived to carry on various intrigues and *liaisons;* supper-parties unknown to her from time to time took place, and it was rumoured that his shooting expeditions were not entirely spent in the pursuit of game in field or forest. In his earlier married life he carried on love-affairs, amongst others, with the

[1] "Marie Thérèse" (Comte de Villermont).

Countess Colloredo, and with Countess Palffy, one of the maids of honour to the Empress.

Afterwards, his chief favourite was the beautiful Princess von Auersperg, who at seventeen had been married to a man twice her age and a widower, and could not resist the fascination of the Emperor's love.

François detested etiquette and stiffness, and would say to different ladies present at some great function :

"I shall stay with you till the court is gone. By the court I mean the Empress and my children; I am here only as a private person." [1]

[1] Vehse

CHAPTER III

The Empress and her children—Betrothal of the Archduchess Johanna to the King of Naples—Joseph, Carl, and Leopold—Death of Carl—Isabella of Parma—Strange romance of her history—Her marriage with the Crown Prince—Her friendship with Christine—Gloomy presentiments—Death of Johanna—"It is the summons"—Death of Isabella—Unhappy second marriage of the Crown Prince—Marriage of the Archduke Leopold—Death of the Emperor.

AMID the weight of cares, occupations, and interests that filled her life, Maria Theresia troubled herself little more about her health than her beauty. Capable of enduring an immense amount of fatigue, she gave herself no rest. When she was tired out with writing and transacting business, she sent for her children by way of relaxation, and this she would often do three or four times in a day.

On one occasion, as the Italian writer of the following notice remarks, her carelessness cost the life of one of her children and endangered her own.

"Diedo, Sept. 21, 1748.—On Tuesday, towards night, Her Majesty gave birth to an Archduchess who died a few minutes afterwards, baptized, however, by a lady among the assistants. Her Majesty was suddenly seized with the pains while walking in the garden, and in a very short time had passed through that ever perilous moment. The evening before she had been at the opera in the city, and drove back, as usual, at a rapid pace. The loss of the infant Princess is attributed to the absolute want of care of her Majesty for her safety, for, although entreated to consider it, she despises everything that might be called even a necessary precaution." [1]

This happened before the death of the Empress Dowager (1750), who had been an invalid for some years, but whose loss was a great sorrow to the imperial family. That same year was born the Archduchess Johanna, the next year the Archduchess Josepha, a year and a half later, Maria Carolina, and after her Ferdinand, Marie Antoinette, and Maximilien. These, the "little ones" of the family, appear to have been all together under the care of their governesses, to whom, when she was absent, the Empress wrote minute details about their lessons, their walks, their health, their conduct, &c.

Four hours' lessons a day, with half an hour's

---

[1] "Diedo, Set. 21, 1748.—Verso la notte del Martedi Sua Majestà diede alla luce un' Arciduchessa, che è morta poche minute dopo del parto, battesimata però da una dama colà assistente. Fu sorpresa S.M. dai dolori mentre passeggiava nel giardino e in brevissimo spazio sortì dal sempre pericoloso momento. Era stata la sera antecedente all' opera in città, valendosi gia di carrozza, è lasciando tenere l'uso solito di un rapido corso. Vien attribuito la mancanza della bambina principessa alla niuna risserva di S.M. nel riguardo della sua preservazione, essa però benchè insinuata ad haversi riflesso, è disprezzante affatto di tutto quello che potrebbe dirsi anche necessaria precauzione."

reading of history, were considered by their mother sufficient for any of the Archduchesses,[1] but if, as historians say, they were made to go oftener to church than their brothers, much time must have been indeed spent there, for it is recorded that one Easter, when the Archduke Joseph was eleven, he was taken to eighteen churches by his father.

According to the fashion of the day, the Empress began to consider their marriages while they were still mere children, and being anxious to ally herself closely with the Bourbon, she resolved to marry several of her sons and daughters to members of that family.

She determined that one of them should be Queen of Naples, and as the King, Ferdinando IV., was too young for her elder daughters, she chose Johanna, who was of a more suitable age, and who was accordingly betrothed to him. For a considerable time negotiations had been going on for the marriages of her three elder sons.

One project was to marry the Crown Prince to Isabella, daughter of the Duke of Parma, and a Bourbon twice over, as her father was the son of Philippe V. of Spain, younger son of the Dauphin, and grandson of Louis XIV., while her mother, now dead, was the eldest daughter of Louis XV.

But there had also been a proposal to marry him to the eldest daughter of the King of Spain, who objected when the next brother, Carl, was substituted for him. Carl was far more attractive than Joseph, and was to succeed his father as Grand-

[1] Arneth.

duke of Tuscany, but of course was not nearly so splendid an alliance as his elder brother.

The Emperor and Empress would have had no objection to change the wives destined for their sons, but the Crown Prince had seen the portrait of Isabella and fallen deeply in love with her, while everything he heard about her confirmed his resolution to marry nobody else.

He remonstrated, implored, and so beset his parents with his entreaties and prayers that they wrote to the King of Spain explaining the state of things, and with many regrets and apologies, representing that they could not in this case force their son's inclinations.

Leopold was to marry the granddaughter and sole heiress of the Duke of Modena, whom he was to succeed, this arrangement having been made when he was six and she three years old.[1]

But at the beginning of 1761 a terrible calamity fell upon the imperial family. The small-pox, that scourge of the seventeenth and eighteenth centuries, broke out amongst them; the two eldest sons and several others were dangerously ill, however—although, considering what the treatment for small-pox was in those days, it is a wonder any one ever survived it at all—most, including the Crown Prince, recovered; but Carl, the idol of his father and mother, the most promising of their sons and the favourite of everybody, had a sudden relapse, and died on the night of January 17, 1761.

"In spite of apparent amendment, all the remedies and all the endeavours made to subdue

[1] Arneth ("Maria Theresia nach dem Erbfolgekriege").

the malignity of the disease, his Royal Highness was seized unexpectedly with a new and violent paroxysm last Saturday after midnight, after a day during which there had appeared better hope than on any other. He died with courage, resignation, and calmness, admirable indeed at his tender age of sixteen years, and which prove the excellent principles of the education given to all this imperial family.

"The bitter anguish of the Sovereigns and of every one of the Princes was indescribable, and indeed the sorrow of the whole city was very similar, for the Archduke was generally beloved for his really extraordinary qualities and gifts." [1]

"Maria Theresia was all the more prostrated by this loss because it was just this son she loved best of all, and especially more than the Crown Prince, as he had always been so much less self-willed, and more obedient to his parents." [2]

---

[1] "Malgrado l'apparso miglioramento, tutti i remedj, e tutta la cura prestata per vincere nell' Arciduca Carlo la maligna forza del male, sorpresa S.A.R. improvisamente da un nuovo violento parosismo, sabato scorso dopo la mezza notte, giorno in cui furono d'ogni altro giorno le speranze maggiori, finì di vivere con una rassegnazione e costanza e tranquillità d'animo, che facendo ammirazione supera da un canto le misure d' una tenera età di sedici anni, e fa dall' altro conoscere li ottimi semi di educazione sparsi in tutta questa imperiale famiglia. Fù qui indicibile l' amara angustia di questi Sovrani e di ognuno dei Principi, e poco dissimile il dolore della città tutta, amata l'Arciduca generalmente per le qualità sue veramente egregie di mente, d'animo e di persona . . . . " (Ruzzini).

[2] " Es war behauptet dass Maria Theresia durch diesen Verlust um so dieser dareinder gebeugt worden sei weil sie gerade diesen Sohn, am meisten, und zwar mehr noch als den Kronprinzen geliebt habe, indem er weniger eigenwillig und gehorsamer gegen seine Eltern gewesen sei alst jener " (Arneth).

In consequence of the death of the Archduke Carl, the Infanta Ludovica of Spain was betrothed to the Archduke Leopold, upon whom the succession of Tuscany was now settled, while his little brother, Ferdinand, was put in his place as the future husband of Maria Beatrice of Modena.

The wedding of the Crown Prince with Isabella of Parma was celebrated in the autumn following the death of Carl. The strange, melancholy romance attached to this marriage, which blighted the life of Joseph II., is related by all historians and well known to all readers familiar with the history of that time. Isabella, eldest daughter of the Duke of Parma, then about sixteen or seventeen years old, was a personality around whom lingers an indescribable charm. She did not possess the beauty of her Austrian sisters-in-law; she had lovely eyes and hair and a graceful form, but her dark face and irregular features contrasted with their bright blue eyes, golden hair, and dazzling complexions; still there was about her a fascination which no one could resist. The Crown Prince, unlike his father, usually cold and indifferent to the attractions of women, was her slave from the first moment he saw her. The Empress adored her; so did her brothers and sisters-in-law [1]; and she returned their affection with all the ardour of a young, warm-hearted girl and an Italian.

Between her and Christine there immediately arose an enthusiastic attachment which never changed. Years afterwards Christine went to

[1] Except the Archduchess Marianne, for whom she never cared (Arneth).

Colorno[1] and wandered sorrowfully through the rooms which Isabella had occupied before her marriage, looking with mournful affection at every object which had belonged to her and recalling the descriptions she had so often given her of the home of her childhood.

Several different explanations and reasons have been given for the strange melancholy and the presentiment of early death, the persistence and fulfilment of which are the only certainties about the whole story. It has, for instance, been declared that Isabella had an earlier attachment which made her marriage with the Austrian Crown Prince the sacrifice of her happiness. But of this there is no corroboration whatever. No person has ever been fixed upon as a possible subject for any such romance, and the Archduchess Christine, who possessed her entire confidence, knew of no entanglement.

Another cause assigned was that Isabella had wished to dedicate herself to the life of the cloister. Of this again there is no proof. She showed no dislike to her marriage with Joseph, though she certainly told the Prince von Lichtenstein, when he came to ask for her hand, that it was useless for her to become the wife of the Crown Prince, as she would not live long.

A third explanation of this mysterious story was that the Duchess of Parma, her mother, whom she adored and by whom she had been trained and entirely influenced, having died a year before, Isabella, overpowered with grief and despair, knelt

[1] Isabella was brought up at the castle of Colorno, in the country.

by her mother's bier and prayed earnestly and passionately that she might die and go to her; that she distinctly heard a voice say the word "three," from which she concluded and hoped that she would die in the third day, week, or month from that time. Finding herself mistaken, she resigned herself to wait until the third year, during which she felt convinced her death would take place.[1]

In the meanwhile she seems to have made herself tolerably happy in her married life. She does not appear to have returned the passionate love lavished upon her by her husband, but to have felt for him the kind of calm affection which many people have considered quite a sufficient and desirable substitute.

As to the assertion that after her death Christine, thinking to lessen her brother's grief, told him that Isabella had never loved him and that that changed his feelings for her and embittered him against all women, this does not seem to be probable. For even if it is allowed that a woman like Christine could make so foolish and so cruel a mistake, the numerous letters of the Crown Prince, long after the death of his first wife, prove that his love and regret for her were never altered.[2] He never ceased to refer to the perfect happiness he had enjoyed with her, and although he was rather fond of the society of women and made various social and intellectual friendships with different members of

---

[1] It must, however, be noted that, as Herr von Arneth remarks, Isabella did not die at the expiration of three years but only before the fourth year was completed

[2] Arneth.

his court, nothing of the nature of a love-affair was ever recorded of him.[1]

They had many pursuits in common, especially music, in which both excelled, but Isabella was altogether an extraordinary woman. A letter to Christine, when one considers that the writer was a girl of seventeen or eighteen, is a proof of her uncommon versatility and intellectual gifts. In it she compares her own head to a cupboard belonging to her, in which she says she keeps a miscellaneous collection of her writings and compositions of all descriptions. A political treatise, a comic opera, a vaudeville, a work on education, a sermon, an essay on the vanity of this world, moral precepts, a composition for the piano, letters from a hundred persons of all sorts, from those of the Empress, which were the joy of her life, to others from persons absolutely indifferent to her. A little philosophy, stories, songs, metaphysics, poems, logic, &c.

Her affection for Christine was the great delight of her life, and often aroused the jealousy of the Crown Prince, who was himself very much inclined to be jealous of this particular sister, only a year his junior and the undoubted favourite of his parents; handsome, hasty, impetuous, proud, masterful, but talented, warm-hearted, true and unwavering either in love or friendship. In 1762 a daughter was born to Isabella, to the delight of both herself and the Crown Prince, but in spite of all the happiness she enjoyed, her expectation of and longing for death was ever in her mind.

In December, 1762, the small-pox again appeared

[1] Vehse.

amongst the imperial family, and this time the victim was the Archduchess Johanna, then about twelve years old.

"I am very happy about my sister Johanna," wrote Isabella to Christine, "and I begin to flatter myself that she will not die. I picture to myself that she will be very happy in that case, and so shall I, for I should be inconsolable at her loss. Why cannot I be in her place? Death is a good thing."

But Johanna grew worse; her sister-in-law goes on to tell of restless nights, delirium, burning fever, and all the sad course of the illness which so soon led to its fatal close.

In many letters and papers of the Crown Princess melancholy but ardent longings for death are to be found, a mystical, dreamy gazing into the future mingling with prayers and communings with God and the unseen world.

As the spring and summer of 1763 wore on she continually spoke to all around her of her approaching death, though her health was extremely good, always declaring that she should die at the end of the year.

When one of her ladies remarked that she was forgetting that she would have to leave her child, she answered:

"Do you think, then, that I shall leave you my little Thérèse? You will not have her more than six or seven years."

In the autumn she left Laxenburg for Vienna, as she was expecting her second confinement. When he carriage reached the top of a hill from which that city was to be seen, she looked towards it with a shudder, exclaiming " *Voilà ma mort !* "

During the night of the 18th of November an alarum was heard to strike suddenly several times, as if out of order. The Crown Princess turned pale, and, on her ladies asking if she were ill, replied :

" It is the summons. It calls me." [1]

Nothing unusual happened next day until the evening when, as Isabella was standing in her room, she suddenly fell upon her knees. She was carried to bed, but that same fatal disease, the small-pox, declared itself; she gave birth to a child which did not live, lingered a few days, and then died, to the despair of the Crown Prince and the rest of the imperial family. Among her papers was found the following :

"Quand donc cette vie finira-t-elle avec ses misères, ses peines, et ses épreuves ? Quand donc mon âme sera-t-elle délivrée des liens qui l'attachent à la machine corporelle ? Quand lui sera-t-il permis de s'élancer vers les demeures éternelles ? "

The Empress nursed the Crown Princess devotedly and mourned for her as if she had been her own child : but now as ever, reasons of state being her first consideration, she pressed the unwilling Crown Prince to agree to a new marriage, which he did with the greatest reluctance ; and it proved a most unhappy one.

For even if Joseph's heart had not been entirely given to his first wife, the unlucky Princess Josepha of Bavaria, in all respects a contrast to her predecessor, was plain, dull, unattractive, regarded with

[1] "*C'est le signal. Il m'appelle.*"

aversion by the Crown Prince and with coldness by the rest of the family, with the exception of the Emperor, who she used to say was her only friend.[1]

In July, 1765, the Emperor and Empress, with their elder children—the Crown Prince, now King of the Romans, the Archduke Leopold, and the Archduchesses Marianne and Christine—attended by a splendid suite and a great number of nobles and courtiers, set out for Innsbruck to meet Leopold's bride, the Infanta Ludovica of Spain.

Josepha, Queen of the Romans, and the younger Archdukes and Archduchesses were left at Schonbrunn.

After getting into his carriage the Emperor sent for the little Archduchess Marie Antoinette, that he might kiss and wish her goodbye again. It was for the last time. The Emperor and his sons made a shooting excursion into Tyrol and then returned by Botzen to Innsbruck, where the wedding was celebrated with great pomp.

A few days afterwards the Emperor was struck down by a sudden seizure and died at the age of fifty-seven, in the arms of his eldest son, who had been with him at the time of the fatal occurrence.

The Empress, bowed down with grief at the loss of the husband whom she had loved from her childhood with a deep, unchanging affection, and whose kindness of heart, good qualities, and attractions had made him universally popular, was at first so crushed by this sudden blow that she relegated the direction of affairs to the King of the Romans and

[1] "Maria Theresia und Kaiser Joseph II" (Berman).

gave herself up entirely to the indulgence of her grief. She even talked of retiring from the world and ending her days as Abbess of the newly founded convent of Salzburg.

But these intentions did not last long. After all, Maria Theresia was only forty-eight; the love of rule, the love of public life, and the interest in state affairs so deeply ingrained in her were too powerful not to resume their sway. And the Emperor Joseph, whom she had made co-regent of her Austrian estates, had begun at once to make all sorts of reforms and changes, many of which were salutary, but all unpopular.

He forbade games of hazard, abolished various sinecures, changed and diminished the state and ceremonial of the court, suppressed most of the holidays, did away with the separate tables of his brothers and sisters declaring that in future there would only be the imperial tables of the Empress-mother and the Emperor, and made economies in all directions.

The court and imperial family in consternation implored the Empress to resume the reins of government, which she very soon did, to such good effect that the Emperor Joseph found his authority and care reduced to the administration of the army.

CHAPTER IV

Grief of the Empress—She resumes the government—The Archduchess Josepha—Marriage of the Archduchess Christine—Her favourite daughter—The small-pox again—Death of the Empress Joseph—Recovery of the Empress-mother—Splendid preparations for the wedding of Josepha—In the Capucine church—A terrible calamity—Death of Josepha—Recovery of Elisabeth—The presentiment fulfilled

MARIA THERESIA lived sixteen years after the death of the Emperor Franz, but she never really recovered from his loss. Her love for her children was not less; she was as much, perhaps even more, absorbed in the business of her government and still more assiduous in the affairs of religion; but she was harder, sterner, more unbending. She, however, allowed the marriage of her favourite daughter Christine with Albrecht of Saxe-Teschen, which took place 1766; and she continued to occupy herself with the establishment of her other children.

The unfortunate wife of the Emperor Joseph died of small-pox, and he would not hear of marrying any more. Leopold, now Grand-duke of Tuscany, was married and Ferdinand engaged to Maria Beatrice of Modena; there was still the question of finding an alliance for Elisabeth, who was two or three and twenty and, as before said, extremely handsome. Resolved that the crown of Naples should on no account be lost for one of the Archduchesses, the Empress substituted Josepha for the deceased Johanna, being the next in age and the most suitable for the young King of Naples, he being only two months her senior.

Josepha was the favourite sister of the Emperor Joseph, who was extremely fond of her; she was very pretty and a universal favourite; Maria Theresia said of her that this daughter had never given her any trouble but only satisfaction, and that the only fault she could see in her was a slight tendency to obstinacy.[1] She was twelve years old when her mother made her take the place of Johanna as the future Queen of Naples, which she did not wish to do, whether from any superstitious feeling about her sister, or from dread of the exile to a distant land, or from anything she might have heard of the character and habits of her future husband.

For whatever was known about Ferdinand was certainly not in his favour; and the Empress herself, bent as she was upon this marriage, could not help feeling considerable misgivings regarding the future prospects of the young daughter she was sacrificing.

She begged the Countess von Lerchenfeld not only to take the greatest possible care of her education, but to promise to accompany her to Naples when the time should come for her marriage; to

[1] Arneth.

which last, however, she does not appear to have consented.

"It is not only a question," she wrote to her, "of the education of one of my daughters, but of one who in four years will be called upon to ascend a throne, and not only to rule a kingdom but to make her husband and herself happy or unhappy. It concerns her happiness, and, what is more, the welfare of her soul. She will have a young husband who from his earliest childhood has known no one higher than himself . . . who has always been surrounded by flatterers and Italians. . . . The court of Spain allows me to send one or two persons with my daughter. . . . And where shall I find them ? . . . My mother's heart is very uneasy. I look upon poor Josepha as a sacrifice to politics. If only she fulfils her duty to God and her husband and attends to the welfare of her soul, I shall be content even if she is not happy.[1]

"The young King shows no taste for anything but hunting and the theatre; he is unusually childish, learns nothing, and knows nothing except bad provincial Italian, and has on several occasions given proof of harshness and arbitrariness. He is accustomed to have his own way, and there is no one with him who can or will give him a good education. . . . They say he is fair, like the Saxon family. I wish he had their good heart. . . ."[2]

[1] "Je regarde la pauvre Josephe comme un sacrifice de politique, pourveu qu'elle fasse son devoir envers Dieu et son époux et qu'elle fasse son salût, dût-elle même être malheureuse je serois contente" (Arneth). Maria Theresia frequently wrote in French, but wrote both that language and German incorrectly.

[2] Arneth.

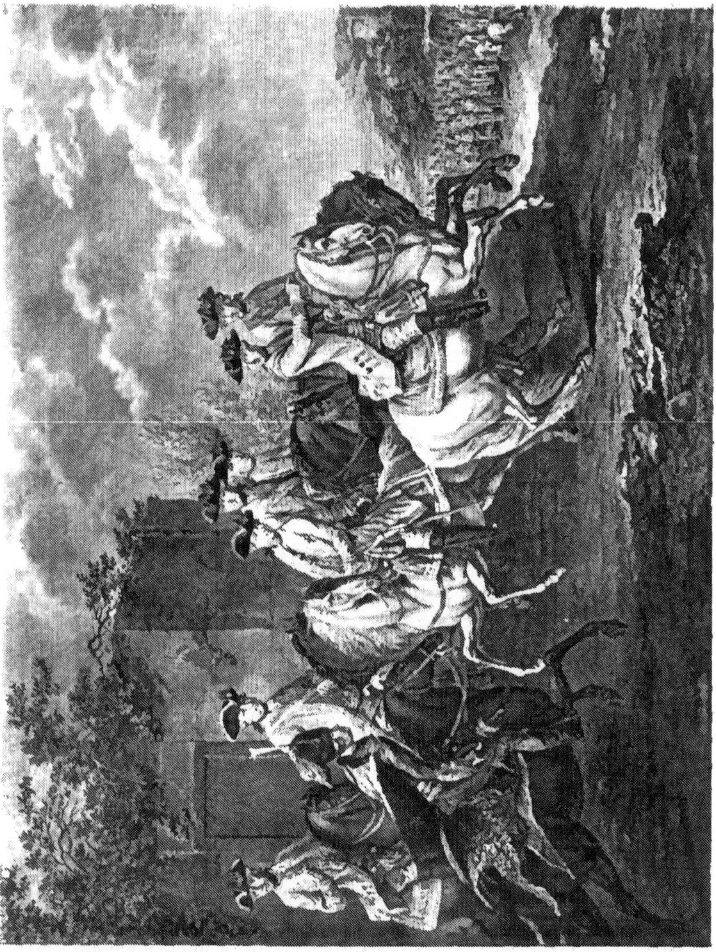

Many directions followed about the education and advice to be given to Josepha, with urgent entreaties to the Countess to go with her to Naples and look after her.

The absence of her favourite daughter Christine was a severe trial to the Empress.

Christine had suffered severely from the death of her beloved sister-in-law, Isabella of Parma, and an early fancy for Prince Ludwig of Würtemberg, which had ended in nothing, had also cast a shadow for a time over her usually high spirits. Her stronger, deeper love for Albrecht of Saxe-Teschen, opposed by her father and eldest brother, but in which she was supported by her mother, had terminated in an engagement to which at last her father had consented. After his death the wedding was celebrated (April, 1766) quietly because of the mourning for him. The Venetian, Polo Renier, writing of this event, says:

"The young Archduchess, who is endowed with more than ordinary beauty, vivacity, and *esprit*, and with charming and gracious manners, appeared, covered with splendid diamonds . . . and caused many to envy her husband."[1]

She departed with him to Presburg, where, as Governors of Hungary, they were to hold their court.

In a letter to her immediately afterwards Maria Theresia says:

[1] ". . . la giovane Arciduchessa, che trovasi fornita di non ordinaria bellezza, di vivacità, di spirito, di accosti e soave maniere si presento sovrabondantemente ornata di brillanti risplendentissimi . . . ed eccito in moltissimi una certa invidia verso lo sposo . . ." (Renier).

"... I believe I am quite well, but not tranquil. My heart has received a blow which it still feels, especially on such a day as this. In eight months I have lost the most adorable husband, a son who deserved all my love, and a daughter who after the loss of her father was my chief object, my consolation, my friend. I was childish enough this afternoon, when I heard your sisters pass through my room, to fancy for a moment that my Mimai was with them: she was then occupied in doing the honours in her own home and rejoicing in the presence of her beloved husband, the result of all the cares that have occupied me for the last two years. I do not know how to thank God enough for having brought them to such a happy conclusion, and I hope from His grace and from you both the continuation of this happiness, which will become greater every day."

Another time the Empress writes:

"C'est un plaisir de voir ces deux mariés ensemble; si je pouvais en gouter, souvent ils me font souvenir des miennes.'[1]

Such letters as these and those written by the Empress to Christine during the time of suspense while the Emperor would not consent to her engagement, telling her to have patience, trust in God, and all would be well, contrast with the sternness and hardness of some other occasions.

Another year of calamity was 1767. In the spring Christine gave birth to a daughter, who only lived a few minutes and nearly cost the mother's life. The disappointment of the loss of

[1] "Maria Theresia's letzte Regierungszeit" (Arneth)

the infant was overpowered by the joy of the Empress at the restoration of the daughter whom she had so nearly lost. But Christine never had any more children.

Before the Empress had recovered from the terror and anxiety of Christine's illness, the wife of Joseph was seized with small-pox. It was a different state of things indeed to the time when the whole imperial family and court watched with intense anxiety and grief the passing away of Isabella of Parma.

The Empress went to see her daughter-in-law and with difficulty persuaded the Emperor Joseph to do the same, and carrying her idea of duty to an imprudent excess, she kissed her, though she saw quite well what was the nature of her illness, which was of a most malignant kind.

She stayed with the Empress Joseph while she was bled, did all she could to comfort her, and then retired, giving orders that the Archdukes Ferdinand and Maximilian and the Archduchesses Elisabeth and Josepha, who had never had small-pox, should be kept out of the way of infection.

For herself it was too late: the malady quickly declared itself, and in a few days the Empress Josepha was dead and the Empress-mother in the greatest danger. Grief and consternation spread through the city; the churches were filled to overflowing with crowds who flocked there to pray for the recovery of their beloved sovereign; but on the 1st of June she asked for the last Sacraments, which were administered to her by the Cardinal Archbishop of Vienna in the presence of the

Emperor Joseph and the Archduchesses Marianne and Amalie.

However, a day or two later the Empress was slightly better, and before long she began with a trembling hand a letter, which was finished by her secretary, to Christine, who had been kept in ignorance of her mother's illness, telling her that she had had the small-pox but was now out of danger, that by her express orders the nature of the illness had been concealed from her, and that she forbade her to make herself uneasy or anxious about her, but she must thank God, as she was now getting well again. But the terrible malady had for ever destroyed the beauty which the Empress had until then preserved.

Vienna was now filled with jubilation: *Te Deums* were sung and splendid services performed in the churches in thanksgiving for the recovery of the Empress; *fêtes* were given, and everywhere signs of rejoicing prevailed. Preparations were made on a magnificent scale for the marriage of the Archduchess Josepha to the King of Naples. Although she was the fifth daughter of Maria Theresia, she was the first whose approaching marriage appeared about to fulfil one of the ardent wishes of the Empress.

Her *trousseau* was ordered with unusual splendour: costly laces and stuffs of all descriptions were chosen, and the Princess Charlotte was commissioned to order a hundred costumes in Paris for her niece. These were shown publicly in Vienna, to the great discontent of the tradespeople there; unfortunately many of the stuffs, especially the velvets, had got damaged during the voyage.

The young Archduchess, now sixteen years old, resigned herself to the fate she could not avoid; the formal demand in marriage was made by the Ambassador of Naples, and her governess, the Countess von Lerchenfeld, fastened the portrait of the King of Naples to her *corsage* in sign of betrothal.

For the first time since the death of the Emperor Franz the Empress-mother appeared in public at the magnificent balls given in honour of her daughter's marriage; the Emperor Joseph declared his intention of himself escorting his favourite sister to Naples, and in August accompanied her in her pilgrimage to the church of Maria Zell, according to the custom of the imperial family, late in the same month.

In the vaults of the Capucine church at Vienna were buried the Emperor Franz and other members of the family, and into those gloomy depths on stated occasions Maria Theresia used to descend with her children to pray at the bier of her husband. She insisted upon Josepha's doing so for the last time before she left Vienna, although the young Archduchess was frightened at the thought of it and entreated her mother with tears not to force her to go there, as she felt a horror which she could not overcome. It was all of no avail; the Empress would not listen, and her obstinate, cruel folly in this matter resulted in the death of one daughter and ruined the prospects of another.

Josepha burst into tears as she got into the carriage and shuddered all the time the gloomy function was going on in the vault, in which was also the bier of the Empress Joseph, who had died four months before of virulent small-pox.

Soon after she returned to the palace the young Archduchess complained of feeling ill, went to bed, and very soon the small-pox declared itself.

The Emperor Joseph, distracted with grief, never left her bedside; the gentle young girl whom every one loved felt she was dying, asked him for the last Sacraments, and passed away patient and resigned, as she had been to the marriage she dreaded. She died in his arms on the 15th of October, 1767, the very day on which they were to have started for Italy.[1]

This terrible event shocked and startled the public. Josepha's illness and death were generally attributed to her enforced visit to the vault of the Capucins, and amidst the universal chorus of alarm and disapproval were heard indignant murmurs against the continued obstinacy of the Empress, who persisted in her foolish, fatal confidence in her favourite doctor, Van Swieeten, from whose deplorable system of treatment it seems astonishing that any one could recover.

The constant bleeding and other stupid, dangerous practices in which Van Swieeten persisted, in spite of the general outcry, were of course fatal to the

[1] This story is told by Vehse, Berman, and other historians. Arneth, in his volume on "Maria Theresia's letzte Regierungszeit," merely states that Josepha paid this visit to the vault according to the pious custom of the imperial house, that she was accompanied by the Emperor Joseph, shortly before the time fixed for her departure, was seized by the small-pox on the 4th of October, and died on the 15th of October. The rest of the story, of her terror and the obstinate harshness of the Empress, he neither affirms nor denies.

delicate girl of sixteen, but when four days after her death the Archduchess Elisabeth was also seized with the same malady, she also was, by the fatuity of her mother, placed under his care. The Emperor Joseph was furious, and swore that he would never see Van Swieeten again.

Elisabeth, however, was four-and-twenty and much stronger than her sister; therefore, wonderful to relate, she survived the treatment, but of her surpassing beauty there remained no trace. Had it not been for this disfigurement she might very possibly have become Queen of France; as it was, no marriage was found for her, much to her disappointment. Elisabeth, who was always very anxious to marry, was certainly unlucky in having no husband found for her. Every proposed match had failed. The Empress, writing of her to Christine, observes:

"Quelques minutes après elle commença à sangloter . . . que tous étoient établies et elle seule étoit délaissée et destinée de rester seule avec l'Empereur, c'est (ce) qu'elle ne faira (ferait) jamais. Nous avions toutes les peines à la faire taire."

The grief of the Emperor for the loss of the sister he loved best excited general sympathy and attention, the despair into which the loss of his first wife had plunged him having been supposed to have deprived him of the capacity to feel so much affection for any one else. But he was certainly especially unfortunate, for the one other person whom he loved so much that he called her his second self, his only child, died, as her mother had foretold, in the following year.

The little Archduchess Theresia returned her father's devotion; she loved him passionately, and in her last illness would take no food or medicine but from his hand. After the last terrible catastrophe caused by the small-pox the Empress, terrified lest she should lose any more of her children, consented to the inoculation of the rest of the imperial family.

PART II

MARIA CAROLINA

CHAPTER V

Carolina and Antoinette—"You are fifteen years old"—Mother and daughter—Carolina or Amalie?—The choice of the King of Naples—Unwillingness of Carolina—The Empress insists—Amalie and the Duke of Parma—The Countess von Lerchenfeld—"Love your husband."

"OF all my daughters," wrote the Empress to Countess von Enzenberg, alluding to the Archduchess Carolina, "she is the one who resembles me the most."

And she seems to have loved her even more than her other daughters after Christine, to whom she wrote some years later of the Queen of Naples: "Vous savez combien m'est à cœur votre sœur et je lui dois cette justice, qu'après vous c'est elle qui m'a toujours marqué le plus d'attachement réel et à suivre et souhaiter mes conseils."[1]

Not that Carolina was by any means a gentle, submissive, sweet-tempered girl like Josepha; no, she was hasty, impetuous, and thoughtless, as appears from certain letters written by her mother at this time.

She and her younger sister Antoinette, to whom

[1] "You know how near to my heart your sister is, and I owe her this justice, that after you she is the one who has always shown me the most real affection and desired and followed my advice."

she was devoted, had been hitherto under the care of Countess Marie von Brandis, with whom Carolina does not seem to have got on very well. At any rate, when it was decided that Josepha's marriage should take place, Carolina entreated her mother to let her have the Countess von Lerchenfeld for her governess instead, after Josepha was gone. The Empress appears to have been of opinion that Carolina and Antoinette had got into idle, careless ways, that they talked nonsense together, and that Carolina, at any rate, was too childish for her age. She therefore decided to separate these two—to place Carolina under the care of Countess von Lerchenfeld, who was very superior to what she called "the Brandis"; and she wrote a long letter of reproof and warning to Carolina, who, now that Josepha was to be married, would take her place and be considered grown up, though she was only just fifteen.

"You wish so much to be separated from 'the Brandis,' and beg so hard to be entrusted to Frau von Lerchenfeld," she writes to her on August 19, 1767, "that I will only hope and believe that it is from esteem for the latter, who has been so successful in the education of your sisters. I do not intend to treat you as a child. You are fifteen years old, and if you make proper use of the talents with which God has so richly endowed you, and follow the good advice which is required by everybody of whatever age, you will earn the approbation of your family and of the public.'. . . To my great astonishment I hear, not only from 'the Brandis,' but from your other women and even from strangers, that you say your prayers very carelessly, without reverence, without attention, and, still more, without fervour. Do not be surprised if, after such a beginning of the day, nothing goes well. Even if representations are made to you they only cause rough words and ill-temper. Besides this, you have lately got into the habit of treating your ladies in a manner which (and this also I know from strangers) has brought great discredit upon you. While dressing you are just as ill-humoured; on this point there is neither forgetfulness nor the least excuse. You must treat your ladies with gentleness, or else you will never be esteemed, much less loved by them; and it is only a bad habit which has led you into this fault. Your voice and manner of speaking are also displeasing. You must take more trouble than others to amend this, and be careful not to raise your voice too much. You must work diligently at your music, drawing, history, geography, Latin, and other studies. Never be idle, for idleness is dangerous for every one, and especially for you, whose head must always be occupied to keep you from playing childish tricks, making improper observations, and longing for unsuitable and unreasonable amusements. As I shall now treat you as a grown-up person, I tell you you will be entirely separated from your sister. I forbid you all secrets, confidences and conversations with her; if the little one tries to begin again you have only to pay no attention or to tell 'the Lerchenfeld' or your ladies. All this mischief-making will then be put an end to at once; for all these secret confidences consist of nothing but speaking against your neighbour, your family, or your ladies. I warn you that you will be strictly watched, and I look to you as the elder, and consequently the most reasonable, to influence your sister. Avoid all discourses and secrets as you go to church, at table, or at home. Attach yourself to your sister Amalie, leave off the childish curiosity which annoys everybody, attend to your own business instead of other people's. . . . Next year you will be as old as your sister Josepha is now . . . you take rank after Amalie. . . . I was pleased with your behaviour at Laxenburg; you said very little, which did not signify. I hope you did the same in your own room. If you will take my advice, which comes from my heart, filled with love for my children and only occupied with their happiness so far as it can be attained in this world, you will be convinced that the only path to follow is that of virtue. With God's help one can do much, but in order to gain it one must lead an innocent life. . . . You will see how much sweeter and more lasting are inward peace and happiness than all the tumultuous pleasures of this world, which only weary one and leave a terrible void behind them. Above all, rely on my help and love; they will only end with my life."[1]

Only a few weeks after this letter was written came the dreadful catastrophe of Josepha's death, by which the future of Carolina was entirely changed. For the grief and shock of this calamity did not cause the Empress to lose sight for a moment of

[1] Arneth

that project of alliance with the house of Bourbon which she considered of supreme importance.

Immediately after the death of the Archduchess Josepha, she directed Count Franz Colloredo, Austrian Ambassador at Madrid, while carefully avoiding taking the first step in the affair, to contrive secretly that a third Archduchess should take the place of her two sisters.

There was no difficulty about this: the King of Spain, equally anxious for the alliance, directly he heard of Josepha's death, wrote to the Empress proposing that another of her daughters should become Queen of Naples, but not specifying any one of them.

As it happened, it would have suited Maria Theresia better at this moment to betroth Amalie to the young King, for she had it in her mind to marry one of the Archduchesses to him and another to the Duke of Parma, and, as the latter was even younger than the former, it appeared to her more suitable to give the elder of her daughters to the elder of the two deplorable boys she had chosen for their husbands. The difference in their age was certainly slight, but the accounts she heard of Ferdinando of Naples made the Empress very uneasy, and although the possibility of giving up the alliance never entered her mind, she thought that Amalie, who was five years older than Ferdinand, might be able to influence him and to hold her own in what was evidently to be a difficult and dangerous position, better than Carolina, a thoughtless, impetuous child, still in the hands of her governess.

The immense importance in former times attached to these alliances, more than the personal ambition of the Empress, must be taken into account when one considers what it really meant. A child whom she had brought up as strictly as a nun, whom she had just been lecturing about saying her prayers, attending to her lessons, obeying her governess, and not playing tricks with her little sister, was to be sent to rule without restraint or protection over a licentious southern court, as the wife of a vicious, uneducated boy of low tastes and uncontrolled passions, whose conversation, ideas, and habits must be equally astonishing and shocking to her.

Not that anything would have made these marriages tolerable to either of them.

A much more suitable husband was proposed for Amalie, namely, Carl von Zweibrücken, cousin and heir-presumptive of the Elector of Bavaria and the Elector Palatine, the former of whom asked for the hand of the Archduchess Amalie and made proposals concerning their establishment. Prince Carl spent some time at the court of Vienna, and as he was good-looking, intelligent, and about the same age as the Archduchess, she was anxious to accept him. Maria Theresia, instigated by Kaunitz, refused her consent, signifying that, his prospects being uncertain, he was not a sufficiently great personage to become her son-in-law. Carl left Vienna in disgust, and was ever afterwards the bitter enemy of Maria Theresia and Joseph II.

The Archduchess Amalie was sacrificed, like her sisters, and it was all the more unfortunate as the

CARLOS III., KING OF SPAIN.
After a painting by Mengs.

Empress and Kaunitz proved to have been quite wrong in their calculations. Carl succeeded to the inheritance upon which Kaunitz declared it was ridiculous to reckon, and Amalie might have been not only a powerful princess but a happy woman had it not been for this mistake.[1]

The Empress replied to the King of Spain's letter, offering him the choice of either Amalie or Carolina :

"Comme je n'ai certainement pas moins d'empressement à unir ma maison à celle de V.M. que celui qu'Elle veut bien me témoigner, je Lui accorde avec bien du plaisir une des filles qui me restent, pour réparer la perte de celle que nous regrettons. J'en ai actuellement deux qui peuvent convenir; l'une est l'Archiduchesse Amélie, que l'on trouve bien de figure et qui est d'une santé à annoncer, à ce qu'il semble, une nombreuse succession, et l'autre est l'Archiduchesse Charlotte,[2] qui est aussi d'une très bonne santé et d'environ un an et sept mois plus jeune que le Roi de Naples. Je laisse à V.M. la liberté de choisir. . . ."[3]

---

[1] Arneth.
Kaunitz said that considering the age of the two Electors, it was absurd to reckon upon their never having male heirs, and that consequently the proposal was almost ridiculous enough to be an offence.

[2] Charlotte was one of the names of the Archduchess.

[3] "As I certainly have no less anxiety to ally my house to that of your Majesty than that which your Majesty is good enough to display to me, I grant with great pleasure one of the daughters remaining to me to repair the loss of her we regret. I have now two who might be suitable, the Archduchess Amalie, who is considered pretty, and whose health appears to promise a numerous succession, the other is the Archduchess Charlotte, who has also very good health and is about a year and seven months younger than the King of Naples. I leave your Majesty at liberty to choose.'.

To the King of Spain it was indifferent which of the Archduchesses his son married, but the King of Naples did not at all like the idea of a wife five years older than himself, and urgently entreated his father, who consulted him on the subject, to choose Carolina.

The King accordingly wrote to Maria Theresia, with many complimentary phrases, saying that although he would be deeply grateful for whichever of her daughters she chose to give him, still, as the Archduchess Amalie was five years older than his son, and as the King of Naples had expressed the strongest desire that Carolina and no other should become his wife, he would, since the Empress gave him the choice, decide upon the latter.

Carolina was no better pleased than Josepha had been when she was told she was to marry the King of Naples. The fate of both the sisters whose place she was called upon to fill might well make the young girl shrink with an almost superstitious dread from the ill-omened engagement.

She remonstrated, cried, entreated, alluded to the deaths of her sisters, and declared that ill-luck followed the Neapolitan betrothals.[1]

And she had heard quite enough about Ferdinand to make her dislike the prospect of him as a husband.

But it was all of no avail. The Empress and Kaunitz had resolved upon the sacrifice of the two Archduchesses to secure the alliance of Naples and Parma, and they were both obliged to submit.

[1] Berman.

Amalie was even worse off than Carolina, for although the accounts received at Vienna of the young Duke of Parma were much better than what was reported of the King of Naples, it was not at all likely that a young woman of three-and-twenty would wish to marry a boy of seventeen; her rank as Duchess of Parma was much below that of her younger sister, the Queen of Naples; while as to their future homes there could be no comparison. Let anyone who knows them compare the little capital of Parma, in the midst of the wide, hot plain stretching away towards the Alps and the Apennines, with the great city of Naples, its blue sea and enchanting scenery, of which the old proverb says "See Naples—and die."[1]

Besides which, the Duke of Parma proved quite different from the cultivated, well-educated youth described to the Empress and her daughter, and when once he was set free from his studies and married, he turned out to be a remarkably stupid, idle boy, who, like his cousin of Naples, was fond of low company, and delighted to amuse himself by roasting chestnuts and winding up clocks.

Amalie, a dull, cold, apathetic girl, the least loved of all the children of the Empress, was both unhappy and unpopular at Parma, and did not get on with her husband nearly so well as Carolina did with Ferdinand of Naples. There were constant quarrels, and she does not seem to have had either the tact, charm, or sense by which she

---

[1] The Bishop of Parma said of that climate that they had "nove mesi d' inverno e tre d' inferno" (Autobiography of Cornelia Knight)

might have succeeded in gaining influence and consideration.

Her wedding did not take place till 1769, the year after that of Carolina, who, when soon after the death of Josepha her marriage was arranged, was allowed to wait for its celebration until the following year, 1768, and was meanwhile placed, as she wished, under the care of the Countess von Lerchenfeld.

That lady, who had spent three years in educating Josepha to occupy the throne of Naples, now did her best to prepare Carolina, in the nine months allowed her, for the same exalted position.

That, short as the time was, she knew how to acquire before it was over the deepest affection and respect from her wilful, thoughtless, but warm-hearted pupil, and to gain a strong influence over her, proves the wisdom of the Empress in her choice. She herself endeavoured by advice and all other means in her power to strengthen and prepare the young girl for the trials, dangers, and temptations of the life upon which she was so soon to enter.

"Never have I undertaken anything," she writes, "which has so deeply interested and occupied me, and given me, at the same time, so much consideration and so much pleasure as the efforts which I am now making to prepare you satisfactorily for your future position," and she goes on to give her most excellent advice on all kinds of subjects—her duties as a queen and as a wife, as daughter-in-law of the King of Spain, as the ruler of the court, &c. "Avoid coquetry," she continues; "you have always seen it despised here. Remember that many things which are harmless in a girl are not so in a married woman, although contemptible in either. . . . Love your husband and be firmly attached to him; that is the only true happiness on earth."

Yes; Maria Theresia's advice was always excellent, but it had this drawback: she required of her daughters more than was possible to any human being. She forced them to marry vicious, unattractive, or stupid boys—perhaps, as in the case of Amalie, years younger than themselves—whom they did not want to marry, and then told them to love their husbands. What could be a greater mockery?

And she could by no means point to her own career as an example, or to the happiness of Christine with Albrecht of Saxe-Teschen. It was easy enough for her to love François de Lorraine, one of the handsomest and most fascinating men of the day, and for Christine to be devoted to Albrecht of Saxe-Teschen, a brilliant soldier and a man of high character and remarkable attractions; but to desire Amalie to love the Infant of Parma was preposterous, and as to Ferdinand of Naples, the only wonder was that he and Carolina should have got on as well as they did.

With the exception of Christine, Maria Carolina was certainly more than all the daughters of the Empress a born ruler, and of this her mother was well aware.

In that extremely interesting and instructive book, "The Queen of Naples and Lord Nelson," occurs the following passage : [1] "Few persons were better qualified to bear testimony to the resemblance of the two sisters [2] and to the intellectual superiority of the Queen of Naples than the Marchioness Solari, who, as the confidential and devoted servant of the French Queen, cannot have come to Maria Carolina's presence for the first time with any predisposition to find her superior to Marie Antoinette. Speaking of her Majesty of Naples as one who in her figure and countenance bore so strong a resemblance to her murdered sister, the Marchioness exhibits the mental and moral difference between the two Princesses in these words : 'For this Princess' (*i.e.*, Maria Carolina) 'really possessed a masculine understanding, with great natural and acquired powers of mind, scarcely inferior to those enjoyed by the profoundest statesman. She had a cool head in council, was capable of forming a just conception of things in general, and had acquired a knowledge of men and manners far exceeding that of her unfortunate sister, Marie Antoinette of France; who, though she had a greater portion of the milk of human kindness in her composition than Carolina, possessed a capacity by no means capable of executing any plan that required firmness or perseverance. She nevertheless had a large share of natural good sense.'"

Yet Maria Theresia undoubtedly loved her children deeply, and had a thorough comprehension

[1] "The Queen of Naples and Lord Nelson" (John Cordy Jeaffreson).
[2] Maria Carolina and Marie Antoinette.

of the character of each of them. Knowing that Carolina was intensely German in tastes and affections, that she loved the grey skies, green meadows, and deep woods of her native land, and that Italy had no attraction for her, she wrote:

"Do not be always talking about our country, or drawing comparisons between our customs and theirs. There is good and bad to be found in every country.... In your heart and in the uprightness of your mind be a German; in all that is unimportant, though in nothing that is wrong, you must appear to be Neapolitan."

Carefully she explained to the young girl that even if she found it impossible to love her husband, she must on no account allow him to perceive it, but must act always as if she were passionately in love with him. Taking into consideration the character and education of Ferdinando, it was evident that if affairs were to go on with even tolerable prosperity, Carolina must not only rule him but rule the kingdom; and the great Empress remembered her own past, considered her young daughter's capacity, and felt that she could do both.

CHAPTER VI

Marriage of Carolina to the King of Naples—Her journey—The Grand-duke of Tuscany—Arrival at Naples—Unhappiness of Carolina—Letters of Leopold to his mother—Of Carolina to her governess—Becomes reconciled to her lot—Her influence over the King—"My wife knows everything"—*Fête* at Naples—Visit of the Emperor Joseph—The King of Naples and the Duke of Parma.

ON the 17th of April, 1768, Carolina was married by proxy at the Church of the Augustines at Vienna, the King of Naples being represented by her brother Ferdinand.

Immediately after her return from the church she put on her travelling dress of blue and gold, and then came the bitter parting from home, country, mother, brothers and sisters and friends, to go for ever into a foreign land, to a strange, perhaps a bad husband, with very little prospect of seeing most of those dearest to her again. One can scarcely realise how terrible all this must have been in those days of difficult travelling and communication, especially to a young, warm-hearted girl, and the prospect of being separated from her German suite made things seem worse.

She was still by no means reconciled to her

JOSEPH II., EMPEROR OF GERMANY, AND LEOPOLD, GRAND DUKE OF TUSCANY, AFTERWARDS EMPEROR, 1782.

marriage, but declared that "they might as well have thrown her into the sea."[1]

The Emperor Joseph would not go with her, as he had intended to do with his beloved Josepha, only promising to pay her a visit the following year. The Empress, therefore, wrote to the Grand-duke of Tuscany, who willingly consented to accompany his sister, and it was arranged that she should be sent to him, under a suitable escort, to Florence. The Countess Renate Trauttmansdorff, sister of Countess Lerchenfeld, and of whom Carolina was very fond, accompanied her on her journey.

With a heavy heart she travelled, by the order of the Empress, through the magnificent Pusterthal and over the Brenner pass to Innsbruck, to visit the room in which her father died before leaving her beloved Austria. Like her sister Antoinette some time afterwards, she grew more and more depressed and unhappy as she came to the last resting-place in their mother's dominions.[2]

At Florence she was received with the greatest kindness by her favourite brother Leopold and his Spanish wife, both of whom prepared to conduct her to her new kingdom.

Leopold was not at all like his elder brother, but resembled his father, François of Lorraine, in his easy-going, kindly nature and fondness for pleasure, magnificence, and women's society. He was much pleasanter than Joseph, and Maria Carolina had all her life a great affection for him.

[1] "Correspondance inédite de Marie Antoinette" (A. Paul Vogt d'Hunolstein).
[2] Ibid.

From Florence she wrote to Frau von Lerchenfeld that although the city was wonderfully beautiful and the palaces splendid, "I remain true to my dear Vienna. Things are more beautiful here than there, but for me they have not the charm and strong attraction of Vienna."

It is very unfortunate that the letters of Carolina to her mother have been lost; she wrote home constantly during her journey.

In her first letter to Frau von Lerchenfeld, written from Innsbruck on the 17th of April, she says:

"Write to me the smallest details of my sister Antoinette, what she says, what she does, and almost what she thinks. I beg and entreat you to love her very much, for I am terribly interested for her. All the kindness you show her will be done for me. Believe me, you will work on a ground that will do you credit and increase and augment the reputation you already have. Write to me all the ceremony of the *übergab* [1]—in which room, what my dear mother, you, she, and the Brandis said."

That the Grand-duke, her brother, was exceedingly kind and sympathetic may be gathered from the letters he wrote about his young sister to their mother.

On the 29th of April, 1768—Florence—he writes:

"The disposition of the Queen is excellent; she has a good heart, she willingly accepts advice, being

[1] Probably the resignation of "the Brandis" in favour of Countess von Lerchenfeld.

anxious to do right, but she is impetuous, a little hasty and thoughtless, and has as yet too little experience of the world."

She was not allowed much time in Florence, but the cavalcade set off on the 3rd of May, and travelled by Siena and Ronciglione to Rome, where Carolina does not appear to have seen much except St. Peter's. Rome, however, excited her deepest interest, and from Marino she wrote to Frau von Lerchenfeld that she envied those who could stay there and have leisure to enjoy it, for it seemed to her so delightful.

"I am well," she continued; "but my heart is sad, for I am so near the place of my destination. In three days we shall be at Terracina, where the separation will take place, and from there it is only nineteen or twenty hours to Caserta. More than ever I long to go back to my fatherland, and see my family and my dear countrymen again. Please tell my sister that I love her dearly."

At the same time the Grand-duke wrote to his mother that the nearer the day of the meeting approached, the more uneasy his sister became; she could not get over the fear that her husband might not be pleased with her and that she might consequently be unhappy.

"She is often so agitated that she scarcely knows what she says. She is dreadfully impatient and quick tempered, but it is over directly. She means to do all we tell her, but advice which she thinks like tutelage irritates her. Her behaviour in public, except a little childishness, is good; and everything depends upon the hands into which she falls. She is extremely young, and if I may say so, has not been educated to be Queen of Naples. She was never intended for it, and her bringing up was not by any means of the best. Frau von Brandis with her roughness irritated her excitable temperament, and she could not bear her; besides which she neither gave nor knew how to give her the instruction necessary for her entrance into the world. I can assure you that the Queen sees all this herself, and if only she could have remained a year longer with Frau von Lerchenfeld the difference would soon have been apparent."

They arrived on the 12th of May at Terracina, the frontier town of the kingdom of Naples, and with intense concern and sympathy Leopold perceived that his sister was seized with such a violent fit of trembling that he feared she would faint, and she seemed broken-hearted at parting from her German suite, especially the Countess Renate Trauttmansdorff.

The ceremony took place that same day, and both Leopold and Carolina were deeply affected. The Queen spoke with such kindness and affection to her departing attendants that everybody was in tears.

During their drive from Terracina to Poztella, the first entirely Neapolitan town, where the King was to meet them, Leopold tried to encourage and comfort his trembling sister.

The King awaited them there, and her first impressions with regard to his appearance were not favourable.

"He is very ugly,"[1] she wrote soon afterwards to Frau von Lerchenfeld, "but one gets used to that; and as to his character, it is all much better than I was told. . . . What irritates me most is that he thinks he is handsome and clever, and he is neither the one nor the other. I must tell you and confess that I don't love him except from duty, but I do all I can to make him think I have a passion for him. I conduct myself with great patience and gentleness. He says that he loves me very much, but he will not do anything I want."

The marriage took place at Caserta the following day, May 13th.

With unusual tact and resolution, Carolina set herself to win the affection of this spoilt, untrained lad, her husband; but the Grand-duke wrote anxiously about her to his mother, saying that she was depressed and unhappy, hated her new life, and that he feared her health would suffer.

"By all the riches in the world," she writes to Frau von Lerchenfeld, "I could not repay the good and excellent service you have done me, for what little success I have here I owe to you, and I envy my sister Antoinette, who, being longer under your care, will become more perfect. . . . I have always had great and especial love for her, and when I reflect that her fate will, perhaps, be like mine, I wish I could write volumes to her about it, and I desire greatly that she may have some one with her like me at the beginning, otherwise I frankly own

[1]. Ferdinando was tall, slight, and his face would have been handsome, but was spoilt by his large, hooked nose, an exaggeration of that of the Bourbon family (Jeaffreson).

that it is desperation, and that one suffers a martyrdom which is all the worse because one has to appear always pleased. I know what it is, and I pity deeply those who still have to make the beginning. For my part, I tell you plainly that I would rather die than suffer what I suffered at first. Now it is all right; therefore I can say, and it is no exaggeration, if Religion had not said to me, 'Think of God,' I should have killed myself, and that to live a week seemed to me like hell, and I wanted to die. I am sure that if once my sister came during the first days of her arrival I should shed many tears, picturing to myself what she would suffer."

This rather confused but pathetic letter was written a few weeks after her marriage (August 13th).

In another letter to the same person, in August, she refers to the arrival of a German lad with some dogs sent by the Emperor to her husband.

"C'était plaisant a voir comme moi, la maison de Kauniz, mes femes et nous tous Allemands se sont empresse a faire tous les honneurs possibles a ce garçon que l'Empereur a envoye avec les chiens, le nom d'allemand suffit et c'est une des plus grandes recomendations ils le méritent bien et on reconait seulment bien la droiture de leurs caracteres quand on et dans un autre pays."[1]

Again the simple letter, with all its faults of composition and spelling, gives one a glimpse of the home-sick girl, half child, half woman, longing for her mother, her governess, and her little sister, yet knowing so well how to charm and fascinate her

[1] Arneth.

strange, unsympathetic husband that he became more and more in love with her, and very soon was her slave, to the dismay of the hitherto all-powerful Tanucci, who had ruled the King and kingdom with an absolute power which he now perceived to be seriously threatened.

And Carolina herself, as time went on, became gradually reconciled to her life. There were no more complaints of her husband, over whom her influence was now unbounded ; her youth, vigorous health, and elastic spirits gradually overcame her depression and sadness, and though her love for Austria remained unchanged, her sentiments towards Ferdinando had so altered that, in a letter to Frau von Lerchenfeld written in the February following her marriage, she says, though acknowledging the surpassing loveliness of her new home :

"I assure you, my dear aja,[1] that for my own taste, and if I could be with the King, I would leave this beautiful paradise and all its inhabitants and be contented to live at Hernals, and that would please me more than all the beauty here, for I love passionately my dear country and my good countrymen, and I have so strongly inspired my dear husband with the same taste that he has a great desire to go there, and if it only depended on him we should be there already."

Ferdinando IV. was the third son of Carlos III., King of Spain. When the latter succeeded his brother[2] upon the Spanish throne, he transferred

---

[1] "Aja," the Spanish name used by the family of Maria Theresia for "governess."

[2] Ferdinand VI., eldest son of Philippe V.

the kingdom of Naples and Sicily to Ferdinando, then nine years old, leaving the government in the hands of a council of eight persons and the Marquis Tanucci Prime Minister.[1]

The then "ajo," or governor, of the young King was the Principe di San Nicandro.

Over the Spanish Bourbons, the descendants of Philippe V.,[2] hung that curse of hereditary insanity which had always been the dread and horror of Carlos III.

His father and his eldest son had both been victims to melancholy, insanity, or idiotcy, and the King of Spain, anxious above all things to preserve his other sons from the same fate, directed that Ferdinando should be kept from any sedentary or serious occupation and lead an entirely outdoor life.

Tanucci and Nicandro, anxious to keep all power and authority in their own hands, purposely exaggerated what, if reasonably carried out, would have been a wise precaution, and the results were as deplorable as could be expected.

Physically, the plan was entirely successful. Ferdinando grew up strong, healthy, and active, an ardent sportsman, but an execrable king.

He had been brought up in the grossest ignorance, knew scarcely anything of any foreign tongue, and could not even speak decent Italian; the jargon of the *lazzaroni* was what he used both in his conversation and his letters to his father, which were filled with nothing but slang and sporting news.

[1] Palombo.
[2] Carlos or Charles III. of Spain, second son of Philippe V., who was grandson of Louis XIV. Philippe was subject to melancholia

Hunting, shooting, and fishing were the occupations by which his whole time was wasted when it was not spent in a still more deplorable manner among low companions or in contemptible amusements. He would dress up as an innkeeper in a country inn, making all his courtiers wear the same kind of disguises, and he and they would amuse themselves by selling wine to customers.

When he heard of the death of the Archduchess Josepha his chief regret was that he could not, for a day or two, go on with his usual games and sports. His courtiers could find nothing to amuse him until one of them thought of acting the funeral of the deceased Archduchess. A girlish-looking boy was chosen to take the part of the Archduchess, his face being marked with chocolate to represent the small-pox; he was dressed in funeral robes, laid on an open bier, and carried in procession all through the state apartments in the palace of Portici, the King following as chief mourner.[1]

An insatiable delight in practical jokes was a characteristic of Ferdinando, and these jokes had sometimes disastrous consequences, as in the case of the Florentine Abbate Mazzinghi, whom he caused to be tossed in a blanket by some of his rough companions, and who, though unhurt by the process, was so scandalised and indignant at such an insult and by not being able to obtain the punishment of its perpetrators that he retired to Rome and died a few months afterwards owing

---

[1] Helfert, however, casts doubt upon this story, which he considers to be most probably one of the many inventions or exaggerations of the political enemies of the King and Queen of Naples.

to the manner in which it preyed upon his mind.

Much better subjects for the King's amusements were his beloved *lazzaroni*, who liked him none the worse for them. One day, as he loitered about the Chiaja, he saw a tall, strong-looking, very ragged and extremely dirty beggar, whom he suddenly seized by the legs, swung round, and flung into the sea. Then, seeing from his struggles that the lad could not swim, he jumped into the water after him and brought him safely to shore.

Ferdinando was kind to the poor, had various good qualities, and if he had been brought up decently, taught self-control, and had proper instruction given him, he might have made a good king.

His great Minister, Sir John Acton, speaking of him in after-years, remarked:

"Ferdinando is a good sort of man, because Nature has not supplied him with the faculties necessary to make a bad one."

He was by no means irreligious, was very patient during illness or adversity, and when he knew him as a middle-aged man, Lord Valentia said that "good-humour was in his appearance and every motion," and that he looked like a country gentleman. That Carolina improved him immensely in manners and habits was, of course, inevitable; he would sing for hours with her and her ladies, and though he sang out of tune it was at least a civilising process; he also played whist well and was fond of dancing. But she had an arduous task before her at the beginning of her life with him.

Even on the morning after his wedding he got up very early and went out shooting.[1]

The absolute contrast between this young half savage and her own father and carefully educated brothers was, of course, at first a continual shock to the young Queen, while to him her beauty, refinement, and intellectual talents were equally surprising. Tall, slight, and handsome,[2] she resembled her mother, the Empress, in her strength of character, but not in her prudence and good sense.

Over Ferdinando, however, she soon reigned supreme. If he displeased her she insisted upon leading a separate life, and would not forgive him without many entreaties and much persuasion.

The Queen of Naples when in the prime of her youth and attractions had a beautiful oval face, very like her sister Antoinette, and if she had rather less beauty, possessed more voluptuous charm and fascination.[3]

For her opinion and capacity the King had the greatest respect and admiration ; he was often heard to say, " My wife knows everything."

She was royally generous, too—one of her first acts at Naples was to devote 20,000 ducats, given her by the city, to provide dowries for a number of young girls, who were brought to kiss her hand, amidst the acclamations of the people, at a great *fête* given in her honour on the 8th of June after her marriage.

Before Leopold left Naples he wrote to his mother an account of a boating excursion they had made,

[1] Vehse. [2] Helfert.
[3] " Marie Caroline, Reine des Deux Siciles " (André Bonnefonds).

during which they had been overtaken by a tempest and nearly drowned. He said they were picked up by a small vessel, but were still in great danger. The King had made himself ridiculous by shouting and crying with terror.

Following the instructions of her mother, the young Queen appeared to enter with sympathy into all her husband's pursuits, compassionating him after a bad day's shooting, admiring his strength and skill. Careful to direct his opinions as she desired, she always made him think that they were originated by himself, and would point out to him, after he had done exactly what she told him, how right and prudent had been his judgment.

The following year, according to his promise, the Emperor Joseph went to Naples to see his sister, of whom he wrote: "In my conversations with the Queen I have always discovered that she has an excellent disposition, good inclinations, remarkable truthfulness, a great deal of cleverness and penetration—in fact, the germ of all that is amiable and estimable; I have no doubt that although she is left to herself she will turn out well. . . . There is not the least atom of flirting about her, although she has plenty of opportunity, being always surrounded with young men; her dress is very simple and without affectation. . . . She always wears a *fichu* and is not at all *décolletée;* her dresses are so long that you cannot see even the point of her foot.

"Her devotion seems to me to be without bigotry; she says her prayers in the morning, hears Mass every day, and has always several German books out of which she prays. . . . In her room and study there seems to me an air of order and neatness. . . . She has grown scarcely at all since her departure, but has become a little fatter, which suits her and makes her prettier. . . ." He goes on to praise her demeanour with the King in public, the reserve and modesty of her manner and the restraint she imposed upon his too demonstrative love-making.

The Emperor Joseph used afterwards to tell many absurd stories of the King of Naples, whom he ridiculed and mimicked, and the mutual jealousy of the King and Queen, their disputes and reconciliations.

He had, besides, many sarcastic anecdotes and recollections of the little court of Parma, which he also visited, and of which he spoke with the greatest contempt.

Some years later he paid another visit to his sister at Parma, and found that Amalie, who was decidedly eccentric, spent nearly all her time in hunting, and often wore a man's dress.

Her husband, who had become very ascetic, used frequently to lead the life and wear the dress of a friar.

One day when he remarked to the Duchess that her headdress was not becoming, she replied:

"Oh! é bello e buono per un frate." [1]

The Emperor, her brother, irritated by this and various other proceedings, said to her that as he was going to join the King of Sweden in Rome,

[1] "Oh! it is pretty and good enough for a monk."

she had better come too, and then they could play an Italian game of cards in which the best hand consists of two kings and a card called "*la matta,*" the fool.[1]

His brother Leopold was introducing important reforms into Tuscany, and the Emperor related with much amusement a conversation he had overheard between him and the King of Naples.

After Leopold telling Ferdinando all about his new laws, edicts, and economies, instituted for the good of his subjects, the latter, who had listened in silence, asked how many Neapolitan families were established in Tuscany; and upon the Grandduke counting up a small number, he replied:

"Well, *mon frère*, I do not understand your people caring so little to seek for happiness. There are more than four times as many Tuscans living in my dominions as there are Neapolitans in yours."

When Carolina had become reconciled to her husband and accustomed to her new life, her active mind sought, as the Empress, her mother, had foretold, for interests and occupations to fill it; and, like a true daughter of Maria Theresia, she found these in the affairs of government and of charitable institutions, and also in society and intercourse with the most distinguished and interesting persons with whom she could surround herself.

The *salon* of Maria Carolina was soon frequented not only by the great nobles and courtiers, but by all the most learned, intellectual, and cultivated people to be found at Naples, old and young, whom she welcomed and protected.

[1] Autobiography of Cornelia Knight

Into the discussions, opinions, and visionary speculations of the *savants*, politicians, literary and scientific men with whom she had surrounded herself she entered with enthusiastic interest, little imagining to what the new philosophy with which she was so delighted was to lead, while she listened to the wonderful plans for regenerating the human race, setting the world to rights and increasing knowledge, set forth by young men of her own age and even younger, who would have been much better employed in pursuing their studies or working at their professions, and also by grey-headed dreamers whose imaginative gifts exceeded their common-sense. Among the latter were Cirillo, the celebrated botanist and physician; Galanti, the author of well-known books on jurisprudence; Conforti, professor of history at the University of Naples, and many others; while the political economist Galiani and Filangieri, the author of a work entitled "La Scienza della Legislazione," were about the same age as Carolina herself; Mario Pagano, author of "I Saggi Politici," was only four years older.

Filangieri had been distinguished by the Queen after a legal success gained [1] when he was only one-and-twenty. Three years afterwards she made him a gentleman of the King's bedchamber and an officer of the volunteers in the marine service, assisted him in different ways in his literary career, and rewarded him for his valuable work on legislation by giving him a lucrative post in the Royal College of Finance.

[1] 1774.

Before the eighth volume of "La Scienza della Legislazione" was published Filangieri died of fever in his thirty-seventh year; after which the Queen provided for his three children.[1] While Ferdinando was fishing, shooting, and amusing himself at Caserta, Carolina governed the kingdom with absolute authority.

Schemes for the reduction of taxes, the reclamation of waste lands, the settlement of disputes amongst the coral fishers, the planting of colonies on uninhabited islands, the establishment of secular schools, reforms and additions to the University, the endowment of more professors, the arrangement of museums and libraries and of a botanical garden were among the matters which occupied the attention of the Queen.

Immediately after her arrival at Naples it was perfectly evident to Maria Carolina that between herself and the then all-powerful Minister, Tanucci, there would be perpetual enmity.

One or other of them would rule the King and the kingdom, and the Queen was determined that this ruler should be herself; and although it was some years before she attained the complete fulfilment of her wishes, she was at length entirely successful.

[1] The widow and children of Filangieri, all of whom had been entirely supported and protected by Maria Carolina, were amongst her bitterest enemies among the Jacobins of Naples

Mon cher Charles je vous souhaite une heureuse nouvelle année et que dans celle
qui va entrer comme le Ciel vous bénisse toujours et vous conserve toutes mes
pauvres souhaits de votre amie ma sœur votre tante et aussi je dois si dois faire vous la et
enfin je que d'apprendre a votre oncle marquis vous discontinuez ou moins ou...
Je voudrais pour la nouvelle [...] au Etats Unis et au Etudes Jeanne [...]

[...] vous vous feu [...] gourvé et d'Espié et avorté dans [...]
Sedam Royer [...] montternul [...] et que je suis de tous [...]

Votre [...]

9 8bre 1790

AUTOGRAPH LETTER OF MARIA CAROLINA

CHAPTER VII

Popularity of the Queen—Tanucci—The dictation of Spain—Correspondence with the Empress—Birth of an heir—The Queen enters the Council—The lazzaroni—Amusements of the King—His love-affairs—Ambition of the Queen—Her life at Naples—Caserta—The King and the peasant woman—The court of Naples—A court intrigue—The Marchesa di San Marco—The Abbé Galiani—Second-sight—Guarini—Birth of Prince Francesco—Death of the Prince Royal.

"QUEEN MARIA CAROLINA of Naples is one of the most shamefully slandered personalities of modern history. There was a time, and a very long time, during which all the world was full of her fame; when she was amongst the leaders of fashion of the day; when her praises were sung by poets and she was surrounded by admiration and flattery."[1]

As a young Queen, Maria Carolina had the reputation of sharing in many of the current ideas of the day; gifted and enthusiastic as she was, this was only probable. Like so many women of high rank in Paris, she sympathised with the "philosophies" of the eighteenth century,[2] little imagining

---

[1] "Maria Karolina von Oesterreich, Königin von Neapel und Sicilien" (Helfert).
[2] Ibid.

that the smouldering fire she and her friends were helping to feed would burst into flame and smoke in which many of those dearest to her would perish.

Under the influence of her new opinions, in the early part of her reign, she favoured the Freemasons in her husband's dominions to such a degree that that body looked upon her and Ferdinando as their greatest protectors.[1]

When Tanucci and San Nicandro perceived the mistake they had made in their calculations with regard to the education of the King, they tried too late to instruct and interest him in State affairs and to induce him to assume the government himself. But their efforts were useless. They had, for their own ends, made Ferdinando incapable of holding the reins of government, which had now fallen, not, as they intended, into their own hands, but into those of a person with whom they had unexpectedly to reckon, and whose ideas and aspirations were entirely opposed to theirs.[2]

During the whole of the King's minority, and afterwards under his nominal authority, Tanucci had governed the Two Sicilies as if they were provinces of Spain and he a viceroy of Carlos III. All orders and directions came from Madrid, Spanish ideas and customs prevailed at court, and Spanish interests were paramount. That this state of things could be upset and altered and the whole policy of the government changed by a young girl

[1] "Maria Karolina von Oesterreich, Königin von Neapel und Sicilien" (Helfert)

[2] "Marie Caroline, Reine des Deux Siciles" (André Bonnefonds)

of sixteen, just out of the hands of her governess, had never occurred to that astute minister.

But so it was.

The dictation of Spain and the power of Tanucci were alike obnoxious to her, and she set to work to overthrow the one and oppose the other, blindly supported in whatever she wanted to do by the King, whose delight in her beauty and admiration of her cleverness increased as time went on, so that before long she was all-powerful in the State, and the influence of Austria was rapidly replacing that of Spain.

That influence was now very strong in Italy. Carolina, Leopold, Ferdinand, and Amalie reigned in Tuscany, Modena, Parma, and the Two Sicilies. From the rest of her family Carolina was divided by a far greater distance, but constant letters passed between the Empress and those of her children from whom she was separated. Three times a week did the imperial couriers leave Vienna to bring letters to Leopold, Ferdinand, Amalie, Carolina, and Antoinette (now the wife of the Dauphin), from their mother, who took the deepest interest in their affairs, health, conduct, and happiness, and who required to be made acquainted with all that went on in their courts and households.

Of her three younger daughters, Carolina was, as before stated, the one of whom she most approved.

From Amalie came little but complaints, quarrels, foolish mistakes to be corrected, offended persons to be conciliated. She did not know how to manage, or to make herself either popular or tolerably happy. Her husband was too young for her, the surroundings amongst which she found herself too uncongenial, her capacity too inferior, and her disposition too cold, dull, and unattractive for her to gain any influence.

Antoinette, on the other hand, was too young, thoughtless, and fond of pleasure and amusement, and, with all her affection and reverence for her mother, often gave very little heed to her counsels.

With Carolina, however, the Empress was so satisfied that in a letter to Mercy, complaining of something which had displeased her in Antoinette, she drew a comparison between her thoughtless conduct and that of her sister, the Queen of Naples. And one of her injunctions to her youngest daughter, on her marriage with the Dauphin, was to write constantly to her sister, the Queen of Naples, whose example she would do well to follow.

The Empress, besides giving her daughter minute instructions as to the way in which she should influence and govern her husband and his kingdom, had stipulated in the marriage contract that Carolina should sit and vote in the State Council when she had borne an heir to the throne. But for the first few years she had no children, greatly to the disappointment of her husband and herself.

One day, when they were walking in the woods of Caserta, they met a young peasant, who told them that a great calamity had just happened to him: his wife had given birth to three boys. He was unfortunate!

"Unfortunate!" cried the King "You are too fortunate! The signora and I have been married for years and have no children. How gladly I would be in your case!" He gave the man some money and a cow, for he was good-natured and kind, especially during the first part of his life, when not enraged and excited to deeds of revenge and ferocity.

However, Ferdinando and Carolina were not destined to suffer from the lack of heirs. In 1772 their first child was born, and although that and the next one were daughters, the third was the much-desired son; and between 1772 and 1794 the Queen had eighteen children, of whom most died in infancy or early youth.

Some, however, lived to grow up, marry, and survive her; and to all Ferdinando was a kind and affectionate father and Carolina a devoted mother—in fact, she used to say that she was "a mother before anything else." She bestowed the utmost care and attention on their education, amusement, and welfare; their tutors and governesses were sent from Austria.

After the birth of the Prince Royal, which was the occasion of great rejoicings, the Queen claimed her right of entering the Council, which Tanucci took upon himself to oppose. It was of no avail; the King supported the Queen, who took her seat, became more powerful than ever, and never forgave the minister who had the audacity to attempt to exclude her, but resolved not to rest until she had obtained his dismissal. He resigned in 1777, after thirty-three years of power.

Maria Carolina cultivated the friendship and confidence of the upper classes, amongst whom she became very popular; while Ferdinando, called "King of the *lazzaroni*," was the idol of this, the lowest order of the populace.

All through his childhood he had been allowed to make them his companions; he spoke their dialect, shared their amusements, and was never so happy as when amongst them.

Of this strange population, during her stay in Naples, about 1791–3, the great artist, Mme. Vigée Le Brun, writes:

"The part of the Neapolitan populace most curious to observe are the *lazzaroni*. These people have simplified life to the extent of doing without lodging and almost without food, for they have no other habitation than the steps of the churches, and their frugality equals their laziness, which is saying not a little. They are to be found lying under the shade of walls or on the sea-shore. They are scarcely clothed, and their children go naked till they are twelve years old. At first I was rather scandalised and very much frightened to see them thus playing about on the Chiaja, where carriages are constantly passing, for this road is the usual promenade of Naples, and that of the Princesses; but I soon got accustomed to it.

"The poverty of the *lazzaroni* does not make them robbers; they are, perhaps, too idle for that, more especially as they require so little to live upon. Most of the robberies are committed at Naples by hired servants, who are generally a very bad lot, the refuse of the great cities of different nations. During my sojourn there I only heard of one theft committed by a *lazzarone*, and that was so restricted that it seemed almost innocent.

"The Baron de Salis, one day when he was going to give a grand dinner, went down to his kitchen. As he came quietly downstairs he stopped short at the sight of a man who, fancying himself alone, approached the *pot-au-feu*, took out a piece of beef, and carried it away.

"The baron only watched him in silence, for all his silver plate was put out on a table; the *lazzarone* saw it perfectly, but yet the poor man limited his theft to the piece of beef which he took."[1]

The *lazzaroni* and the rest of the lower classes loved Ferdinando, who was good-natured and easy-going, whose strength and sporting achievements they admired, and to whose vices and ignorance they had no objection; while the Queen, finding it useless to try to alter him, left him at liberty to follow his low pleasures and undignified amusements and *liaisons*, while she led her own life, supported by his authority, he remaining, as ever, a tool in her hands.[2] And with this arrangement he was quite content.

The care and affection she bestowed upon her children, of whom, after the birth of the eldest, she had one nearly every year, occupied a great deal of her thoughts, in spite of the political affairs in which she was absorbed.

The relations between Spain and Naples became strained, for the Queen would permit no foreign dictation nor interference; in fact, she found

---

[1] "Souvenirs de Mme. Vigée Le Brun."
[2] André Bonnefonds.

Naples and Sicily too narrow for her ambition as she recalled the days of her childhood in her Austrian home, and the vast dominions, power, and magnificence of her mother, the great Empress.

Although she had now become accustomed to the King, and adapted, or rather resigned, herself to his ways, his society was, of course, not amusing to her. They had not a taste in common, and he was generally in the country, at Portici and Caserta, the latter the favourite summer palace of the royal family.

Here he hunted, shot, and fished to his heart's content, and carried on the love intrigues which the Queen, unable to prevent, ignored to a certain extent when they concerned obscure persons not likely to give any trouble, but put an end to if the object of the King's fancy happened to be a woman of rank and education, likely to influence him or interfere in the slightest degree in political or social matters.

For herself, freed at so early an age from all restraint, she desired the excitement and ambition of public and the freedom and enjoyments of private life, all of which she found no difficulty in obtaining. She had inherited the ambition of her mother without her austerity; from her father, François de Lorraine, came the love of pleasure and magnificence, the fondness for society, with its interests, amusements, friendships, and flirtations. Flattered and admired by all around her, thoughtless, hasty, and inconsiderate by nature—these qualities, which her mother had endeavoured to correct, and of which her brothers had spoken with regret, saying that "all depended upon the hands into which she fell," were fostered and exaggerated in the position to which she had been called, not only by the pleasures, but by the sorrows which filled her stormy life.

Carolina had never been insensible to the surpassing loveliness of her Italian home, and as time went on she became more and more attached to it—" my beautiful Naples" as she called it sadly in later years of exile.

And Caserta was an enchanting place in the still, hot, brilliant days of the long, radiant summer of Italy. Schönbrunn and Laxenburg could not rival the vast palace, with its spacious, lofty halls and corridors and saloons of marble, cool and delightful during the burning heat, the deep woods that surrounded it, the gardens, with their statues, cascades, and fountains, where Carolina made what she called an "English garden," while Ferdinando pursued his sports and pastimes in the forest, which was full of game.

One day, while the royal family were at Caserta, the King, walking about by himself, bought a turkey from an old woman whom he met not far from the palace, but who did not recognise him. He turned back to walk to the palace, accompanied by the old woman carrying the turkey. As soon as they approached drums began to beat and the guard turned out. The old woman stopped, seized hold of him, and pulled him back.

"Take care!" she exclaimed. "Get out of the way! Here is the mad King[1] coming! He would

[1] "Lou Re pazzo."

think nothing of trampling us under his horses' feet!" And she proceeded to grumble against him that he was always running about instead of minding his business, and so everything went to the devil; there was no law, no justice, and everything was very dear. While she talked in this strain the King led her through the great gates, where the manner in which he was received showed her who he was.

The old woman was dreadfully frightened, but Ferdinando, delighted with the adventure, took her to the Queen, to whom he made her tell the story, and who, equally amused, comforted her and gave her money.[1]

The twenty-two years following their marriage were spent by Ferdinando and Carolina in the greatest splendour, luxury, and prosperity.

"In our day," writes the Marchese Ulloa,[2] "no one can form an idea of what an Italian prince was, who sat peacefully on his throne, with no responsibility except to God and his conscience, beloved by his people, in the midst of a splendid court, surrounded by art, magnificence, and pleasure."

Swinburne, who spent some time at the court of Naples, expatiates on the splendour of the festivities that perpetually went on; every day brought some entertainment. He describes the magnificence of the court balls, the fairy-like illuminations constantly to be seen lighting up the great palaces, the streets, and the calm bay, where ships and fishing boats lay at anchor, while the burning mountain

[1] "Memories of the Courts of Europe" (Swinburne, 1777).
[2] Helfert.

towered above, at intervals sending forth its volume of smoke into the starry night; the races through the narrow streets, between tall houses and palaces hung with costly stuffs, their balconies filled by all the society of Naples; the drive on Sundays to Posilippo by the Chiaja, thronged with carriages; the sumptuous liveries of the servants, and the splendid sedan chairs in which the ladies went about the streets. He describes also a magnificent procession through the Toledo of sledges and sportsmen of different nations, splendidly dressed, and watched from open windows thronged with spectators leaning upon tapestries and silken hangings.[1]

There seemed to be no end to the balls and the *fêtes* of different kinds. The taking the veil by a daughter of a Neapolitan house was an occasion of great ceremonial and expense; it often cost more than a marriage, including the function and the pension paid afterwards to the nun.

Large families prevailed at Naples; the Duchessa di Monterolando had more than twenty children, and when one of her daughters took the veil the music and ceremonial expenses cost a thousand pounds.

The nuns in and about Naples were very rich, and enjoyed a great deal of liberty. Every summer the Queen would visit each convent in turn and be entertained by the nuns, with the large suite by which she was accompanied.

Swinburne describes the King as boyish, good-natured, and boisterous, telling amusing stories

[1] "Memories of the Courts of Europe" (Swinburne).

and always carrying on intrigues with women—chiefly *contadine*.[1] The opera dancer Rossi, one of his favourites, afterwards married to an Italian noble, always came to her balcony when the King was on his, to see the masquerades. Ferdinando was also very fond of music and danced well.

Amongst others he carried on an intrigue with a beautiful dancer named Bretella, with whom a certain Austrian, Baron Ambrosius von Leykam, was also in love. One day the Baron, while visiting her, was nearly surprised by the King, and in his haste to escape from the house slipped upon a polished floor and lamed himself for life. However, he married La Bretella and took her to Vienna. Their second daughter, Antonia, born in 1806, was so lovely that Prince Metternich, then a widower, became passionately in love with her, and married her, to the utter astonishment of all Vienna. For, besides the scandal of the Bretella, the Leykam were à *parvenus* family who had risen in the postal service; and such a marriage was opposed to every sentiment, principle, and idea which that haughty and illustrious statesman had entertained and professed during his whole life. But he adored Antonia, and for fifteen months their marriage was a romance of love. Then Antonia bore a son, Richard, his heir; and after thanking him for the unspeakable happiness of her short wedded life, died in his arms. He never left her, and in his grief and despair offered the doctors all the treasures and favours of the monarchy if they could save her.

[1] Peasants.

His first marriage had been one entirely of convenience; his third wife, Mélanie, of the great Zichy family, he never loved; the portrait of Antonia always hung before his writing-table, in spite of the jealousy and anger it aroused in her successor.

It was not so much to these dancers and *contadine* that the Queen objected—she considered them too far beneath her notice; but when the King's attention was attracted by any one of a different class she at once interfered.

The Duchessa di Lucciana, daughter of the Marchese Gonzuela, Secretary of State, was at one time an object of her suspicion; so much so that on the night of a State ball at the palace, being displeased by the flirtation between her and the King, she stopped the ball, and every one had to leave.

It was remarked that this was jealousy of power, not of love,[1] but it was quite necessary for her to be watchful in order to guard against the plots from time to time organised to get the King under another influence.

In one of these conspiracies the Marchesa di San Marco, one of the beauties of the court, arranged a plan, with the assistance of the Prince della Rocca and one or two others, to captivate the King, and by using many precautions and carrying on the intrigue at Caserta while the Queen was at Naples, to prevent her knowing anything about it.

At first it was successful; the King was, of course, only too delighted, but after a time the Queen found out what was going on. She appeared at Caserta very angry and at once put an end to the

[1] "Gelosia d' impero, non gelosia d' amore."

affair. She brought back the King to Naples, and forgave him on his promising to give up the Marchesa di San Marco, whom she exiled from Naples. The Prince della Rocca prudently retired to his estates in the country. Some time afterwards the King sent him the ribbon of San Gennaro, in consequence of which he returned to court, waited on the King and Queen to thank them, and was graciously received by both their Majesties. When he was gone Ferdinando told Carolina that he had been an agent in the San Marco affair, to which she replied :

"You have told me too late."

A witty story is told concerning this same Marchesa di San Marco, whose evil reputation was well known at Naples.

A conspicuous figure at the Neapolitan court was the Abbé Galiani, who had lived much in Paris, where he belonged to the philosophical set, was a friend of Voltaire, and frequented the *salons* of Mme. du Deffand and Mme. Geoffrin. He was clever, amusing, a favourite with the King of Spain,[1] and consequently an object of the jealousy of Tanucci.

A dispute was going on one day between the Abbé and some others, in which the former was endeavouring to prove that the Gospel of St. Mark (San Marco) was an abstract of that of St. Matthew (San Matteo). Some one, tired of the subject, tried to change the conversation, and began to speak of the beauty of certain women of Naples—amongst others of Signora di San Marco.

[1] Carlos III.

"Eh! what is the use of it?" he exclaimed. "Have not I told you twenty times that *San Marco* is the epitome of *San Matteo*." Now San Matteo was the name of that quarter of Naples usually inhabited by the *demi-monde*.[1]

A very different ecclesiastic sometimes to be met there was a Scotchman, the Abbé Grant, who had been concerned in the rising of 1745. He was arrested and sent to London in the same ship with Balmerino, Kilmarnock, and other unfortunate adherents of the Stuarts. During the voyage a Scotch servant, said to possess second-sight, remarked to him, "You will be saved."

"I fear not, my friend," replied the Abbé, shaking his head.

"You will," reiterated the man; "but you will be the only one."

The Abbé did not believe him, as he had no friends to intercede for him and he knew the court party was bitter against him. By the merest chance, however, no proofs were forthcoming and no witnesses appeared against him. He was accordingly acquitted and retired to Italy, where he spent the rest of his life—chiefly in Rome.

Gossip, it need scarcely be said, did not spare the Queen, who was incautious, fond of admiration, and eager to amuse herself; and the King was always glad to seize the opportunity to retort when she complained of his proceedings.

A young officer named Guarini was at one time foolishly distinguished by her, and, what was more

---

[1] "Eh! à che serve? non vi ho detto già venti volte che San Marco è l' epitome di San Matteo?"

foolish still, she made confidences about him to her friend the Duchess of San Severo. Afterwards she quarrelled with the Duchess, who, out of revenge, persuaded her husband to tell the King of the flirtation between the Queen and Guarini.

The King was delighted, and next time the Queen was jealous he retorted with some remark about Guarini which showed her that she had been betrayed. And at a grand supper at Posilippo Ferdinando led Guarini up to the Queen and made him sit next to her, saying that was his place.

The Queen, though very angry, could say nothing, and the King considered it an excellent joke; but Carolina's vexation gave her an attack of fever. She sent Guarini away to Turin, where she gave him a house, and the affair was at an end.

In 1777 the Queen, who was expecting another child, caused a sensation by dismissing her doctor, Viventor—a corrupt, ignorant, brutal fellow, who had obtained his post by marrying one of her favourite maids—and engaging an Englishman named Pears in his place. Viventor had somehow acquired the King's favour, meddled in everything, even in naval affairs, did infinite mischief, and made himself generally odious.[1]

Carolina was at a ball when she suddenly felt ill and retired, soon after which the roar of cannon announced the birth of a prince. The King on this occasion gave the Queen 100,000 ducats and an allowance of 50,000; all of which she spent in a year. This prince was Francesco, soon by his brother's death to become Prince Royal. One

[1] Swinburne.

FERDINAND IV. AND MARIA CAROLINA (KING AND QUEEN OF NAPLES) AND THEIR FAMILY.

of the few sentiments shared by Ferdinando and Carolina was their love for their children, especially for the little Prince Royal, a pretty, engaging child, of whom Christine's husband, Albrecht of Saxe-Teschen, wrote with much approval during a visit to Naples.[1]

But the following year the little Carlo, who had always been delicate, died of small-pox, to the inexpressible grief of his parents.

The King, though devoted to his children, seldom if ever gave them any presents himself, but let them have everything they wanted through the Queen. One day, however, he gave his eldest daughter a gold piece, with which the child was so delighted that she threw her arms round him and hugged him.

On the Queen asking why she was so overjoyed, when she herself gave her so many presents, the child replied:

"Ah, mamma, but this is the first I was ever able to get out of papa!"

Upon which the King became quite affected and cast down.

Too much money was squandered in the costly revels and extravagant life of the court to leave anything to continue the improvements begun by Carlos III., who had built the palaces of Portici and Caserta and the great hospital, begun the excavations at Pompeii and Herculaneum and the great road along the sea, made other roads, the Strada Nuova, and the Mola.

[1] "Er hat eine offene, freundliche Physiognomie."

CHAPTER VIII

The Queen's Government—Acton—Death of the Empress Maria Theresia—Scandalous reports—Jealousy of the King—Violent scene—Reconciliation—Visit of the Archduchess Christine—Scenes in an earthquake—On board the fleet—Death of the King of Spain—Of two children of the Queen—The eve of the French Revolution—Mme Le Brun—Journey to Vienna—Death of the Emperor Joseph—Marriages of two daughters of the Queen—Coronation of the Emperor Leopold—Stay in Austria—Rome—Marie Antoinette—Varennes—Escape of the Comte and Comtesse de Provence—The Archduchess Christine.

THE military forces of the kingdom having fallen into neglect, the Queen turned her attention towards their improvement, and, what was still more necessary, to the consideration of the unprotected condition of the coasts, in constant peril not only from the attacks of the enemy in time of war, but at all times from the ravages of the corsairs from Barbary, Morocco, and all along the North Coast of Africa.

It was obvious that a proper fleet was necessary for the protection of the seaboard towns, villages, fishing, and trading vessels; but the fleet must have an admiral, and Carolina looked in vain amongst the Neapolitans for a suitable person.

Finding nobody who was at all possible, she turned her attention and inquiries to other countries, and fixed her choice upon an officer named Acton, at that time head of the Tuscan navy, whom she persuaded her brother Leopold to give up to her.

Acton was of English[1] parentage, but born at Besançon; he had been for a time in the French navy and afterwards entered the Tuscan service, in which he had rapidly distinguished himself.

He had invented certain light, swift sailing ships, by which the Tuscan *renfort* had protected the retreat of the Spanish fleet during an expedition against Algiers; had rendered invaluable service to the Tuscan navy, and was evidently just the sort of man required to take the direction of naval affairs at Naples, where the Queen, delighted to have secured him, made him Minister of Marine and set him to reorganise the fleet (1779).

Subtle, penetrating, intelligent, capable, he was the ideal Minister of her dreams. Very soon he was made Minister of War, was loaded with honours, and before long was the most powerful personage in the country.

His influence with the Queen became unbounded; gradually he helped her to throw off the Spanish yoke; the navy was increased and reorganised, and various changes and projects carried out according to the desires of the Queen.

The death of her mother in 1780 was a severe

---

[1] Son of an English Jacobite who emigrated to Besançon, where he practised as a physician. In 1791 he succeeded his distant cousin, Sir Richard Acton, of Aldenham Hall, Shropshire. Of his two sons, Ferdinand Richard Edward succeeded to the baronetcy, Charles Januarius Edward entered holy orders and became a Cardinal. Sir Ferdinand's son was made Baron Acton, December, 1869.—" The Queen of Naples and Lord Nelson " (Jeaffreson).

sorrow and calamity. The Empress was only sixty-four, and ever since her daughter's marriage had kept up a constant correspondence with her; her counsels and influence could not be spared by the excitable, wilful young Queen, who, in her, lost the only being in the world who had the right to blame or advise her in every circumstance of her life, and to whom she looked up with love and reverence as her superior.

That the Neapolitan navy should be, as it soon became, more than strong enough to protect the country without having recourse to Spain, did not suit the Spanish King, who was imprudent enough to desire his son to dismiss Acton, by which interference he only estranged Ferdinando and infuriated Carolina. Not only the fleet but the army was increased and made efficient, Acton inviting foreign officers and drill-sergeants to fill the posts for which the Neapolitans were utterly incompetent, and thereby incurring the jealousy and hatred of the latter.

When Acton arrived at Naples he was about forty or forty-two years of age, by no means handsome, but a courteous, agreeable man of the world, with all the knowledge and experience acquired in a varied and adventurous life.

Carolina was about twenty-eight, in the height of her beauty, supreme in power, rash and inconsiderate in character, with a husband altogether her inferior intellectually and morally, with whom she had scarcely an idea in common.

The court of Naples was at that time a remarkably scandalous one, but in any case it was impossible that the intimate friendship which arose between the Queen and the Minister should not have caused considerable comment.

The position of women at Naples was widely different from the way in which they were regarded in Austria, and Carolina was not at all likely to act with prudence or caution, nor to escape calumny even if she had been more circumspect, considering her exalted position, the party she represented, and the enemies with whom she was surrounded. When one remembers the outrages and infamies circulated by the radicals and revolutionists about her sister, the unfortunate Marie Antoinette, and the disgraceful slanders and lies deliberately fabricated and spread abroad by Napoleon for political reasons against the gentle, saintly Queen Louise of Prussia, one cannot be surprised that these same radicals and revolutionists should pour forth their spite and fury upon a woman who was not only the sister and aunt of their victims but herself a queen, and a leader and protector of royalists, *emigrés*, and conservatives; or that Napoleon should vent his rage upon a princess who dared to oppose him and whose kingdom he wanted for one of his own family.

The friendship between the Queen and Acton, and the constant intercourse which their joint government of the State rendered absolutely unavoidable, accordingly gave rise after a time to a considerable amount of gossip, as may easily be imagined at the court of the Two Sicilies. It even spread to various foreign courts, and the jealousy of the King was aroused.

That there was any harm in this friendship there

has never been the slightest proof, nor is there the least reason to suppose so. The fact of the affairs of the kingdom being conducted by a young and attractive woman, whose high spirits and love of society, amusement, and admiration were as conspicuous as her talents, and a man who, besides being a capable minister, was an extremely pleasant, cultivated person, was certain to give rise to scandalous reports. The malignity of her enemies was gratified by making and circulating the unjustifiable statements on this subject and many others which are to be found in the writings of her revolutionary assailants.

The jealousy of Ferdinando, in spite of his own conduct, was continually causing those shortlived though violent quarrels which, with their frequent occurrence and rapid reconciliation, so amused the Emperor Joseph.

There were stormy scenes at first about Acton, in one of which Ferdinando flew into a rage and exclaimed:

"I am trying to surprise you together. I will kill you both, and have your bodies thrown out of the windows of the palace!"

Carolina retorted, as well she might, and they set spies upon each other. But very soon a reconciliation was patched up; Acton left Naples, but only for Castellamare, from whence he returned in disguise two or three times a week for the audiences which the Queen continued to give him, and gradually matters drifted back into their usual course.

The English traveller, John Moore, records his impressions of Naples at this time in a series of letters, in which he describes the beauty of the scenery, climate, &c. "No street in Rome," he says, "equals in beauty the Strada di Toledo at Naples; and still less can any of them be compared with those beautiful streets which are open to the bay. . . . The Neapolitan nobility are excessively fond of splendour and show. This appears in the brilliancy of their equipages, the number of their attendants, the richness of their dress, and the grandeur of their titles.

"I am assured that the King of Naples counts a hundred persons with the title of prince, and a still greater number with that of duke, among his subjects. . . . When we consider the magnificence of their entertainments . . . we are surprised that the richest of them can support such expensive establishments.[1] I dined, soon after our arrival, at the Prince of Franca Villa's. There were about forty people at table. It was a meagre day. The dinner consisted entirely of fish and vegetables, and was the most magnificent entertainment I ever saw, comprehending an infinite variety of dishes, a vast profusion of fruit, and the wines of every country in Europe. I dined since at Prince Isacci's. I shall mention two circumstances from which you may form an idea of the grandeur of an Italian palace and the number of domestics which some of the nobility retain. We passed through twelve or thirteen large rooms before we arrived at the dining-room. There were thirty-six persons at table; none served but the Prince's domestics, and

[1] It had just been mentioned in the same letter that the richest of them had not more than twelve or thirteen thousand a year.

each guest had a footman behind his chair. Other domestics belonging to the Prince remained in the adjacent rooms and in the hall. We afterwards passed through a considerable number of other rooms in our way to one from which there is a very commanding view.

"As there is no opera at present, the people of fashion generally pass part of the evening at the Corso on the sea-shore. This is the great scene of Neapolitan splendour and parade, and on occasions of grand parade will strike a stranger very much. The finest carriages are painted, gilt, varnished, and lined in a richer and more beautiful manner than has yet become fashionable either in England or France. They are often drawn by six, and sometimes by eight, horses.

"It is the mode here to have two running footmen, very gaily dressed, before the carriage, and three or four servants in rich liveries behind. . . . The ladies or gentlemen within the coaches glitter in all the brilliancy of lace, embroidery, and jewels. The Neapolitan coaches for gala days are made with very large windows, that the spectators may enjoy a view of the parties within. Nothing can be more showy than the harness of the horses; their heads and manes are ornamented with the rarest plumage, and their tails set off with ribands and artificial flowers. . . .

"We may have what opinion we like of the whole race of Bourbon, but it would be highly indecent to deny that the reigning Kings of Spain and Naples are very great Princes. . . . His Neapolitan Majesty seems to be about the age of six or seven and twenty. He is a prince of great activity of body ... very fond, like the King of Prussia, of reviewing his troops, and is perfectly master of the whole mystery of the manual exercise. ... This monarch is also a very excellent shot ... possesses, I am informed, many other accomplishments. I particularise only those to which I have myself been a witness. No king in Europe is supposed to understand the game of billiards better. ... In domestic life this Prince is generally allowed to be an easy master, a good-natured husband, a dutiful son, and an indulgent father.

"The Queen of Naples is a beautiful woman, and seems to possess the affability, good-humour, and benevolence which distinguish, in such an amiable manner, the Austrian family."[1]

At this time Maria Carolina had the happiness of a visit from her sister and brother-in-law, the Archduchess Christine and Prince Albrecht of Saxe-Teschen, who were making a tour in Italy. Of them also the Englishman, John Moore, writes in one of his letters from Naples:

"The King and Queen lately paid a visit to four of the principal nunneries in this town. Their motive was to gratify the curiosity of the Archduchess and her husband, Prince Albrecht of Saxony. ... We had the honour of seeing them frequently in Rome, where they conciliated the affection of the Italian nobles by their obliging manners as much as they commanded respect by their high rank. The Archduchess is a very beautiful woman, and more distinguished by the propriety of her conduct

[1] J. Moore.

than either by birth or beauty. Conscious from her infancy of the highest rank, and accustomed to honours, it never enters into her thoughts that any person will fail in paying her a due respect. . . . A smile of benignity puts all who approach this Princess perfectly at their ease, and dignity sits as smoothly on her as a well-made garment. . . .

"As nobody is permitted to enter those convents, except on such extraordinary occasions as this, when they are visited by the Sovereigns, the British Minister seized this opportunity of procuring an order for admitting the Duke of Hamilton and me. We accordingly accompanied him and a few others who were in the King's suite. I have seen various nunneries in different parts of Europe, but none that could be compared even with the meanest of those four in this city for neatness and conveniency. Each of them is provided with a beautiful garden. . . . These four nunneries are for the reception of young ladies of good families, and into one in particular none but such as are of very high rank can be admitted, either as pensioners or to take the veil. Each of the young ladies in this splendid convent have both a summer and a winter apartment, and many other accommodations unknown in other retreats of this nature. The royal visitors were received in them all by the Lady Abbess at the head of the oldest of the sisterhood. They were afterwards presented with nosegays and served with fruit, sweetmeats, and a variety of cooling drinks by the younger nuns. The Queen and her amiable sister received all very graciously, conversing familiarly with the Lady Abbesses, and asking a few obliging questions of each.

"In one convent the company were surprised, on being led into a large parlour, to find a table covered, and every appearance of a most plentiful cold repast, consisting of several joints of meat, hams, fish, fowl, and other dishes. It seemed rather ill-judged to have prepared a feast of such a solid nature immediately after dinner, for these royal visits were made in the afternoon. The Lady Abbess, however, earnestly pressed their Majesties to sit down, with which they complied, and their example was followed by the Archduchess and some of the ladies. The nuns stood behind to serve their royal guests. The Queen chose a slice of cold turkey, which, being cut up, turned out to be a large piece of lemon ice of the shape and appearance of a roasted turkey. All the other dishes were ices of different kinds, disguised under the forms of joints of meat, fish, and fowl, as above mentioned. The gaiety and good-humour of the King, the affable and engaging behaviour of the royal sisters, and the satisfaction which beamed from the plump countenance of the Lady Abbess threw an air of cheerfulness on this scene."[1]

In the year 1783 a fearful earthquake devastated parts of Calabria and Sicily, by which Messina was almost destroyed. It began just at the hour when most of the inhabitants were at dinner, and after the first terrible shocks flames broke out in different parts of the city. The cathedral, the royal and archiepiscopal palaces, the hospital, most of the convents, churches, and houses were in ruins;

[1] "A View of Society and Manners in Italy" (John Moore, M.D. 1780).

numbers of people were killed, while robbery, violence, and panic increased the scenes of horror which everywhere prevailed.

There were, however, instances of unselfish heroism which contrasted with the darker incidents of this calamity, as, for instance, the conduct of the young Marchesa di Sparpara, daughter of a Provençal gentleman. Having fainted with terror, she was carried out of her tottering house by her husband and hurried down to the port, when, just as she was about to step into a boat, she perceived that in the confusion her child had been left behind. Her husband was too busy to see what she was about, and leaving the boat, she rushed back to the house, snatched the baby from its cradle, and hurried to the staircase. Just as she arrived there it fell in ruins before her; the rooms were falling as she ran from one to another with the child in her arms, and finally appeared upon the balcony calling desperately for help. But no one could get near her; the house fell, and mother and child perished in the flames and ruins.[1]

Horror-stricken by this terrible calamity, the King and Queen did their utmost to help the sufferers, straining every resource to collect money to mitigate the famine and distress that followed. But the next year another scourge, namely, a great pestilence, spread through those afflicted provinces, bringing new terrors, dangers, and miseries in its train.

During this second year of misfortune (1784) the Emperor Joseph arrived for the second time on a visit to his sister. On this occasion he travelled

[1] "Histoire de Marie Caroline, Reine de Naples" (Sérieys).

incognito, and represented to his sister that, as he wished to pass his time with the learned men of Naples, and to study the antiquities of the country, he would rather not stay in the Palazzo Reale. He therefore lodged elsewhere, and the learned Luigi Serio was appointed by the Queen to be his *cicerone* during his sojourn there.

The fleet for which Naples had to thank the Queen and Acton was a source of deep satisfaction and pride to the former, who, in the spring of 1785, persuaded the King to accompany her in a magnificent progress to display it to some of the other Italian Princes.

On the 30th of April, therefore, the royal family embarked on the flagship, which was luxuriously arranged, splendidly decorated, and followed by twelve warships, all crowded with the Neapolitan court and nobles, with bands of music, flags, and every sign of festivity. Their first destination was Livorno, where they were met by the Grand-duke Leopold and the Tuscan Princes, who escorted them to Florence, where, as on her former visit, Maria Carolina was magnificently received, and enjoyed herself much more than when, as a frightened, homesick girl of sixteen, she first beheld its gates and towers. They visited Pisa, Milan, and Turin, everywhere received with festivities; and at Genoa went again on board their own ships, and sailed homewards over the bright summer sea attended by numbers of warships of other nations—English, Dutch, Maltese, &c.—and with this imposing escort entered the Bay of Naples.

Carlos III. of Spain, father of Ferdinando, died in

1788, and was succeeded by his son, Carlos IV., a weak, miserable prince.

Not long afterwards the small-pox, which had been fatal to so many of the Habsburg children, and to which the Queen's eldest son had already fallen victim, broke out again amongst her family.

Francesco, now the heir and about eleven years old, escaped; the next boy, Gennaro, who was two years younger, died. The Queen, half wild with grief and terror, had all the rest of the children inoculated, but this was the middle of winter, and the youngest was a baby of five months old, which also died. The Queen added to her sorrow by reproaching herself bitterly for having perhaps caused the child's death by having him inoculated when he was too young to bear it or the weather too cold.

The Austrian Ambassador writes to Vienna, January 3, 1789:

"The royal family and court have lately been in great distress. Scarcely had they had time to recover from the ... death of his Catholic Majesty,[1] when the second Prince, the Infant Don Gennaro, died in a few hours, after a sudden relapse, of small-pox, January 2nd, at four o'clock in the morning. His royal parents, whose especial love his precociously developed intelligence had gained, are plunged in grief. . . ."

The writer goes on to relate the death a few days later of the little Don Carlo, and to say that much anxiety was felt for the health of the Queen, who seems really to have been almost out of her senses

[1] Carlos III.

with the violence of her grief. The frantic, unreasonable state into which she threw herself was certainly very unlike the way her mother the Empress had borne sorrows of this kind, and her brothers Joseph and Leopold, while pitying and sympathising with her sorrow, said to each other that they feared the impatience and rashness of their "crack-brained sister" would bring trouble upon her some day. The immediate consequences of her folly might have been serious, for in her frenzy she declared the small-pox came through the Spaniards, whom she actually accused of having designs against the lives of her sons.

Fortunately no notice was taken by Spain; these outrageous and senseless accusations being attributed to the state into which her grief had thrown her. When she recovered her right judgment she apologised, saying that the loss of her children had made her lose her senses and suspect every one.

She had afterwards two more sons—Leopold, born 1790, who survived her and was her especial favourite and consolation, and Albert (1792), who died young.

The King of Spain, anxious to be on friendly terms with his Neapolitan relations, now proposed that the Spanish fleet should go to Naples to salute the King and Queen, and that a Spanish infanta should be betrothed to the Prince Royal of Naples. Ferdinando might have consented, but the Queen would not hear of it. She was quite as eager to marry her children into the family of Habsburg as her mother had been for alliances with that of Bourbon, and this arrangement would have frustrated her favourite plan.

The health of the Emperor Joseph was failing; the Grand-duke of Tuscany, her favourite brother, was the next heir. He had offered his daughter, the Archduchess Clementine, for the Prince Royal, and his second son for her eldest daughter.

The fleet of Spain paid its proposed complimentary visit to Naples, but the Spanish marriages were declined, and the elder children of the King and Queen were betrothed to their Austrian cousins.

Maria Carolina was as anxious as her mother had been for the early and exalted marriages of her children.[1] For her two eldest daughters and her eldest son to marry the children of her two brothers was her most cherished plan; besides which she had formed another one of marrying her fourth daughter, Amélie, to the Dauphin, son of her sister Antoinette, with whom she had corresponded upon the subject and who was delighted with the idea. The Dauphin was born in 1780 and Amélie in 1782; therefore their ages were suitable; they both shared the blood of Bourbon and Habsburg; their mothers resolved that this alliance should some day take place, and the Princess Amélie was taught to consider herself the future wife of the Dauphin.

But the eldest son of Marie Antoinette, fortunately for himself, died in 1789, and the little Princess of

[1] The daughters of Maria Carolina who lived to grow up became the Empress of Germany, the Grand-duchess of Tuscany, the Queen of Sardinia, the Queen of France, and the Princess of the Asturias, who, if she had lived, would have been Queen of Spain.

MARIE ANTOINETTE
"FAISANT UN BOUQUET."
After the painting by Mme. Vigée Le Brun at Versailles.

seven years old took his death very much to heart and cried bitterly when she was told of it.

When she was an old woman of eighty, Amélie, in speaking of this recollection, said :

"*Je pleurai beaucoup mon petit cousin ;*" adding with a smile, "*Vous voyez que j'avais toujours été destinée à être Reine de France.*"[1]

If it occurred to the two unfortunate Queens to substitute their two next children, the Duke of Normandy (now Dauphin) and the Princess Antoinette, events soon put an end to the possibility of uniting these two ill-fated children, whose tragic destiny contrasted so terribly with the brilliant prospects to which they were born.

The event just recorded was a severe disappointment to the Queen of Naples, besides her sympathy with the grief of her sister.

The child destined to be Queen of France was the first born after the death of the Empress Maria Theresia, whose name was added to the others chosen for her. Marie Amélie Thérèse de Bourbon was born at Caserta in the full height of her parents' happiness and prosperity (1782). She was so delicate a baby that she had at first to be kept wrapped up in cotton-wool. But if her health in her childhood was delicate, her intelligence was so remarkably and early developed that at two years and a half old, although she had as yet no teeth, she was beginning to read; and the King of Spain, her grandfather, was so pleased with her precocious attainments that in 1785 he wrote to her himself to encourage her.

Often in later years she would talk to her children

[1] "Vie de Marie Amélie, Reine des Français" (Auguste Trognon).

and grandchildren of this letter of Carlos III., and also of an old priest to whom she used to say the catechism, and who was so fond of her and so delighted with the facility with which she learned and understood his religious lessons that he used to call her "*fata mia.*"[1] At that time Naples and all Italy were filled with admiration of the sanctity of S. Alfonso di Liguori, and the Queen on one occasion when she went to see him took all her children with her and asked him to bless them.[2]

Mme. Campan, in her "Mémoires de Marie-Antoinette," says that the Queen of Naples was at one time anxious to marry the Prince Royal, her son, to Madame Royale, eldest daughter of the King and Queen of France, and that she well remembered a secret messenger coming from Maria Carolina to Marie Antoinette and asking her, she being one of the ladies of the Queen's household, to use her influence with her royal mistress in favour of the plan; that she explained that such an interference in State affairs on her part was out of the question; and that the Queen afterwards spoke to her on the subject, declaring that Madame Royale would be in a much better and happier position married to her cousin the Duc d'Angoulême than she could be in any foreign country even as Queen. That she went on to say that there was no court in Europe to be compared with that of France, and that if a French princess was to be married to a prince of any other nation she ought to leave Versailles when she was seven years old, to be brought up at the court which

---

[1] "Vie de Marie Amélie, Reine des Français" (Auguste Trognon).
[2] Ibid.

was to be her future home; that at twelve years old it would be too late, for the recollections she would then have and the comparisons she would make would destroy the happiness of her life.

For in the days of her splendour and prosperity Marie Antoinette thoroughly appreciated the superior magnificence of her position to that of any of her sisters, and would often allow this to appear in her conversations with Mme. Campan.

On one occasion she showed her some letters from the Queen of Naples, in which the latter related to her sister the annoyance then being caused her by the interference and impertinence of the court of Spain respecting her minister, Acton, about whom reports and suspicions which both Maria Carolina and Marie Antoinette declared to be outrageous appeared to be rife.

Her father-in-law, Carlos III., had actually sent an insolent Spaniard named Las Casas to persuade her to dismiss a minister who was invaluable to her and to the country, and when she had condescended to explain to this emissary the real state of affairs, and declared that, in order to prove to the Spanish King that the superior capacity of Acton as Prime Minister could alone be the reason for the favour she showed him, she would send his portrait and his bust to Spain, he had dared to reply that that would be useless trouble, for it was well known that a man's ugliness did not prevent his success, and that the King of Spain had too much experience not to know that the caprices of a woman were inexplicable. This insolence had thrown Maria Carolina into such a paroxysm of agitation and anger that a miscarriage had been the result; and by the request of his sister-in-law Louis XVI. had intervened as mediator between the courts of Naples and Madrid.

The time was now rapidly approaching when Maria Carolina should attain the triumph of her most cherished plans for the exaltation of her children; but amidst her rejoicings were mingled the uneasiness and fear which foreshadowed those terrible calamities so soon to change the brilliant sunshine of her life into darkness and ruin.

They were on the eve of the French Revolution; indeed, it had already begun by the sack of the Bastille and the murder of its brave defenders, the horrible scenes at Versailles, and the return to Paris of the King and Queen, prisoners in their own capital.

Still, nobody at Naples realised or dreamed of the fearful tragedies that were to follow, and Maria Carolina, deeply sympathising with her most dearly loved sister, reviled the weakness and cowardice of Louis XVI.

Already the stream of fugitives which later on poured out of France into every other country had begun to flow. Many who were especially marked out for the hatred of the revolutionists foresaw the times of peril at hand, and, wishing to get away before it was too late, were already leaving France, and kept arriving with gloomy accounts of the state of affairs there. Amongst others, the beautiful and gifted artist, Mme. Vigée Le Brun, whose royalist principles and sympathies had begun to excite the sinister attention of the brutal mob, had fled disguised as an *ouvrière*, with her child, a single attendant, and only just money enough to take her to Rome. Having spent some months there and having easily restored her financial prosperity by painting the portraits of all the most distinguished people in Roman society, she arrived at Naples, where, delighted with its enchanting life and surpassing beauty, she decided to remain for a time. Mme. Le Brun was fêted, admired, and popular at Naples, as she had been at Paris and Rome, and it was, as usual, the supreme fashion to have a portrait painted by her.

The Queen desired the French Ambassador, the Baron de Talleyrand, to announce that she wished her to paint those of her two eldest daughters, which command she of course hastened to obey.

The well-known devotion of the great artist to the unfortunate Marie Antoinette was an additional passport to the favour of Maria Carolina, who must have felt the deepest and most melancholy interest in one who had so lately been with the sister whom, in spite of all the long years of separation, she still loved with unchanging affection.

The death of the Emperor Joseph had just taken place, and the Queen was now preparing for a hurried journey to Vienna in order to arrange with her second brother, Leopold, the marriages they had planned for their children. Mme. Le Brun says that when on her way through Italy she was presented to another sister of the Queens of France and Naples, Amalie, Infanta of Parma, she was in deep mourning for their brother, the Emperor Joseph. She remarks that "the Infanta, sister of Marie Antoinette, was much older than our Queen and possessed neither her beauty nor grace. Her rooms were all hung with black, and she looked like a shadow; all the more as she was very thin and pale. She rode every day on horseback; her way of living and her manners were like those of a man. Altogether I was not charmed with her, although she received me extremely well."

Of Maria Carolina she says:

"The Queen of Naples, without being so pretty as her younger sister, the Queen of France, reminded me very much of her; her face looked tired, but one could still see that she had been beautiful; her hands and arms were perfect in form and colour. This Princess, of whom so much evil has been said and written, was of an affectionate nature, very simple in her private life; her generosity was truly royal. . . .

"The Queen of Naples had a lofty character and superior talents. She alone bore all the weight of the government. The King would not reign; he was nearly always at Caserta, where he occupied himself with manufactories, of which the work-women employed were said to compose his seraglio."

"I recollect," she continues, "that when the Queen returned [from Vienna] she said to me: 'I have made a successful journey. I have just settled with great satisfaction two marriages for my daughters.'"[1]

During the absence of the Queen, Mme. Le Brun painted the Prince Royal and the Princess Térésa; she began also a portrait of the second Princess, Ludovica, but found her so plain and the grimaces

[1] "Souvenirs de Mme. Vigée Le Brun."

she made so ugly that she never finished the picture.

Maria Carolina had indeed made a successful journey and splendid provision for the future of her children. Her eldest daughter was to marry the eldest son of the Emperor Leopold, as that young Prince had now become a widower; while the second son was to marry her second daughter and succeed his father as Grand-duke of Tuscany. A daughter of the Emperor, the Archduchess Clementine, was to be affianced to the Prince Royal of Naples.

As she passed through Rome on her way back the Queen met Mme. Le Brun, who had just returned there after finishing all the portraits she had engaged to paint at Naples. But as she wished to have her own picture done by that celebrated artist she insisted upon her returning there at once, which Mme. Le Brun consented to do, and the result was the magnificent portrait now in the Museo Nazionale of Naples, in which the likeness to the unfortunate Queen of France may be clearly traced. The heat was now so great that during one sitting both Mme. Le Brun and the Queen fell asleep.[1]

Late in the summer the King, the Queen, and the whole of the royal family set out on their journey to Austria for the weddings of the two eldest Princesses and the coronation of the Emperor.

The King and Queen travelled as Count and Countess di Castellamare; as they left Naples

[1] Ibid.

the *lazzaroni* crowded their way, reproaching Ferdinando with cries of disapproval, and entreating him not to stay long away from them. On August 28th they arrived at Fiume amidst the thunder of guns and every sign of public rejoicing, and were met there by Leopold, King of Hungary, Bohemia, &c. (for his election to the imperial throne had not yet taken place), and by the Archduchess Elisabeth; the Archduchess Marianne had died the year before.

After this meeting the royal family and court proceeded to Trieste and thence to Vienna, where they arrived on September 14th, and five days later the betrothal of the Archduchess Clementine to the Prince Royal of Naples[1] and the marriages of his sisters to the Crown Prince Franz and the Grand-duke Ferdinand of Tuscany were celebrated with great pomp and splendour at the Hofburg Capelle, all Vienna being illuminated in their honour.[2]

Next came the imposing ceremonies and festivities connected with the election and coronation of the Emperor, which had never before been so magnificent as for this, the last but one of the Emperors elected to bear that ancient title.[3]

While the election was going on, Leopold waited at Aschaffenburg, and on October 5th made his entry into Frankfort with the imperial family, the Electors and the court. Sumptuous banquets were

[1] The Prince Royal of Naples was then thirteen years old.
[2] Helfert
[3] The dissolution of the old German Empire took place under his successor, who was henceforth only Emperor of Austria.

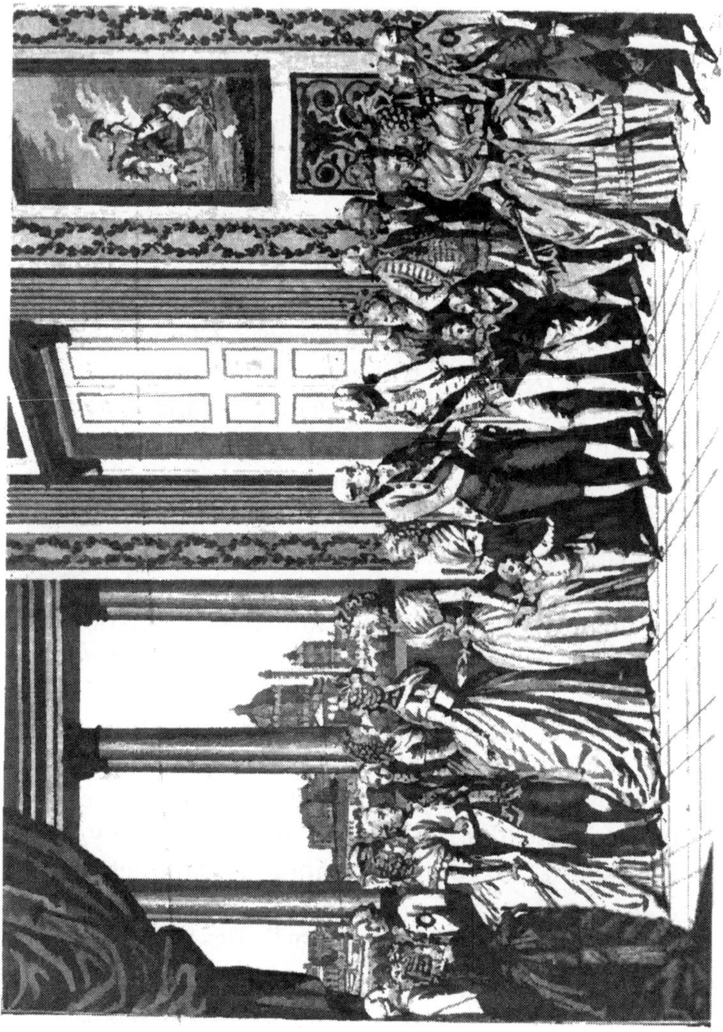

offered to the imperial family and royal personages, amongst the most splendid of the entertainments being the great supper and *déjeuner* given by the Elector of Treves on board his state barge, moored on the river Main, and, as well as that of the Elector of Cologne, brilliantly illuminated.

The coronation took place on October 12th, and on the 16th the Emperor, his family and court returned to Vienna. The King and Queen of Naples remained for eight months with their Austrian relations, and this time was to Maria Carolina one of much happiness, though disturbed by anxiety about her sister Antoinette, disquieting rumours respecting the state of affairs in France and doubts as to the prospects and even safety of the royal family continuing to reach Vienna. But to be in her beloved Austria, amid the scenes of her childhood, was always delightful to Carolina, and although she missed so many of those who had been dear to her, there were others remaining to welcome her in those familiar haunts. She had still her sisters Christine and Elisabeth, her favourite brother was now on the throne, and her own position as a reigning sovereign and mother of the future Empress was more powerful and illustrious than ever.

Her son-in-law, the Crown Prince, was very fond of her; he used to call her "mother-in-law and threefold aunt."[1] The happiness, exalted position, and splendid future of the most beloved of her daughters seemed secure; the Grand-duchy of Tuscany was a magnificent provision for Ludovica,

[1] "Dreifache Tante."

and she had the Austrian daughter-in-law she desired instead of the Spaniard to whom she objected.

The Emperor Leopold was much more popular, especially in Hungary and Bohemia, than his brother Joseph had been; the unpopular rule of the latter, who had never been crowned King of those countries, had nearly lost them both to the house of Habsburg. The Netherlands were in revolt and must be won back; in fact, the throne of the Emperor was beset with anxieties and difficulties from which he had been free during the twenty-five years of his wise and peaceful government of his grand-duchy of Tuscany.

The King and Queen of Naples accompanied him to Presburg, where he was crowned King of Hungary, and in that country he was received with an outburst of loyalty; the popularity of the Emperor and imperial family including Ferdinando and Carolina, whose reforms at Naples were known and appreciated, especially the industrial colony established by the latter at San Leucio, near Caserta.

This colony was an experiment of the Queen's on the new philanthropic plan — to establish silk-weaving. She had built factories, cottages, a church, a hospital, and a little villa in which she could stay when she came to visit the settlement. Foreign workmen were engaged to teach the best way of working the silk, and excellent though somewhat minute regulations made for the welfare and good behaviour of the inhabitants of the colony, extending into the arrangement of marriages, the disposition of property, and even dress. It was, in fact, a community the organisation of which combined a sort of Christianised republic of Plato with the grandmotherly government of Maria Theresia. For many years the colony prospered exceedingly; the manufactures were excellent, the people happy and contented, their numbers increasing steadily.[1]

Many and anxious were the consultations held between Leopold and Carolina respecting the measures to be taken for the rescue of their sister Antoinette. Their hope was in a coalition of nations against France. They could among themselves reckon on the Empire and the principal Italian Powers; the King of Spain, weak and contemptible as he was, could scarcely refuse to join in assisting the elder branch of his own family; other allies might for various reasons be induced to enter the coalition, while the *emigrés* dispersed all over Europe would flock into their ranks.

So long as Carolina was by his side her courage, high spirit, and resolution spurred on her more peaceful and vacillating brother.

But the time came when she must return with her husband to their own dominions, and passing through Venice on their way home they stayed for

---

[1] It was to this manufactory that Mme. Le Brun referred (p. 120). The colony of San Leucio was established after a visit paid in 1784 by Ferdinando and Carolina to the Emperor Joseph at Vienna. The credit of it is always given by the calumniators of the Queen to Ferdinando, because the edict ran in his name, but it was organised and maintained under the supervision of Maria Carolina.

a short time in Rome, where it was important for them to have an interview with the Pope, and where also were to be found Mesdames Adélaïde and Victoire de France, the two last surviving daughters of Louis XV., who had made their escape from the dangers and horrors of their own country and taken refuge there.

To part from her favourite daughter was hard for the Queen, for of all her children this one, her firstborn, had always been her especial joy and pride; and in her she now saw the fulfilment of all her most ardent wishes and plans. This daughter was one day to wear the crown of the mother she had so adored, obeyed, and reverenced; and as she had loved the great Empress, so Térésa loved and trusted her, and would in the same way be guided by her influence.

She had now six children living, and was expecting another before long.[1] The Prince-Royal, who was too young to be married, returned with his family to Italy.

The relations between the Vatican and Naples had not of late years been cordial, and Carolina was anxious to place them on a more satisfactory footing.

During the pontificate of Clement XIII. the King, then barely of age, had incurred the indignation of that Pontiff by expelling the Jesuits from his dominions and confiscating their property, under the influence of Spain, then paramount at his court. Clement XIV. confirmed this proceeding by a brief, and thus patched up a reconciliation which only

[1] Leopold was born 1790 and Carlo Alberto 1792

Pius VI.

lasted a little while, as his pontificate was a short one, and with Pius VI., whose election Maria Carolina had opposed, a constant succession of disputes and quarrels had gone on about the choice and investiture of bishops, about ecclesiastical laws, &c., culminating in the refusal of the King to continue the payment of the annual tribute of seven thousand golden ducats and a richly caparisoned white horse by which Naples acknowledged herself a vassal of Rome.

Maria Carolina, however, was now resolved that this state of things should cease, and accordingly arranged that not only should they go to Rome and visit the Pope, but that additional emphasis should be given to their arrival by its being pretended to have been so hastened by their eagerness that they should reach the Vatican earlier than they were expected. All went smoothly; the King and Queen appeared, passed through the private entrance into the Vatican, and penetrated into the private apartments of Pio VI., who rose in feigned astonishment to receive them. The audience passed in the greatest harmony: the apologies and protestations of the Queen were graciously accepted, and anxious deliberations were held concerning the ominous and gloomy prospects that already overshadowed the horizon.

The King and Queen of Naples were delighted with Rome and the splendid manner in which they were entertained there.

But the Romans had a caricature of a conversation supposed to have taken place between the Pope, the King and Queen, General Acton, and the

Queen's confessor, with the devil in the corner of the picture:[1]

What the Queen learned from Mesdames de France was anything but reassuring, and only increased the anxiety she already felt for the safety of her sister and her family. Mesdames Adélaïde and Victoire had only just come away in time; as it was, they had had the utmost difficulty, first in getting permission to leave at all, then in their journey. They had been stopped more than once on the road, and had been in constant danger and terror until they got over the frontier into the dominions of their nephew and niece, the King and Queen of Sardinia. Their youngest nephew, the Comte d'Artois, with his wife, had emigrated before them, and they bitterly regretted the obstinacy of their niece, Mme. Elisabeth, who, notwithstanding their entreaties, had refused to come with them, but persisted in remaining with her eldest brother, Louis XVI., to whom she was devoted.

All this was very alarming, and the *emigrés*, with whom Rome, and indeed every great city in Italy,

[1] *Pope* Io concedo tutto
King. Io voglio tutto quel che vuole la Regina
Queen · Io voglio tutto.
Acton Io rubo tutto.
Confessor Io assolvo tutti.
Il Diavolo. Io porto via tutti.

Pope: I yield all.
King · I wish all the Queen wishes.
Queen. I want all.
Acton I rob all
Confessor. I absolve all
The Devil: I carry away all.
            (Autobiography of Cornelia Knight

LA COMTESSE DE PROVENCE,
WIFE OF MONSIEUR (AFTERWARDS LOUIS XVIII.)

was now crowded, increased her fear and horror by the terrible histories of their sufferings and perils, and the misery which most of them were experiencing.

Many were in agonies of suspense about the fate of their nearest and dearest relations; others were mourning for the murder of those they loved best in the world; most of them had lost the whole or the greater part of their fortune, and in many cases were in absolute destitution.

That the King, Queen, and royal family should escape from France was the one aspiration of Mesdames and all the *emigrés,* and though this was becoming more and more difficult and dangerous, it is probable that it might have been accomplished and that all, or at any rate some of them, might have been saved, had it not been for the folly, obstinacy, and mismanagement which characterised their plans and their way of carrying them out.

The Comte and Comtesse de Provence had just escaped separately, and the Comte and Comtesse d'Artois had emigrated while it was tolerably easy to get away, but the King and Queen had put off their flight until it was well-nigh impossible, having thrown away one opportunity after another which offered them safety.

Already in the early days of trouble and danger Marie Antoinette had ordered Mme. de Tourzel to make preparations quietly for a sudden start from Versailles which would have saved them, but the King changed his mind and they stayed.[1]

Again, after the banquet of the *gardes-du-corps* at

[1] "Mémoires de Mme. de Tourzel."

Versailles and the outburst of loyalty it called forth, when they were protected not only by the *gardes-du-corps* but by the *chasseurs de Lorraine*, the faithful Swiss guards, and a great part of the *régiment de Flandre*, what could have hindered their leaving Versailles that night, gaining the coast, and embarking for England? Afterwards, when the furious, bloodthirsty mob was pouring into Versailles, as the King was out hunting, and the horses were actually being harnessed to the Dauphin's carriage, if the Queen with her children and Madame Elisabeth had had the presence of mind to get into the carriage and drive away, they could have joined the King and fled together. They would have had a start, as it would have been some time before it was discovered that they were really not going to return.

But they never thought of it!

Between the 20th of June and the fatal 10th of August there was a project for their escape separately. It was well arranged; they were to be saved one at a time by those responsible for its execution. But it was put an end to by Marie Antoinette, who refused to be separated from the King and the Dauphin,[1] a decision which destroyed what must have been a very good chance of the latter being saved, and probably his sister, if not Madame Elisabeth, even supposing the King and Queen did not succeed in reaching the frontier unrecognised. They were, of course, so well known that they were less easy to disguise, but one cannot

[1] "Mémoires de Louis XVIII., recueillis et mis en ordre par M le Duc de D——," t. v. p. 176

believe that, especially in those days, innocent of telegraphs, railways, and motors, it would not have been perfectly feasible to hide two children and smuggle them out of the country without their being discovered.

The tissue of mistakes and follies which led to such fatal results must have been maddening to Maria Carolina, who bitterly inveighed against the cowardly, contemptible indecision and obstinacy of her brother-in-law, Louis XVI., and when at last the attempt to escape was made and failed—as so ill-arranged and ill-executed a proceeding might be expected to do—her terror and indignation knew no bounds.

The whole thing was a succession of errors and mismanagement, and yet it had almost succeeded, which certainly seems to prove that with proper care, reasonable precautions, and promptitude, they would have been saved.

Of all the tragic stories in history there is none more pathetic and, one may say, none more provoking than that of Varennes.

It was undoubtedly essential that those who had sufficient foresight to perceive what was coming, and had decided to save themselves and their families while there was yet time, should also save what was possible of their property, and consequently should make preparations beforehand by placing as much of their fortune as they could in foreign securities, and taking with them all their most valuable possessions that could be packed up and easily removed.

But for those who had deferred their flight until

the last moment, when their lives were in immediate danger—when, especially if they were in a conspicuous position, they were surrounded with spies and every movement watched—it was too late for all such considerations. It was better to arrive penniless in a foreign country than to fall into the hands of the fiends whose thirst for murder, outrage, and cruelty spared neither men, women, nor children.

Therefore, the all-important matter was to avoid suspicion, which was certain to be aroused by the slightest appearance of preparation for a journey.

But when, after waiting until their flight was most difficult and dangerous, the King resolved to attempt it, Marie Antoinette insisted upon making extensive preparations for their journey and residence abroad. In March, 1791, she began to give orders for a complete *trousseau* for herself and her children, which was to be packed and sent to one of her ladies, to whom she gave leave of absence to go to her estates in Arras. As this lady had also property across the frontier in Austrian territory, she was to hold herself in readiness to cross on pretence of going to her other estate and take the trunks with her, which, as she was in the habit of going from one property to the other, need not, the Queen said, excite any attention.

In vain Mme. Campan, *première femme de chambre de la Reine*, represented to her royal mistress the additional and most unnecessary risk she was running. "The Queen of France," she observed, "would be able to get dresses and chemises wherever she might be."

It was useless. The Queen insisted, and Mme. Campan went out almost in disguise to buy the things, ordering six chemises here, six there, six elsewhere, and so on, trying so to break up and distribute the numbers of garments required as to avert suspicion.

The eldest daughter of Mme. Campan's sister, who was about the size of Madame Royale, was measured for her clothes, and those of the Dauphin were made to fit the little son of Mme. Campan. When they were ready Mme. Campan packed and sent them addressed to the lady in question, who was to be ready at a moment's notice to start for Brussels or any other place indicated.

The Queen also declared she must take her *nécessaire de voyage,* or at least she must send it to her sister, the Archduchess Christine, who with her husband was now governing the Netherlands, and that to prevent suspicion she would pretend to send it her as a present.

To this Mme. Campan opposed arguments and entreaties in vain. Nobody, she said, would believe the *nécessaire* was given to the Archduchess, for all the Queen's household, which was full of spies, knew how fond she was of that "piece of furniture," which she had often declared would be most convenient in travelling. The only concession she could obtain was that the Austrian *chargé d'affaires* should be told to present himself at the Queen's toilet, and ask her in the hearing of her ladies and servants to order a *nécessaire* exactly like it for the Archduchess Christine, who wanted one.

The Queen accordingly gave the order as arranged.

A month afterwards Mme. Campan went to inquire for the *nécessaire* and found that it would not be finished for six weeks; upon which the Queen told her she could not wait for it, as they were to set off in June—it was now May—but that, having taken the precaution to order it in the presence of her household, there was no danger in declaring that the Archduchess was impatient, and that she would send her own instead.

Again Mme. Campan remonstrated in vain. The *nécessaire* was a large thing, cost 500 *louis*, and attracted attention,[1] but finding it must be sent, Mme. Campan went about it as openly as possible, ordering all the contents to be taken out and no trace of perfume left, which the Archduchess Christine might not like. It was then sent to her.[2]

She also helped the Queen pack up her diamonds, which were given to Léonard, the Queen's *coiffeur*, who took them to Brussels.[3]

All this time there was a spy in the Queen's household, a *femme de garde-robe*, to whom Marie Antoinette had shown particular kindness, and who had long been in the pay of the radicals.

She secretly possessed a second key to the private rooms of the Queen, by means of which she opened the door locked by the latter before the arrange-

[1] It contained a whole silver toilet service, even a warming-pan. The Queen had it made in 1789 " in case of sudden flight."
[2] Directly it was sent, a spy informed the Mayor of Paris that the Queen was preparing to depart; her *nécessaire* had already gone.
[3] These were the Queen's private jewels, and were afterwards restored to Madame Royale, Duchesse d'Angoulême (Campan).

ment of the diamonds was finished and saw them lying about half-packed. She did not believe the story of the *nécessaire* for the Archduchess, and not only reported all these things to Gouvion, the *aide-de-camp* of Lafayette, whose mistress she was, but made a denunciation which was shown by the Mayor of Paris to the unfortunate Queen after her capture.

The whole deplorable tale is well known, with its catalogue of mistakes and mismanagement and folly.

The time necessary for the journey to Montmédy was miscalculated by M. Goguelat, who when making the journey reckoned the time in which it was performed in a light postchaise with no *courrier*. When it was too late, they discovered to their cost that a large, heavy travelling carriage with a *courrier* took more than two hours longer. This was probably fatal, and was added to first by the carriage being kept waiting nearly an hour, and then by the King insisting upon getting out and walking up a hill, which delayed them still further. When the cumbersome party, which included not only the five royal fugitives but two or three ladies of their household, arrived at the place where M. Goguelat and his escort of hussars was to have met them they were three hours late, and no one was to be seen.

Goguelat and his troop had come to the appointed place, but after waiting in vain for the arrival of the royal party, finding their presence was attracting the attention of the peasants, Goguelat formed the fatal resolution to retire with his men, with whom he left the highroad and went by lanes and bridle-paths back to Varennes, in consequence of which he missed the fugitives, who, finding nobody there, drove forward hoping to meet them.

At St. Menehould the King put his head out of the window and began to question the postmaster, and this act of supreme folly sealed their fate.

The postmaster, Drouet, recognised him by his likeness on the coins and *assignats*, looked into the carriage, thought he recognised the Queen, saw by the numbers and ages of the party that the royal family must be there, and hurried before them by cross roads to Varennes, where he gave the alarm.

At Varennes was Goguelat with his hussars, and here, it is said, fresh mistakes were made. If a message had been sent to M. de Bouillé, who was waiting a little further on with a troop of horse, he would have rescued them and carried them safely over the frontier, now so near.

Or Goguelat might have charged the hostile but not very powerful crowd at Varennes and carried them safely through, instead of consulting the King, who, of course, would not allow it.

Of the miserable failure of the attempt and the captivity and danger of her sister and her family, Christine, Governess of the Netherlands, heard at Brussels, where she was hoping and waiting for them, and where Mme. Thibaut, one of the Queen's ladies who was to meet her there, arrived quite safely.

The Comte and Comtesse de Provence, whose plans and proceedings had been so much more prudent and so much better managed, also arrived, overjoyed to meet each other, but filled with grief

BOUILLÉ.

and consternation at the catastrophe of which they immediately heard. The Archduchess Christine received them with the greatest kindness and sympathy, would not hear of their going to an inn, but lodged them in a *dépendance* of her palace, from which latter, in consequence of the alarming state of things, she had removed most of the furniture. She lent them her *grand appartement* in which to receive the *emigrés*, of whom Brussels was full, and who crowded to pay their respects to the Princes, for the Comte d'Artois, on hearing of the escape of his second brother, hurried to Brussels to see him.

Besides Brussels and Coblentz, another great refuge of the *emigrés* was Cologne, of which Maximilian, youngest brother of Maria Carolina, was Elector.

He had latterly been the favourite son of his mother, the Empress, although anything more utterly unlike his brother Carl, their mother's first favourite, cannot well be imagined. For Maximilian, though merry, jovial, and good-natured, was stupid, plain, and very fat.

When he went to visit his sister Marie Antoinette his awkwardness and mistakes made him perfectly ridiculous. When the great naturalist Buffon offered him a copy of his works, he said that he would not deprive him of it. When the pupils of a college were brought to perform their exercises before him, he said he would not give them that fatigue. Every one laughed at him, and he was called at Paris " L'Archi-bête d'Autriche." He was, however, liked by the *emigrés*, to whom he showed kindness and friendship at Cologne.

CHAPTER IX

Return to Naples—Leopold and Maria Carolina—State of Tuscany—Of Naples—The Queen's society—Awakening—Change of policy—The secret police—Warlike preparations—The French Ambassadors at Naples and Venice—Mme Le Brun—Slanders against the Queen—San Gennaro—Lady Hamilton.

WHEN Maria Carolina returned to Naples after a long sojourn in Austria, her ideas and policy had undergone an entire change.

Hitherto it had been on philanthropic and philosophical principles that she had governed the Two Sicilies. Her government, like her brother Leopold's, was to a great extent a benevolent despotism, such as might have been expected from the children of Maria Theresia.

They both believed implicitly, as they had been taught to believe, in the divine absolute right of the monarch over the people he was born to rule, and also in his responsibility for their welfare and happiness—that God had committed them to his charge, and to God alone he was accountable for the manner in which he exercised the authority placed in his hands.

And under the paternal rule of Leopold the Tuscans were prosperous, contented, and happy.

The Italian historian, Botta, thus speaks of him :

"In 1765 the Grand-duke Leopold ascended the throne of Tuscany. This Prince can never be praised so much as to equal nearly what he deserved. . . . Before his time the Tuscan laws were partial, intricate, inconvenient, and improvident . . . the criminal laws were insufficient and cruel, commerce was ill-protected, agriculture neglected, the soil was pestilential, property insecure, the public debt serious, taxes ruinous. To all this the good Leopold applied remedies. He abolished sinecures and privileged or incompetent officials, and amongst other prerogatives some of those of the crown. . . . He suppressed the privileges of individuals, courts, and corporations; to everyone he gave equal rights and justice. . . . The result was in conformity to his pious intentions, for after the reforms of Leopold life was perfectly happy in Tuscany, manners and customs were good and cultivated, crimes were rare, and if committed were immediately punished; the prisons were empty; everything flourished."[1]

[1] "Era stato assunto nel 1765 al trono di Toscana il Gran-duca Leopoldo. Questo Principe, il quale non si potrà mai tanto lodare, che non meriti molto più . . . Erano prima di Leopoldo le leggi di Toscana parziali, intricate, incommode, improvvide . . . Erano altresì leggi criminali crudeli, o insufficienti, un commercio male favorito, un' agricoltura non curata, un suolo pestilenziale, possessione mal sicure, coloni poveri, debito publico grave, dazj onerosissimi. A tutto pose rimedio il buon Leopoldo. Annullò i magistrati o superflui o poco proficui. . . . Fu l'effetto conforme alle pie intenzioni; poichè fu in Toscana una vita felicissima dopo le novità di Leopoldo; i costumi non solo buoni ma gentili; i delitti rarissimi, nè si tosto commessi che puniti; le prigione vuote; ogni cosa in fiore.—"Storia d'Italia," t. i. pp. 14, 16 (Botta).

In no part of Italy were the feudal rights more oppressive, the taxes more ruinous, and the laws worse than in the kingdom of the Two Sicilies.

The arbitrary power of the nobles was a curse to the whole country, which was impoverished and crushed by the burden of extortion pressing upon it. The *dîme* (or *decime*), the *gabelle*, the feudal service, the amount of taxation upon all crops, the tyrannical rights not only over every kind of game, but over the ovens, mills, and many other necessaries of life, the *dazio* exacted on entering their estates, the power of appointment of magistrates and officials in town and country, all these made the nobles formidable not only to the people but to the crown.

Such was the state of things until the middle of the eighteenth century, when Carlos III., an enlightened monarch, anxious to improve the condition of his subjects, began to introduce certain reforms by means of his minister Tanucci, which continued to progress after the majority of his son, Ferdinando IV., and when Tanucci resigned had been eagerly carried on by the young Queen, who was anxious to follow in her government the example of her mother and her favourite brother, the Grand-duke of Tuscany.

To none of them would the idea have occurred of granting their subjects any kind of self-government or voice in the conduct of affairs, their view of the relations between a ruler and his people being very much the same as those subsisting at that period between parents and children. On the one side affection, care, absolute authority, and the assumption that they must in all respects know better upon every subject than their sons and daughters, no matter of what age, and had the right to control and dispose of their lives and affections as they thought best. On the other side, love, reverence, implicit obedience, and unquestioning submission at any age to any command, however unreasonable and whatever misery it might cause.

Thus the children of the great Empress had obeyed her, and such was their idea of the proper relations between themselves and the people over whom they were called to reign.

The new ideas so rapidly spreading not only in France but in Italy, where Filangieri, Pagano, Conforti, Cirillo, and others were high in the favour and confidence of the Queen, inspired her with an ardent desire to relieve the sufferings and improve the material and moral condition of her subjects ; but, like many others, she had failed to perceive any but the plausible, benevolent side of all this new philosophy, until her eyes had been rudely opened to the real meaning of the specious arguments and insidious doctrines of the set she had admired and protected.

It was a terrible awakening, and, especially with a character like that of Maria Carolina, the reaction was sure to be proportionably violent. So these were the results to which all the cant and jargon about the worship of nature and humanity and the rights of man were to lead. Within the last year or two the radical party had increased and advanced with fearful rapidity, the unpractical philanthropists and visionary theorists who really believed in the sentiments and ideas they proclaimed were contemptuously brushed aside by the mass of their followers, to whom fraternity and equality meant getting possession of other people's property and a state of riot, spoliation, and destruction; while liberty, as understood by its ardent votaries, was an unrestrained course of outrage, violence, lust, and murder.

Already France, the headquarters of the radical and revolutionary party, was such a scene of bloodshed and crime that any decent person would have been safer in the most savage countries in Africa than there; already the Queen trembled for the lives of her beloved sister, her stupid, well-meaning brother-in-law, and their innocent children; already in Italy, in Naples itself, there was a growing party holding the blasphemous and infamous doctrines which threatened her own family, kingdom, and life.

Henceforth her opinions and views were absolutely changed; her chief endeavours were to protect herself, her kingdom, and those dear to her from the horrors which threatened them, and, so far as she could, to avenge the sufferings of her friends and punish the wretches who had inflicted them.

After her return to Naples, where she was welcomed back with delight and rejoicing, the liberal leaders found their influence at court was at an end. Radical and philosophical professors of the university, socialist lawyers, doctors, and writers were no longer invited to the palace. The discussion of the theories and principles which were leading to the destruction of religion, property, and life was not permitted in the society of the Queen.

The bishops appointed to vacant sees were now men of strong conservative and Catholic principles; the authority of the Church was supreme over the schools, whose secular tendencies, which the Queen had hitherto in some degree encouraged, were now sternly repressed.

It was evident that a strong party in favour of the revolutionary doctrines already existed in Naples; and that this party, as in France, comprised, besides professional men, merchants, and other members of the middle class, a certain number of nobles and gentlemen, mostly young, enthusiastic, and credulous; some actuated by benevolent and fantastic visions of a Utopian, impossible future, others thirsting for the saturnalia of plunder and bloodshed which would be the obvious fulfilment of their principles and projects.

In order to discover and counteract their plots Maria Carolina placed each of the twelve wards of the city under a police-magistrate chosen by the government, instead of aldermen formerly elected by the citizens, the Chief Commissioner being the Cavaliere Luigi dei Medici, a young noble of courage, energy, and ambition, of whose loyalty she felt confident. She also organised a numerous body of secret police belonging to all classes, from those highly placed at court and in society to the lowest frequenters of the popular resorts. Those of rank and social position brought their intelligence to the Queen herself at night, and were received by her in a room called the *sala oscura;* by these means she was kept informed and warned of the conspiracies, seditious proceedings, and various dangers with which she was beset.

The philosophers and radicals whom she had ceased to favour joined in these agitations, their uneasiness and alarm being increased by the various decisive measures taken by the Queen, and most of all by the evident preparation for war going on vigorously under her superintendence and Acton's in docks and arsenals. Ships were fitted out and manned, new regiments formed, a corps of Swiss and Dalmatian soldiers joined the army of Naples; everywhere in pulpit and confessional were to be heard denunciations against the murders and blasphemies going on in France.[1]

Except by the members of the radical party, France was at this time hated at Naples. French subjects complained of the difficulties made about their passports and the persecutions of the police, and the relations between the two governments became more and more strained.

Louis XVI. was known to be a mere cipher in the hands of the Jacobins; but when the news of his arrest arrived at Naples it was decided to break with France, and this resolution was announced by Acton to the French Ambassador, the Baron de Talleyrand, brother of the famous Archbishop of Reims of revolutionary celebrity, but absolutely opposed to him in principles and politics.

He had sent in his resignation on learning what had taken place at Paris, and wisely decided to remain as a private person at Naples, where he

[1] "The Queen of Naples and Lord Nelson" (Jeaffreson).

joined the camp of the *emigrés* and was fêted and caressed by the court and royal family.

The Neapolitan government refused to receive Cacault as *chargé d'affaires*, and that individual refused to leave Naples.

Maria Carolina was beside herself with anger and apprehension. She cursed the Revolution, showed more and more intense sympathy and affection to the *emigrés*, and wrote to the Comte de Bombelles, French Ambassador at Venice, who had refused to sign the new Constitution, and by his disinterested loyalty had reduced his family to poverty and difficulties. She congratulated him on his noble conduct, and, adding that all sovereigns were bound to recognise such fidelity, she begged him to accept from her a pension of twelve thousand francs. Nor did her gratitude stop there; the future of his children was secured, and Mme. Le Brun, who relates this anecdote in her "Souvenirs," remarks:

"Three of the children of M. de Bombelles now occupy brilliant positions in the world. The eldest, Count Louis de Bombelles, is Austrian Minister in Switzerland; the second, Count Charles, is Grand-Master of the household of Marie Louise; and the third, Count Henri, is Austrian Minister at Turin.

"Besides this generous action of the Queen of Naples," continues Mme. Le Brun, "I have known various others which do honour to her heart; she loved to relieve misery, and would not hesitate to climb to a fifth floor to bring help to sufferers. . . . This is the 'virago' about whom, under Bonaparte, the most infamous and obscene engravings were exhibited in the streets. They must needs calumniate her, they wanted her crown. It is well known that she was betrayed even by those whom she had always honoured with her friendship and confidence. The woman she loved most corresponded with the conqueror, who, by vile means, succeeded at last in dethroning the sister of Marie Antoinette to put Mme. Murat in her place. . . .

"When the Queen heard that I was preparing to return to Rome, she sent for me and said, 'I am very sorry Naples cannot keep you.'

"Then she offered me her little house on the seashore; but I was longing to see Rome again, and I declined with all the gratitude with which her great kindness inspired me. At the last, when she had paid me magnificently, and when I went to take a final leave of her, she gave me a beautiful old lacquer box with her cipher in diamonds, worth ten thousand francs.

"Magnificent as is the country I was leaving, I should not have liked to spend my life there. In my opinion Naples ought to be seen, like an enchanting magic-lantern, but to pass one's days there one must have become accustomed to the idea, one must have overcome the terror inspired by the volcano. One also reflects that all who inhabit the regions around live in constant expectation of an eruption or an earthquake, without speaking of the plague, which in the hot weather exists only two or three leagues off; and that the lakes in which they steep the flax give forth a pestilential air which brings fever and death to the inhabitants of this beautiful land.

"All these are serious drawbacks, it must be

admitted ; but if they did not exist, who would not wish to live in this delicious country ?

"The Chevalier Hamilton, who had been English Ambassador at Naples for nearly twenty years, was perfectly well acquainted with the manners and customs of the best society of that city.

"I must confess that what he told me was not at all favourable to the Neapolitan *noblesse*, but since that time everything is doubtless much changed. He told me a thousand stories of the greatest ladies, which, as they were too scandalous, I refrain from repeating. According to him, the Neapolitan women were surprisingly ignorant : they read nothing, although they pretended to read ; for one day, when calling upon one of them and finding her with a book in her hand, he saw as he approached her that she was holding it upside down. Destitute of any kind of instruction, many of them, he said, did not know that any country but Naples existed, and their only occupation was love, the object of which most of them frequently changed.

"What I could judge of myself was that the Neapolitan ladies gesticulate very much in speaking. They take no exercise, and only go out in a carriage, never on foot. Every night they go to the theatre, where they receive visits in their boxes; as they only listen to the *aria*, it is there that conversations are carried on ; much less comfortably, it seems to me, than in a *salon*.

"If one wishes to observe the expression of Neapolitan faces, one should go on to the road that leads to the church of San Gennaro, the day of the miracle of the *sainte ampoule*. The inhabitants of Naples and its environs flock in crowds along this road; carriages are stationed on the right, pedestrians on the left. Anxiety and impatience were so strangely depicted upon their countenances as the miracle was a little delayed, that I could scarcely prevent myself from laughing, when fortunately I was warned to keep calm, if I did not want to be stoned by the crowd. At last it was announced that the miracle had taken place, after which not a face was to be seen that did not express joy and rapture with such vivacity and vehemence that it is impossible to describe the scene." [1]

Into the life of Maria Carolina about this time came another and a very different woman from the gifted, brilliant, charming and high-souled Mme. Le Brun.

So much has been lately written about Lady Hamilton, formerly known as Emma Hart, but whose real name, according to the careful and exhaustive account in that interesting work, "The Queen of Naples and Lord Nelson," [2] was Amy Lyon, that it is unnecessary here to go into much detail respecting her very reprehensible early career, which in no way concerns the present history.

It is enough to say that she was the daughter of a blacksmith in Cheshire, that she went as a young girl into domestic service, that she was extraordinarily beautiful, and became the mistress of Sir Henry Fetherstonehaugh, with whom she led a rackety life, during which she is supposed to have had other lovers; that she quarrelled with Sir

[1] "Souvenirs de Mme. Vigée Le Brun."
[2] J Cordy Jeaffreson.

Henry Fetherstonehaugh, spent two years as model for "Hygeia." in the lecture-rooms of a certain Dr. Graham, and then became the mistress of Mr. Greville,[1] to whom she was really and strongly attached, and with whom she led a quiet life for four years, during which he tried to educate her; not, it would seem, with much success, for she could never write a letter even tolerably correctly, and in other respects remained ignorant and uncultivated in mind. So at least she appears to have been, judging from her letters, of which many exist, and none of which, either in spelling, expressions, or composition, are in the least like those of a refined, educated person.

During the time she lived with Charles Greville, however, her musical talents were cultivated, greatly to her advantage, as she had a beautiful voice; she was also accustomed, while under his protection, to associate with his friends, for the most part men of the world, distinguished, intellectual, and artistic, in whose society she acquired a certain amount of polish and good-breeding, which completed the attraction of her astonishing beauty and grace and the natural vivacity of her manners.

To Romney, who was a friend of Charles Greville's, she sat frequently, and that great artist appears to have been fascinated not only by her loveliness but by the charm of her manner and disposition. She had, says Mme.-Le Brun, a wonderful power of acting, and not only copying the gestures and voices of the actors she saw on the stage, but of giving to

[1] Second son of Francis, first Earl of Warwick of the Greville family.

her features the expression of joy, grief, remorse, &c., and of posing in attitudes exactly in accordance with any character or sentiment she desired to portray.

Except as regards her extraordinary beauty, Mme. Le Brun, however, does not appear to have shared the somewhat unreasonable admiration for Lady Hamilton which appears in the pages of some of her modern biographers. On the contrary, at the time when she painted her portrait at Naples she remarks in her " Souvenirs " :

" Lady Hamilton n'avait point d'esprit, quoiqu'elle fût excessivement moqueuse et dénigrante, au point que ces deux défauts étaient les seuls mobiles de sa conversation ; mais elle avait aussi de l'astuce, et elle s'en est servie pour se faire épouser. Elle manquait de tournure et s'habillait très-mal, dès qu'il s'agissait de faire une toilette vulgaire." [1]

At the end of four years Charles Greville, having become tired of the state of affairs, sent Emma, accompanied by her mother, a harmless, unpretentious woman, who lived with her, to his uncle at Naples, on pretence of giving her a better opportunity of studying music, promising to join her there during the autumn.

Sir William Hamilton lodged the mother and daughter at the British Embassy until the apartment he had engaged for them was ready, placed a carriage, boat, and servants at their disposal, loaded them with presents and attentions, and soon made it very apparent that he was deeply in love

[1] " Souvenirs de Mme Vigée Le Brun."

with Emma. But being much attached to Charles Greville, whom she hoped to marry, and in whose love she believed, she refused the offers of his uncle, and wrote many urgent letters imploring him to come to her.

Finding her entreaties disregarded, Emma had recourse to threats. She declared that she would never become the mistress of Sir William Hamilton, as Greville soon tried to persuade her to do; but that "It is not your interest to disoblige me, for you don't know what power I have *hear*. Onely I will never be his mistress. If you affront me, I will make him marry me."

Greville, however, neither came to Naples nor answered the letter, and about a month after having written it Emma became the mistress of his uncle, over whom she used her influence to such effect that when a few years had elapsed Sir William Hamilton married her during a visit to England, and in 1791 she returned to Naples as his wife.

CHAPTER X

Early career of Emma Hart—Arrives at Naples—Her life there—Marries Sir William Hamilton—Prosperous and splendid career of the Queen—The turn of the tide—Death of the Emperor Leopold and of the King of Sweden—Danger to Naples—Disputes with France—The French Ambassador—Evil news from Paris—On the brink of war—A patched-up peace—The Ambassador of the Republic—Threatened bombardment of Naples—Life at Naples—News of the murder of Louis XVI.—Outrageous conduct of French Ambassador—His reception at a *fête* at court—He is recalled—Attempt to save the Queen and Madame Elisabeth

THE strange intimacy which arose between this adventuress and the Queen of Naples did infinite harm to the reputation of Maria Carolina, gave colour to the infamous slanders and calumnies which her enemies delighted to invent and circulate, and aroused no lasting gratitude in the woman herself, who, after professing for years the most vehement attachment to the Queen, by whose notice she was so flattered and delighted, changed her mind when she found she could not get a pension from her, and in after years made an abominable and absolutely groundless accusation against her simply to obtain a small sum of money.[1]

[1] "The Queen of Naples and Lady Hamilton" (Jeaffreson) Years after the death of Nelson, Lady Hamilton, reduced to poverty by

LADY HAMILTON AS "NATURE."
After the painting by Romney.

Emma Hart arrived in Naples in 1786, and spent five years and a half there before marrying Sir William Hamilton, living under his protection, but in an apartment with Mrs. Cadogan, as she called her mother, and being generally supposed to be studying for the stage.

Her remarkable beauty made a great sensation in Naples, and the Queen was anxious to see her, more especially because the King had taken a fancy to her, and besieged her with attentions which she was too prudent to encourage, as her great desire was to be received, or at any rate noticed, by the Queen.

Maria Carolina gratified her curiosity by desiring a Neapolitan prince, who was a friend of Emma Hart's, to walk with her during a promenade one Sunday, so near that she might see her, and was greatly impressed by her beauty. She gave no cause for scandal except by her connection with the English Ambassador, but lived quietly and harmlessly, occupying herself with music and the society of the many men and few women who visited her, and continued to behave with entire discretion towards the King, in spite of his open admiration.

He would sit in his boat with his hat off while his musicians serenaded her, but even if she had

---

her own extravagance and folly, declared on one occasion that her daughter Horatia was the daughter of the Queen of Naples. There was not the slightest ground for so atrocious a slander. There had never been the slightest idea of love between the Queen and Nelson, and over and over again, in speech and letters, she had asserted her to be her own child. Both she and Nelson spoke of and to the child as father and mother.

been so inclined, Emma Hart was far too astute not to perceive that to be the mistress of Ferdinando, with his never-ending love intrigues and his subservience to the Queen, would not be nearly so much to her advantage as the approbation of Maria Carolina, the protection of Sir William Hamilton, and the probable achievement of becoming his wife.

She played her part so well that the Queen gradually proceeded to show her some distant signs of favour, and to encourage the great ladies of the court to do the same, and even to notice her privately. To many of them her want of instruction would, according to what is known of their own ignorance and frivolity, have been no drawback, but she could not, of course, be presented at court until after her marriage.

For some time after she and her mother removed into the English Embassy very few either Neapolitan or foreign ladies were to be seen at her partics, but gradually she became the fashion; the Duchess of Argyll, *née* Elizabeth Gunning, took her up, Lady Elcho did the same, and it began to be said, especially by those who wished to think so, that she was secretly married to Sir William Hamilton. To the Queen it was a matter of the greatest importance to secure the friendship of the English Ambassador, and to do so she would have made much greater sacrifices than to receive a beautiful, attractive woman, whatever might be her morals; for England was her great hope in the crusade against France, in which her whole heart and soul were now chiefly absorbed.

In January, 1791, while the King and Queen were still in Austria, Sir William Hamilton made the experiment of a great concert and ball at the English Embassy, at which the honours were done by Emma Hart. It was a complete success, being attended by all the diplomatic and court set, and Emma Hart felt that she had attained one, at any rate, of the three objects for which she had been working: she had become a "personage" at Naples; she had also probably effected her second project, and made herself capable of winning a position in the musical and theatrical profession in case she were again thrown upon her own resources. This, however, did not appear to be likely; on the contrary, she was about to realise her crowning ambition and triumph.

After the return of the royal family in the spring, Sir William Hamilton left Naples for a visit to England, before which he had long and important consultations with the Queen upon the threatening aspect of political affairs. The European Powers were gathering slowly for the overthrow of the French revolutionists. The Emperor Leopold, the King of Prussia, the Duke of Saxony, the Grandduke of Tuscany, the Empress of Russia, were preparing their forces, and the chivalrous Gustavus III., King of Sweden, eagerly offered to lead the allied host to Paris.

How Maria Carolina pushed on her own preparations, how ardently she sympathised and longed for the strife and victory, for the rescue of her sister and the punishment of her persecutors, and how she pleaded for the help of England, for the fleet of England, in the coming crisis, one can well imagine.

Sir William left Naples in the early summer, as also did Emma Hart, who returned with him as Lady Hamilton, and as such was formally presented to the Queen.

She had had plenty of gaiety, admiration, and social success in London, where her old friend Romney had been delighted to see her again, but where Queen Charlotte had refused to receive her; but what was of the deepest interest to Maria Carolina, she had stopped in Paris and had been admitted into the presence of Marie Antoinette.

Shortly after her return she dined at the palace of Caserta in company with Lady Malmesbury, who wrote to her sister, Lady Elliott, that the Queen had received Lady Hamilton very kindly and that all the English meant to be civil to her. And this was the beginning of her friendship with Maria Carolina.[1]

Hitherto the life of the Queen of Naples had been a long course of uninterrupted splendour and prosperity.

Daughter of an Emperor and Empress, brought up by devoted parents in state and magnificence under the shadow of the mightiest throne in Christendom, surrounded by young brothers and sisters, carefully and religiously educated under the supervision of such a mother as the great Empress, called at sixteen to wear a crown and rule a kingdom, at thirty-eight she could look back upon such a career of enjoyment, success, and splendour as falls to the lot of few women.

[1] "The Queen of Naples and Lord Nelson" (Jeaffreson).

To the marriage she so dreaded she had quickly become reconciled; the husband forced upon her was almost immediately her slave, and in spite of the difference in their tastes she had soon found she could get on very well with him. Her home was in one of the most enchanting regions of the earth, her court a constant scene of pleasure, gaiety, and luxury, her life filled with occupation and interests of the highest importance, her government wise and successful, she herself admired and popular, her children a source of unfailing delight to her; and now the splendid marriages of the three eldest had fulfilled her dearest wishes and satisfied her loftiest ambition. But she had reached the turning-point: from henceforth the tide of prosperity which had flowed so steadily began to ebb, and the clouds which for some time had hung threateningly upon the distant horizon gathered around until they overwhelmed her in a flood of calamities as extraordinary as the happiness and magnificence of her former life.

The King of France, having signed the Constitution which reduced him to the position of a puppet, and recovered a semblance of liberty, sent circulars to stop the movements of the foreign armies collecting to deliver him. The King of Naples declared that he would suspend his opinion until the King was free, and the rest of the sovereigns replied in the same strain. But there were differences and dissensions amongst them: Venice and Lombardy would not join the Italian league; Spain hung back; the Emperor Leopold, after the communication of the King of France, sent back to their quarters the army he had collected;[1] England and Russia held aloof; Prussia would not act alone; only the gallant King of Sweden and the Queen of Naples were now as ever ready and willing to fight.

But they were powerless alone, and as the months passed on, amidst the cares of government, the perils surrounding herself, her husband, and children, and the gaieties and excitements which, in spite of everything, went on perpetually at the Neapolitan court, Maria Carolina's heart and mind were filled with terror, indignation, and anxiety for her sister Antoinette, and a passionate longing to deliver her.

In March, 1792, the death of her favourite brother, the Emperor Leopold, came upon the Queen as a crushing blow. Six weeks after him died the Empress Ludovica, who declared she could not survive the husband whom she had always loved passionately, in spite of the numerous infidelities in which he resembled his father, the fascinating Emperor Franz.

The gallant King of Sweden was murdered by his subjects in the same month.

Furious at not being received by the court and government at Naples, Cacault had used all his endeavours to induce France to attack the Two Sicilies, representing that the coasts of Sicily were exposed, and that Naples was built on the sea-shore; with its royal palace, government stores, and public buildings so near the water's edge it would be the easiest thing in the world to bombard and destroy the whole place if a French squadron were sent to the bay of Naples.

[1] Colletta.

To the revolutionary government, however, other considerations presented themselves. However willing they might have been to gratify the spite of their worthy envoy, they could not but perceive that the destruction of Naples might entail consequences too serious to be risked for such a satisfaction.

The injury to commerce would be enormous, and it was not to be supposed that the maritime Powers, headed by England, would allow such an outrage to pass unpunished. It would be better to try by all possible means to keep Naples neutral, and with this object a more decent, respectable envoy was selected, to receive whom the Queen was induced to consent.

It was with the greatest reluctance that she yielded, but there seemed no alternative. Naples was not strong enough to protect herself; the exposed situation of both the Sicilies was only too apparent.

The envoy chosen by Dumouriez was a certain Mackau, who, though a radical, was not a furious Jacobin, but supposed to be a moderate member of the revolutionary party. He had decent manners and habits, being the son of a *diplomate* and of a *sous-gouvernante* of the children of France, and had himself been Minister at Wurtemberg.

He received instructions to address himself to the Queen, as it was useless to talk to the King. He was to calm her uneasiness, to point out to her the dangers the Neapolitan fleet and commerce would incur in a war with France, and to assure her of the peaceful intentions of the French government. Armed with these instructions, Mackau set out for Naples, passing through Rome, where he had so little *savoir-faire* as to propose to pay his respects to Mesdames de France, who, of course, refused to receive him.

Then, he forgot to get a passport before leaving Rome, in consequence of which, when he arrived at the Neapolitan frontier he was refused permission to cross it. He persisted, threatened to declare it an act of hostility, and at last was allowed to proceed on his journey; but the officer on guard was punished for not carrying out his *consigne*.

This incident shows the state of feeling prevailing at Naples, which was crowded with *emigrés*, and where his arrival was anticipated with disgust. The *emigrés* declared he was a dangerous revolutionist; everywhere he was avoided, or received with coldness and contempt.

Before long the news of the attack on the Tuileries and all the horrors of the 10th of August filled the court with consternation.

The King and Queen, in the first frenzy of grief and indignation, refused to recognise Mackau and directed Acton to communicate their decision to him, and there was a stormy scene between the Neapolitan Minister and the French envoy on the 3rd of September. Those of the French residents in Naples who belonged to the revolutionary party begged Mackau not to leave them, as they were afraid of the *emigrés* and the overwhelming numbers who sympathised with them. He himself was especially anxious to remain, and declared his intention of doing so, requesting permission to wait, at any rate, until after the confinement of his wife, which was expected to take place before long.

Every *salon* was now closed to him; he was closely watched by spies of the police, and in every way his position became intolerable.[1]

War appeared to be imminent, and it was only the terribly helpless and isolated position of Naples which prevented the King and Queen from instantly breaking off all relations with the nation for which they now entertained the profoundest hatred and horror, but which was so powerful that it must be conciliated almost at any cost.

The King of France was deposed, the Republic proclaimed, and Mackau announced that as the French nation had decided upon a republic he would serve that as he had served the King when under his orders, but that he had never been properly received and treated as Ambassador of France, and that now he wished to know whether, being the accredited representative of the Conventional Government, he was to be recognised as French Ambassador to Naples or not.

The court put off the decision as long as they could by evasions and temporising, until matters were brought to a crisis by the Convention sending orders to their representative to leave Naples at once.

Mackau requested an interview with Acton, and began to prepare for his departure, upon which the Neapolitan court, yielding to a cruel necessity, changed the line of conduct hitherto observed, and requested him to remain.

[1] "Marie Caroline, Reine des Deux Siciles" (André Bonnefonds).

There was no help for it. The allies and *emigrés* under the Duke of Brunswick had indeed begun the campaign so ardently longed for by Maria Carolina, who, watching with breathless anxiety the progress of their arms, had, with all her court, family, and *emigrés* friends, rejoiced and exulted when the news arrived of the capture of Longwy. But their joy was soon turned into despair by the evil tidings which followed this short lived success.

There had been a great battle at Valmy. The Duke of Brunswick had been defeated by Dumouriez; the allies were driven back. Dumouriez had invaded Nice and Savoy, and the ferocious mob at Paris, terrified and infuriated by the news of Longwy, had perpetrated the awful September massacres which sent a thrill of horror through the civilised world and inflicted an indelible stain upon the honour and fair fame of France.

Everything looked black and threatening: the allied forces were disunited and incompetent; England, whose powerful fleet could have swept the seas, still held back; the ferocious republic was everywhere victorious; its representative must be received with consideration. Concessions, political and social, were therefore reluctantly made. The Queen consented to receive Mme. Mackau; the *salons* were opened to her husband and herself, who now presented themselves at the balls and dinners of those by whom they were loathed and despised.

The bloodstained republic was not only a serious danger and curse to every country in Europe, but an annoyance in many lesser but intolerable ways. It sent brutes and ruffians of infamous character and low, coarse manners as ambassadors and plenipotentiaries to other powers, especially if they were not strong enough to resist. These scoundrels were not only objectionable from their odious habits and customs, and as the suitable representatives of the gang of murderers their masters, but they were also exceedingly mischievous, taking every opportunity of disseminating amongst the ignorant populace the murderous, rapacious, and blasphemous principles of their own party.

One of these ruffians, named Basille, was sent to Rome, where he behaved in a manner so offensive and outrageous that the Romans rose up and killed him in a riot. The French writer, M. Bonnefonds, in relating this circumstance, exclaims with horror and indignation at the well-deserved fate of this violent caitiff, apparently supposing that the emissaries of the French republic had a right to oppress and annoy, even in their own cities, the people of other countries, but that those persons had no right to defend themselves or retaliate.

Another of these pestilent fellows was sent to Genoa, where he busied himself in translating into Italian, and spreading in Italy, the doctrines of the wretches now terrorising France. Acton, who considered this agent of the revolution a danger to the country, managed to get rid of him. The King of Sardinia, to whom it was attempted to send him, refused to receive this Semonville, who was then sent to Turkey. Acton, however, wrote to the Neapolitan plenipotentiary at Constantinople, and gave him an account of the proceedings of Semonville in Italy. The plenipotentiary showed this letter to the Sultan, who thereupon declared he would not have Semonville in his dominions.

The Convention were enraged at all these rebuffs, which they attributed to Acton and the King and Queen of Naples, and on the 17th of December, 1792, a squadron of French ships of war appeared in the bay of Naples. The largest of them dropped anchor within half a gunshot of the fortress of Castel dell' Ovo, and the French admiral, La Touche, having drawn up the rest of his ships in line of battle across the port, sent a messenger to demand reparation or disavowal of the insult offered to France in the person of her ambassador, declaring that unless such apologies, retractation, or disavowal were made within an hour he would lay Naples in ruins.

The republican writer, General Colletta, blames Maria Carolina for yielding to this demand, but, in common with all the radical writers, especially the French and Italian ones, he was tolerably certain to blame whatever she did. If she had refused the demand, and her refusal had resulted in the destruction of Naples and the massacre of its inhabitants, no words would have been strong enough for him to inveigh against her folly, cruelty, and obstinacy in sacrificing her capital and her people to her pride and vengeance. As it was, he accuses her of weakness and cowardice, neither of which faults belonged in the least to her character.

The danger was immediate and terrible. The

Neapolitans had been taken unprepared. Both the Queen and Acton were aware of the numbers and violence of the Jacobin party in Naples, and believed they would revolt and assist the French, even if they were not already in conspiracy with them.[1] Whether their suspicions were right or wrong, it was unanimously decided at a hurried meeting of the Council, by a vote agreed to by the King, Queen, and Sir John Acton (who was not a person to be suspected of cowardice), that they had not the power to resist, and therefore there was no choice but to comply with the demands of the stronger force. The letter was disavowed. The King promised to treat Mackau as the ambassador of the republic and to remain neutral, which last promise the Queen had no intention of keeping. The hostile fleet weighed anchor and sailed away.

Their narrow escape from the catastrophe which had only just been averted filled the society of Naples with alarm, but neither that nor the fearful anxiety of the royal family for their relations in France seems to have influenced the festivities of the court. It was a strange life just then at Naples: a whirl of excitement, in which terrible suspense, continual danger, acute sorrow, and anxious watchfulness mingled with perpetual entertainments, music and dancing, theatres, mas-

[1] The violence and disloyalty of this party were a serious danger. Even as the messenger from La Touche, bringing his threat to bombard Naples, passed through the street, he was greeted with shouts of welcome from these traitors. "Courage, brave Frenchmen! Go on! Fifty thousand men will stand by you" (Helfert).

querades, and pageants, fairy-like illuminations reflected at night from the stately palaces and ships into the calm waters of the lovely bay, picnics and hunting parties in the shady woods and delicious gardens of the enchanting country outside, now and then disturbed by a shock of earthquake, the rumour of an approaching enemy, or a dangerous conspiracy; while from time to time the great volcano poured streams of burning lava down its steep sides, and smoke and flames burst forth, their lurid light to unaccustomed eyes like watchfires in the still Southern night.

Lady Webster, writing from Naples, where she was staying at that time, to Lady Sheffield, says:

"In the course of one month we might either have been Bombarded by the French, Smothered by the Mountain, or Swallowed up in an Earthquake.... Our Mountain blazes in a Grand Style, and I mean to ascend it amidst torrents of red-hot lava and showers of burning stones.... All the English except the Palmerstons and those who stay the summer here have flown. The Gaieties, however, go on merrily. To-morrow we have a *Fête* at Portici, which consists of Breakfast, Dinner, Concert, Ball, and Supper. Of the Day, sufficient is the Evil thereof.... I wrote you a very pretty history by M. la Flotte, who carried the news of the massacre at Rome to the Convention.—16 March, 1793."[1]

The royal family and court were, however, in mourning when this letter was written, for on the

---

[1] "The Girlhood of Maria Josepha Holroyd" (afterwards Lady Stanley of Alderley).

Louis XVI.

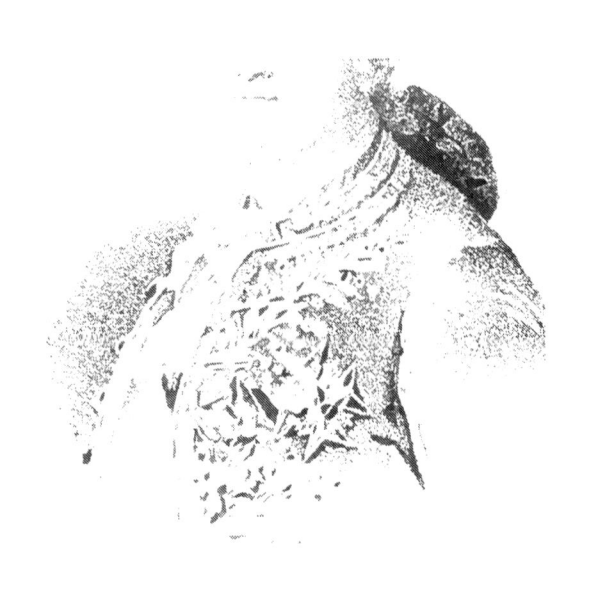

7th of February the news of the murder of Louis XVI. had come upon them like a thunderbolt, just as they were preparing for the *fêtes* of the Carnival. Balls and concerts were put off, a general mourning was ordered, and a grand funeral Mass, attended by all the court and *élite* of society, was celebrated with great pomp and solemnity.

The King and Queen were plunged in grief and longing for vengeance. To them the crime was so monstrous as to be almost incredible.[1]

On some one remarking shortly afterwards that this was the second instance in history of the execution of a king by his subjects, Ferdinand exclaimed in astonishment:

"The *second* time?"

"Yes, your Majesty; in England——"

"A king put to death in England?"

"Charles I., your Majesty."

"No!" cried Ferdinando indignantly, "you have been misinformed. The English are far too brave and loyal a people to commit such an abominable crime."

Then, after a pause, he continued:

"You may be assured that it is a pure invention of the Jacobins at Paris, which they have set about in order to make their own crime appear less by the example of the great English nation. They may succeed in deceiving their own people, but I hope we know better than to be taken in."

The French ambassador, Mackau, was, to do him justice, horrified at the murder of his King. Like many of his party, he had never expected things to

[1] Helfert, "Konigin Maria Karolina," &c.

be carried to such extremities. Though a miserable creature he was a gentleman, and his early instincts and associations made him recoil from iniquities which came naturally enough to many of his colleagues. He had known Louis XVI. from childhood, had received many kindnesses and benefits from him, and although he was requiting them with the blackest ingratitude, this catastrophe caused him both grief and consternation. He shut himself up with his wife and gave way to tears and lamentations, which did not, however, prevent his refusing to wear the general mourning ordered and writing a cringing letter to Lebrun, assuring him that he had not done so.[1]

His despicable weakness and self-interest, however, did him no good, and pleased nobody.

Acton sent the usual notice of general mourning to him as well as to the other ambassadors, and he ought in decency, if he did not intend to observe it, to have sent in his resignation.

In consequence of his conduct his position at Naples became intolerable. He met with nothing but slights and insults. Every one turned away from him with horror as identified with the assassins.

Still, he clung to his post in spite of it all, and put the finishing stroke to his folly and baseness two or three months later.

Early in May the Empress of Austria, eldest daughter of the King and Queen of Naples, gave birth to a son, an event which, in the midst of their sorrow and anxiety, gave them much consolation and happiness. In honour of the Archduke their

[1] Bonnefonds

grandson they ordered the general mourning to cease, and issued invitations to a *fête* to be given in celebration of the occasion.

As a matter of course, all the ambassadors received invitations, including Mackau, who could not, as French ambassador, be excluded, but who was, of course, under the circumstances, expected to understand that it was only a formality of which he could not possibly avail himself. That he should have actually done so was all the more unexpected and outrageous, as he was not only the son of a *diplomate*, but had been himself Minister at Würtemberg, consequently the excuse of ignorance could not be his.

Nevertheless, on the evening of the *fête* he arrived at the palace and appeared in the presence of the King and Queen.

A thrill of disgust and indignation ran through the whole assembly. That the representative of the regicides should present himself at a *fête* in the family of him they had murdered was so shocking that it called forth a chorus of horror and contempt.

Mackau approached the sovereigns, who, without deigning to return his salutation, turned their backs upon him, while gibes and sneers and whispers all around showed him clearly the enormity of his offence.

He understood; retired profoundly mortified; and, resolving to leave Naples at once, he wrote to Cacault to ask for a French ship from Livorno, as the Papal States were closed.

It is satisfactory to know that, far from deriving any advantage from his contemptible conduct, it in fact ruined him.

From Lebrun and the Executive Council he received severe censure for the incident.

Considering, they declared, that the object of the *fête* to which he was invited should have indicated to him that he could not attend it without impropriety, he ought to have excused himself from what was only a matter of formality. And since his inconsiderate conduct had exposed him to a slight which compromised the office with which he was invested, they took this opportunity to recall him. He therefore departed in disgrace and returned into the Terror, through which he passed without losing his life; but his career was closed. That he never learnt either sense or dignity is evident from his having had the impudence to ask Louis XVIII. for a pension.

Maret, afterwards Duc de Bassano, was appointed to succeed him, but never occupied his post, for two very sufficient reasons.

Maret and Semonville were seized in the Grisons, July 22, 1793, by the emissaries of Austria, who carried them secretly to Mantova, and then to Hufstein, in the Tyrol, where they were imprisoned. In his Memoirs, Louis XVIII. relates this circumstance, which he declares to have been most unfortunate:

"After the death of the King, the courts of Naples and Tuscany attempted to save the Queen and Madame Elisabeth, offering their mediation with the revolutionary government. This proposition having for a moment appeared of a nature to be admitted, it was decided at Paris to charge Maret and Semonville with this mission. The latter had just been named Ambassador at Constantinople; he was secretly directed to stop at Florence on various pretexts to confer with the Minister Manfredini, charged to treat with him; while Maret should go to Naples for the same purpose. Perhaps a fortunate result might have crowned this enterprise if Austrian policy had not ordained otherwise. On the 22nd of July, Maret and Semonville were seized in time of peace, in the neutral territory of the Grisons, by emissaries of Austria. This veritable trap had disastrous consequences. In vain the two diplomatists explained the object of their journey: no one would listen to them; they were sent first in secret to Mantova, then to Hufstein, in the Tyrol. Not only that, but the Grand-duke was forced to disgrace Manfredini, and these measures were followed by the death of the Queen and Madame Elisabeth."[1]

[1] "Lui (Semonville) et Maret avaient été arrêtés dans le cas suivant: après la mort du Roi, les cours de Naples et de Toscane avaient essayé de sauver la Reine et Madame Elisabeth, en offrant leur médiation au gouvernement revolutionnaire. Cette proposition ayant un instant paru de nature à pouvoir être admise, on se décida à Paris à charger Maret et Semonville de cette mission. Le second venait de recevoir le titre d'Ambassadeur à Constantinople: on lui enjoignit secrètement de s'arrêter à Florence sous divers prétextes pour s'y concerter avec le Ministre Manfredini, chargé de traiter avec lui, tandis que Maret se rendrait à Naples dans le même but. Peut-être qu'un heureux résultat aurait couronné cette entreprise, si la politique autrichienne n'en eût ordonné autrement. Le 22 juillet, 1793, Maret et Semonville furent enlevé en pleine paix à Novale, sur le territoire neutre des Grisons, par des émissaires de l'Autriche. Ce véritable guet-apens eut de funestes conséquences. Vainement les deux diplomates firent connaître l'objet de leur voyage, on ne voulut rien entendre; ils furent d'abord envoyes secrètement à Mantoue, puis à Hufstein, dans le Tyrol. Ce n'était pas assez, le Grand-duc de Toscane dut disgracier Manfredini, et ces mesures furent suivies de la mort de la Reine et de Madame Elisabeth."—"Mémoires de Louis XVIII.," t. vii. pp. 76–7.

CHAPTER XI

The Queen's popularity declines—Her proceedings give offence—The Neapolitans—Faults and virtues of Maria Carolina—Violence and calumnies of her enemies.

FOR the last two or three years the popularity of Maria Carolina had been rapidly declining, to a much greater extent than she at all suspected. The discovery she made by means of her police spies, who penetrated everywhere, high and low, of the numbers of her enemies, their ingratitude for all she had done for them, and the atrocious slanders they were spreading about her, was at once painful and astonishing.

For even her bitter enemy, the historian Colletta, admits that for more than twenty years, until 1790, she had governed the kingdom well and wisely, although he tries, like all her detractors, to give the credit of her reforms and beneficent institutions to Ferdinando, who they know perfectly well was a man incapable of originating or carrying them out, besides being entirely occupied with his own pleasures at Caserta.

So far was he from wishing to take any part in the government or in any kind of business, that he would not even allow inkstands to be in the

Council chamber, for fear he might have the trouble of writing anything.

One day at Caserta, where a Council was being held, a most important matter was under discussion. Suddenly the crack of a whip was heard three times in the courtyard. The King started up, and turning to the Queen, exclaimed, "My dear, take my place, and conclude the affair as you think best." So saying, he left the Council chamber and went out hunting.[1]

In spite of her many good qualities, however, Maria Carolina was a person certain to make enemies, even if her position had not been one of such extreme difficulty.

The active brain, always busy about something or other, and the hasty, impetuous disposition against which the Empress, her mother, had so strongly warned her, as well as the generous heart and deep interest in her subjects by which she was so strongly characterised, caused her to be too eager and too vehement in carrying out her plans and reforms, and too resolved to push them on in spite of all opposition.

Young, enthusiastic, and full of good intentions, during the first part of her reign she had been carried away by the doctrines which then seemed as beneficent as in later years they became abhorrent to her. She tried to do too much at once, as eager, enthusiastic young people are apt to do, and being not only an impetuous young girl, but the daughter of an Empress and herself a Queen with absolute authority, she swept away all obstacles to the ful-

[1] Helfert.

filment of her plans, and treated those who disliked or disagreed with them with disdain and contempt.

This was all the more unfortunate as most of her projects and reforms, righteous and excellent though they might be, were calculated to irritate one class or other of her subjects who were affected by them.

The corruption that prevailed in the law courts was iniquitous, and the inquiries and reformations she caused to be made in them infuriated the lawyers, especially the edict obliging every judge to state the reasons of his decrees.

Her reduction of the oppressive privileges of the nobles had angered many of them, and the numerous party amongst them whose sympathies were with Spain were alienated by the substitution of Austrian for Spanish influence at the court of Naples.

Carlos III. had been a capable and excellent King; his rule over Naples had been just and benevolent; the only mistake he made was his attempt to exercise, after his abdication, a control which made it virtually a province of Spain. But he had been deeply incensed by the independent policy of his son and daughter-in-law, and had died, not in open hostility, but without having forgiven what he considered to be undutiful conduct on their part.

The clergy resented the Queen's secular schools and the part she took in the distribution amongst educational and secular institutions, such as hospitals, museums, and the University, of the confiscated property of the Jesuits; although it was not she who had either quarrelled with them or seized their possessions, but Carlos III. and Ferdinando, before her marriage.

The army reforms furnished another ground for contention, although she had restored it from the miserable state in which she found it to discipline and efficiency. But although there was not a single Neapolitan officer capable either of commanding a battalion or organising a corps of artillery, the nobles were furious because the Queen sought for and employed competent officers from other countries.[1]

With the navy it was just the same; in spite of their unprotected coasts, the miserable Neapolitans, like a certain party in our own country and in the present day, grudged the necessary money to pay for the magnificent fleet she had created, which ought to have been their pride as well as their safeguard.

The new laws for the regulation of the coral fisheries and the planting of waste lands with olives, though benefiting many people, made enemies of others whose profits were injured thereby. Her attempt to prevent the insanitary custom of burying in the churches was so obviously right that even the people of Naples subscribed quickly for the new *campo santo;* but the nobles, though they gave money for this object, continued to bury their own dead in the churches, as they had always been accustomed to do.

The Queen completed the palaces and buildings left unfinished by Carlos III. and built the theatres of the Fondo and San Ferdinando. She also carried

[1] "The Queen of Naples and Lord Nelson" (Jeaffreson).

on the work of the royal archives of Naples originated by Ferdinand of Arragon (1477) and carried on by some of his successors. It was finished under her government (1786).

Jeaffreson justly remarks that Colletta, in stating that this work was completed by *Ferdinando the Bourbon*, gives "a good example of the way in which Maria Carolina is deprived of the glory due to her for her good deeds even by historians who admit in a roundabout way that Ferdinando was in no degree personally accountable for the virtuous achievements of his reign. Caring for nothing but his pleasures, Ferdinando was wholly indifferent to the work under consideration. Had it related to the game in the royal chases, instead of the parchments in the royal archives, the matter would have received a proper share of the King's attention." [1]

But, especially when one considers that at the same time Maria Carolina was a devoted mother to her numerous children and entered with the keenest enjoyment into the pleasures and excitements of her gay, luxurious court, one cannot fail to be astonished at the immense amount of business that, with the authority of Ferdinando and the assistance of Acton, she managed to transact, and the varied scope of her exertions; more especially if one realises the time, place, and circumstances.

Coming as an inexperienced girl of sixteen from the highly civilised, cultivated, and decorous court of Vienna; accustomed to a society regulated by the strictest ideas of religion and refinement and a

[1] "The Queen of Naples and Lord Nelson."

family celebrated throughout Europe for the exceptional talents, education, attractions, and superior qualities of all its members; and living amongst a people like the Austrians; what could be more astonishing, perplexing, and incomprehensible than such a husband as Ferdinando and such a court and people as those of Naples?

Any one who has lived in Italy even in our own day knows the extraordinary difference in civilisation between the north and south of that country, not only among the lower classes, but in ranks which in other lands are not affected by geographical position. The further you go south in Italy, the more Oriental are the aspect and the atmosphere around you. Women are more secluded, children more spoilt and ill-behaved, servants more dishonest, animals worse treated, the pursuits, amusements, and conversation both of men and women more unintellectual and frivolous, the ideas, habits, and customs less civilised.

That in every department of the state corruption prevailed was not surprising; at that time and in the different Italian states it was a matter of course. For an experienced man it would have been difficult enough to purge the administration of the government of the Two Sicilies from the malpractices and abuses which abounded in every department; for a girl or young woman it was impossible.

Still, she did what she could; and if she did it in an autocratic way, that was only following the precepts she had always been taught and the example of her mother and brother, who had gained the love of their subjects and the approbation of the world in general.

For many years she had been very popular, except with the Spanish party, at the court she had made so attractive and splendid; with the poor, to whom she showed such constant charity and kindness; and with the liberals, to whom she gave so much encouragement and sympathy.

But now her popularity was everywhere disappearing, and these last, from her ardent admirers and devoted friends, had not only turned into her bitterest foes, but were doing all they could by the blackest calumnies, the most wicked and monstrous inventions, to ruin her reputation, and by their secret conspiracies to undermine her government.

Maria Carolina had the virtues and the faults of a strong, undisciplined character. Under happier circumstances, or if she had died after the first three or four and twenty years of her reign, she would have always been looked upon as an excellent queen. But fate was against her; the latter part of her life was beset with misfortunes, sorrows, and injuries which embittered her mind and exaggerated her faults. Jeaffreson, in speaking of her, remarks:

"In her best time she had the ordinary failings of an ambitious, aspiring, and supremely beautiful woman. In her later years, when multitudinous troubles and griefs that sharpen with time had changed her moral nature, and so affected her mind that its sanity was sometimes questionable, she became a woman whose claim to pity was stronger than her title to admiration. But the beautiful Queen of Naples, with her delight in splendid vanities and her keen appetite for every enjoyment befitting a personage of her high degree, could not have been so steadily considerate for the poor and ignorant, and so perseveringly thoughtful for the higher interests of her people, had she not been a conscientious and good woman. The story of Maria Carolina's humane and glorious government of the Sicilies up to 1790 would by itself discredit the monstrous inventions of the much later libellers, who, without a single scrap of sound testimony for the justification of their revolting statements, require us to believe that her private life during this same period was no less vile and loathsome than her public life was bright and admirable. . . .

"At the close of 1790 Maria Carolina had for more than twenty years been carrying out her laudable schemes for the welfare of her people. In the execution of these schemes she had (to use one of Lord Beaconsfield's many felicitous expressions) spent some twenty years in harassing interests. No wonder, then, that by the end of 1790 Naples abounded with people who thought and spoke ill of the meddlesome Queen, and were ready to believe tales to her discredit. Amongst the people thus ready to believe defamatory tales of Maria Carolina there were equally furious and credulous simpletons who would have swallowed the monstrous invention had any malicious gossip accused the Queen of having poisoned her own mother. I am not aware that this particular charge was ever made against Maria Carolina by her calumniators. But at the close of 1790 the time was approaching when quite as wild and hideous things began to be whispered of her by the revolutionary fanatics, whose monstrous and utterly baseless slanders found their way to the pages of deplorably indiscreet but not intentionally wicked writers of history."[1]

I have quoted this in full, because Mr. Jeaffreson, who, from the large collection of documents concerning Queen Carolina, Lady Hamilton, and Lord Nelson that came into the possession of Mr. Alfred Morrison, and to which he so recently had access, gained therefrom a considerable amount of valuable information, hitherto inaccessible to the public, which throws light upon many transactions and circumstances otherwise obscure. The value of the details and explanations we thus obtain does not, of course, consist in anything new that we learn about Lady Hamilton, whose life and character are well known, but in the evidence it brings forth respecting a woman of far different position, character, and importance—the much-maligned Queen of Naples. English readers are, for the most part, well acquainted with the history of the adventuress who, after leading a disreputable life as model or mistress to one person after another, enjoyed for a few years a brilliant social career and then disappeared into obscurity. But with regard to the illustrious daughter of the great Empress, the daughter, sister, mother, and grandmother of emperors, empresses, kings and queens, herself a queen, for many years practically an absolute ruler,

[1] " The Queen of Naples and Lord Nelson "

distinguished for her talents, beauty, and misfortunes, most of them know little or nothing; many have no idea who she was at all, or confuse her with her unworthy supplanter, Caroline Buonaparte.

It is from certain German writers that a clear estimate of Maria Carolina should be gained. The French and Italian works about her are written for the most part by violent radicals and revolutionists who, as in the case of Marie Antoinette and Queen Louise of Prussia, thought no infamy too atrocious to invent or spread against a woman who was the enemy of their party or their nation. English writers read and believed these calumnies, or received as truth the slanderous reports circulated by her enemies during her later years, especially when at the climax of her misfortunes she was opposed to the English in Sicily.

In the graphic, exhaustive, and deeply interesting volumes of Freiherr von Helfert,[1] who has devoted to the history of Maria Carolina—as did Herr von Arneth to that of Maria Theresia—all the learning, research, and study necessary to produce works so voluminous, so powerful, and so invaluable to the student of the history of those times, we find the true and carefully given account of the life of this brilliant but most unfortunate Queen.

With painstaking accuracy he traces out the different incidents, showing the absolute impossi-

[1] "Königin Karolina von Neapel und Sicilien im Kampfe gegen die franzosische Weltheerschaft, 1790-1814" (Freiherr von Helfert, Wien, 1878); "Maria Karolina von Oesterreich, Königin von Neapel und Sicilien. Anklagen und Vertheidigung" (Freiherr von Helfert, Wien, 1884).

bility and the preposterous nature of various charges made against Maria Carolina, and shows that whatever might be the faults of her later years, immorality was certainly not amongst them; while of the malignant scandals circulated about her relations with various persons in her younger days there has never been the slightest proof, and the object and motives for their invention were perfectly evident.

The raving fury of her revolutionary assailants makes their statements ridiculous; as, for instance, those of the Milanese Gorani, who remained in Paris during the Terror and shared in many of the excesses and infamies going on, although at last he was anxious to save the Girondins, destroy Robespierre, Marat, and Danton, and place Louis XVII. upon the throne under a regency of radicals.

He hated Maria Carolina as an Austrian as well as a queen, and countless specimens of his writings show the venom and blindness of his fury against her:

"Elle a les passions aussi fortes, les mêmes vices, les mêmes inclinations que sa sœur Antoinette de France. . . ."

"Ce n'est point une Reine, une épouse, une mère, que l'Autriche nous a donnée; c'est une furie, une Mégère, une Messaline qu'elle a vomie dans sa colère et lancée parmi nous."

"La Reine de Naples ressemble à ses sœurs. Elle chérit la famille dont elle descend, méprise son mari, et déteste le pays sur lequel il a la faiblesse de la laisser régner."

"Ah! j'aime à penser que Marie-Caroline est l'unique monstre de cette espèce," &c.

Such are some specimens of the less violent of his ravings against the Queen; others are too disgusting and outrageous to record.

CHAPTER XII

Return of the French fleet—Treachery of La Touche and Mackau—The Jacobin supper—Conspiracies—Disguised as porters—The secret police—A secret treaty—Capture of Toulon—Alliance with England—Nelson—Splendid reception at Naples—The Queen and Captain Nelson—Departure of the *Agamemnon*—The Queen and her daughters—The Princess Amélie—The murder of Marie Antoinette—The Office for the Dead—The Marchesa Solari—Vows of vengeance

NOT long after the departure of La Touche and his ships, but before the breaking out of hostilities between the Two Sicilies and the French Republic, the fleet which had caused so much terror and threatened so much evil had returned in a deplorable state, all battered and damaged by a violent storm by which it had been overtaken, the Admiral asking to be allowed to repair the ships in the port of Naples, so recently threatened with bombardment by its guns.

As the two nations were still on friendly terms this request could not be refused, and the ships accordingly were put under repair and supplied with provisions, much to the disgust and grief of the Queen, forced by a terrible necessity to give assistance to the murderers of her brother-in-law and the oppressors of her sister, and wishing with all her heart that they were at the bottom of the sea.

She urged Acton to press on the work so that they might be got rid of as soon as possible, for she dreaded the mischief they might do in Naples; but Neapolitan workmen being in those days very much like what they are now, it is easy to understand that his orders, remonstrances, and reprimands were useless; the work dragged slowly on, and the republican officers, as the Queen expected, took every opportunity of doing all the injury possible to the government whose hospitality and assistance they were receiving.

They spread about everywhere the doctrines of the revolution; the revolutionary leaders, many of whom were students at the University, young professional men, or cadets of noble houses, vied with each other in showing them attention and admiration, constantly visiting them on board their ships and listening with avidity to the abominable precepts poured into their ears.

La Touche himself, regardless of the most elementary principles of honour, which would have made him recoil from the treachery of secretly working injury to those whose guests he and his officers were, advised the young Jacobins to organise secret societies for the dissemination of revolutionary principles, and taught them how to arrange and carry on their meetings and conspiracies with the least possible harm to themselves and the greatest amount of danger to other people.

The spies of the secret police, who penetrated into every resort of all classes of the city, soon discovered that treason and danger were rife, and brought their reports to the Queen.

Sheltered by the darkness, they were cautiously admitted in the dead of night to the royal palace, where, in the stillness and seclusion of the *sala oscura*, the Queen was waiting for them in deep anxiety and dread. For she knew that not only her crown and kingdom, but her life and the lives of her husband and children were threatened by the same miscreants who were urging on the destruction of her beloved sister, whose image was seldom absent from her heart. At last the repairs were finished, the French ships provisioned, and the fleet weighed anchor and departed.

But before they left they had joined the leaders of the Neapolitan Jacobins in a supper, at which, amid inflammatory and treasonable speeches, the conspirators in a frenzy of disloyalty and fanaticism fastened to their breasts the red caps of the Terrorists.

General Colletta, in the account he gives of this transaction, illustrates amusingly the bias with which he in particular and his party in general regard different actions according as they are committed by their own adherents or by their opponents.

" Many of the Neapolitan youth, enthusiastic for the new doctrines, held communications with the officers of the fleet, with Mackau and La Touche; *and as it was the policy of the French government* to incite the people to liberty, and thus associate them in their dangers and struggles, *the Admiral inflamed their youthful minds still more, and advised them to hold secret meetings."*

These two worthies, it must be remembered, who were thus secretly stirring up sedition and conspiracies in a friendly State, and inciting rash boys to treason, were the Ambassador accredited to that country and the Admiral of the fleet now accepting its protection and hospitality!

Of the proceedings at the supper Colletta remarks, as if it were the most ordinary and unimportant matter in the world, that "in the intoxication of their hopes and wishes, *it happened* that the Neapolitans hung at their breasts a little red cap, at that time the symbol of the Jacobins in France."

For such a thing to "happen," however, especially at that time of peril and commotion, was by no means a trifling matter. Little or big, the red cap was the badge of the Terrorists, and was no trifle at all; it meant that the young men who "happened" to hang it to their breasts were pledging themselves to preach and take part in treason, plunder, and bloodshed. It would be interesting and curious to know what, under these circumstances, General Colletta and his friends would have thought it right and reasonable for the government of Naples to do.

Was it complacently to allow dangerous conspiracies to be organised amongst its subjects, and to refuse to protect itself and the loyal portion of the people from the attempts of those who were preparing to attack them?

Such, apparently, was the opinion of the radical historian, who, while he saw no harm whatever in an ambassador (if republican) taking advantage of his position secretly to arouse rebellion against the government to which he was accredited; was horrified and indignant that in order to discover how far he was mixed up in the conspiracy, to what extent it existed, and who were the persons concerned in it, the Queen, having been informed of what had taken place and what was still going on, should have availed herself of the services of one of her spies, one Luigi Custode, who was living in the house of Mackau, to get hold of certain papers, which he accordingly brought to her.

Nothing was found in the papers, however, and another grievance against the King and Queen was that when Mackau accused Luigi Custode and nothing could be proved against him, he was not only acquitted by the judges but afterwards rewarded by the court—that is to say, by the King and Queen, who, having made use of him, did not choose to desert him.

It was no wonder they were alarmed. Only a short time before the supper in question two copies of the French revolutionary statute of 1791 had been picked up in the apartments of the Queen, where they had been purposely placed by some one whose name could not be discovered. But it was found that two thousand of these documents had "happened" to have been printed by a secret club of Jacobins in Naples, who, when they had got these compromising productions, did not know what to do with them. Their courage failed when they reflected upon the probable consequences to themselves if they carried out their original intentions and distributed them about the city; so, after giving away by night a few copies to their immediate sympathisers, they decided that the rest had better be destroyed, and that the safest way to do this would be to drop them into the sea.

Two sacks were therefore filled with these valuable productions, and two young nobles dressed as porters carried them on their backs to the rocks of Chiatamone. In order to arrive at their destination they had to pass through the most populous part of the city; but they started just after sunset, that they might avoid both daylight and the night watch, and they effected their purpose in safety and were applauded by their companions as if they had done some noble and heroic deed.

This story is also related by General Colletta, who calls the cowardly insult offered by these young men to the Queen in putting the papers in her rooms and then hiding themselves "a spirit of youthful defiance."

To other people this useless outrage would seem to have more fear than defiance about it, and rather to resemble an anonymous letter, which is usually supposed to be what a schoolboy would call "a blackguard thing." And an anonymous insult on that subject directed against a woman who, as they well knew, was at that moment in an anguish of suspense about the fate of her sister, then a helpless prisoner in the hands of the ruffians in question, would appear to ordinary persons not sharing the political opinions of General Colletta not only cowardly but brutal.

It is scarcely surprising that the King and Queen, exasperated and alarmed by these incidents and proceedings, should have become embittered, stern, and not too scrupulous or lenient about the measures they took to defeat the machinations of their traitorous subjects and protect the lives and property of those who were loyal, as well as the safety of themselves and their children.

The *coup d'état* prepared by Maria Carolina was most carefully arranged so that no innocent person should be molested;[1] and when information had been gained of the names of those who had had treasonable intercourse with the French, or of whose treasonable actions or conspiracies there was sufficient proof, orders were given to the police, and the conspirators and Jacobin leaders were seized in one night and carried to the underground cells of the strong fortress of St. Elmo, there to await their trial before the special tribunal to be appointed to judge them.

It was all done so swiftly and silently, they were so utterly taken by surprise, that in the morning nothing was known except that during the night many houses had been visited by the police and many people taken away. Where they were nobody knew, and no statement, explanation, or allusion to their fate appeared.

How many and who were missing was not immediately known, as some few of the Jacobin party had, after the departure of the French fleet,

---

[1] This does not mean that during the arrests now beginning no innocent person was involved, but only that the Queen was most anxious that no one but the guilty should be taken. It was, of course, impossible, at such a time of terror, exasperation, and confusion, deplorable mistakes should not occur.

escaped to France, Genoa, Milan, and Venice, and the families of some of those taken were either afraid to compromise their own safety by making any stir, or else so furious and so much ashamed that a member of their house should be a traitor and a Jacobin that, far from wishing to proclaim the matter, they did all in their power to hush it up.

This measure spread terror and uneasiness amongst the Jacobin party and all those who in any way sympathised or associated with them, but reassured the loyal and peaceable inhabitants, who regarded them, their doctrines, their principles, and their aims with fear and abhorrence.

While the emissaries of the French republic were occupied in inciting to rebellion the subjects of an ostensibly friendly power, the King and Queen on their part, not considering themselves bound by an agreement forced violently upon them against their will under threats of massacre and destruction, were secretly arranging a treaty with England. By this the King of Naples was to send four men-of-war, four frigates, and four lesser vessels, with six thousand soldiers, to the Mediterranean to join an equal number of ships and soldiers from England, secure the dominion of the sea, and protect the commerce of the Two Sicilies, which, besides the danger threatened by the French fleet, was perpetually subject to the attacks of light ships from Barbary. These pirates devastated the coasts, seized on merchant vessels, and did an immense amount of mischief.

Towards the end of August Lord Hood took

Toulon, and the Neapolitan fleet hastily set sail to join him, as did the Spaniards and Sardinians.

The French declared, as they always did and still do, whenever they experience a reverse, that they were betrayed, and, as usual, sought for a victim upon whom to lay the blame. General Colletta, following their lead, declares, as they did, that General Count de Maudet, who commanded at Toulon, had voluntarily yielded the fortress committed to his charge to the enemies of his country.

Nelson, however, wrote to England:

"Famine has accomplished what force could not have done: not a boat has got into Toulon since our arrival, and we literally starved them into a surrender."

The Comte de Maudet, who knew what was likely to be his fate if he trusted to the tender mercies of the Jacobin government of Paris, accompanied the fleet to Naples, and received a small sum, just sufficient for the subsistence of his family, which gave rise to the assertion of the French that he had betrayed his country for gold.

In fact, it was the fault entirely of the republican government, which, although well aware of the scarcity of food in Toulon, would not send supplies there when it would have been perfectly easy to do so.

The alliance was now openly signed between the Two Sicilies and the rest of the coalition against France, *i.e.*, England, Russia, Austria, Prussia, Spain, Portugal, and Sardinia.

Acton announced the definite rupture by the following communication to Mackau: "La cour de

Naples, ne pouvant plus supporter la faction qui a usurpé le pouvoir en France a pris la determination de faire savoir à M. de Mackau qu'il doit dans le terme de huit jours quitter les États de S.M. Sicilienne."

Shortly afterwards Captain Nelson, on the *Agamemnon*, appeared at Naples to request that assistance might be sent to Lord Hood, who with a ludicrously inadequate force was holding Toulon.

An outburst of enthusiasm welcomed the English hero, then in his thirty-fifth year, to the southern capital, where he and his officers and men were entertained with lavish honours and hospitality by high and low.

Whenever the English sailors passed through the streets shouts and cheers broke from the people who crowded to see them; at court and in society Italians and English vied with each other in the splendour of the entertainments given to the officers; at theatres, banquets, and balls they were fêted and flattered by the most beautiful women in southern Italy; the three weeks they spent in Naples passed like a dream of enchantment. Captain Nelson was, of course, lodged at the British Embassy; but Mr. Jeaffreson declares positively that it was not on this occasion, and in fact not until five years later, that his passion for Lady Hamilton began.

"Extant documents prove conclusively that the passion had its birth no earlier than the moment of his departure from Sicilian waters in July, 1798, for his second expedition to Egypt, and that the grievous and reprehensible part of the entanglement did not begin before the year 1800." [1]

[1] "The Queen of Naples and Lord Nelson," i. pp. 254-5.

His acquaintance with her and his friendship with Sir William Hamilton began, however, during this, his first visit to Naples, when he was treated by them both with the greatest distinction. The suite of rooms he occupied at the British Embassy had been prepared and decorated for a prince, and his stepson, a young midshipman named Josiah Nisbet, received especial kindness and attention from Lady Hamilton. He himself was received by the King and Queen almost as if he had been a royal visitor; at the great banquet at the palace he sat on the right hand of the King, above all the Ambassadors and nobles present; he was constantly in the society of Ferdinando; and Maria Carolina, who looked upon the English as her last chance, poured into his ears her impassioned hopes and longings that by their help even yet she might save her sister, avenge the murder of Louis XVI., and set her nephew on his father's throne. As the Queen could not speak English, or at any rate not well enough to carry on a long conversation in that language, and Captain Nelson, like many of his countrymen, could speak nothing else, Lady Hamilton was employed on all occasions by them as interpreter. Sir William Hamilton had for many years been the trusted and intimate friend both of the King and Queen, and the friendship with which Maria Carolina now regarded Lady Hamilton, and that has given rise to such wild, incredible, and monstrous fabrications on the part of her enemies and traducers, can be easily accounted for by the exceptional circumstances by which they were both surrounded.

LORD NELSON.
After a painting by Abbott.

The Queen looked upon the alliance of England not only as the one and only hope of saving the sister whose life now hung on a thread, but also of protecting her own children, her husband, and herself from the perils with which they were threatened; the friendship and assistance of the English Ambassador were absolutely essential to her, and to neglect an obvious way of securing and strengthening it, by showing favour and consideration to the woman whose influence over him was all-powerful, would have been out of the question, even if Lady Hamilton had been a woman more objectionable and less pleasant or attractive than she happened to be.

Her wonderful beauty and grace, however, fascinated the Queen, and by this time she had acquired a superficial cultivation and to a certain extent the usages of society. She had learned to speak French and Italian fluently, although in all languages her grammar and spelling were fearful and wonderful, especially in writing. She had given much attention to the study of music, and her singing was much admired. The Queen also liked her lively good spirits, which cheered her when, as now so often happened, she was anxious and unhappy.

- Lady Hamilton for her part had certainly at this time, and for long after, a real affection for the Queen, whose notice and protection were all-important to her, whose friend she was immensely flattered to consider herself, and in whose trials and griefs she warmly sympathised.

That she had sense enough always to speak of

and behave to the Queen with the profoundest deference, never presuming upon the kindness and favour shown to her, is evident.

"I had been with the Queen the night before alone *en famille,* laughing and singing, &c.," she wrote Mr. Greville, June 2, 1793, "but at the drawing-room I kept my distance, and paid the Queen as much respect as if I had never seen her before, which pleased her very much. But she showed me great distinction that night, and told me several times how she admired my good conduct."

And many things had happened which drew the strangely incongruous friends nearer together. In the November of 1792 Sir William Hamilton had been dangerously ill at Caserta, and much sympathy had been shown to his wife by the English residents. Lady Plymouth, Lady Webster, and others used to send twice a day to inquire for him, though Caserta is sixteen miles from Naples; they also offered to help nurse him. The Queen, to whom his death would have been a most serious calamity, also sent a messenger every morning and evening until he was out of danger, and the concern and sympathy she displayed increased the gratitude and affection of Lady Hamilton for her royal protectress.

The three weeks' stay of the *Agamemnon* at Naples had just drawn to a close, and Captain Nelson had invited a large party to a grand farewell *déjeuner* on board his ship. The King had promised to arrive at one o'clock; but before that hour the news was suddenly brought that a

French man-of-war, with three ships under convoy, was at anchor off the coast of Sardinia.

It was enough for Nelson. At once he gave orders to sail, and before King or guests were to be seen or heard of the *Agamemnon* was disappearing out of the Bay of Naples in pursuit of the enemy.

Owing to the gaps made by the death of so many of the children of the King and Queen of Naples there were great differences in the ages of those remaining.

The Empress of Germany and the Grand-duchess of Tuscany were now about twenty-one and twenty years old, the Prince Royal fifteen, Marie Christine, and Amélie fourteen and eleven, Marie Antoinette ten, Leopold four, and Carl Alberto three years of age. In their education while under her care, and in her constant correspondence with them after they were married, the Queen followed the example of her mother and the system to which she had been accustomed during her own early life.

Like Maria Theresia, she strongly desired to obtain a lasting influence over her daughters and to possess their entire confidence. She never allowed a day to pass without their spending at least an hour with her. To a certain blue *salon* at Caserta, therefore, the young Princesses were expected to come to her every day, which they did very often with some anxiety, if not alarm, for their mother was in the habit of questioning them about their studies and conduct, and administering advice and reproofs concerning both.

The King used also every now and then to appear in the blue drawing-room, where the children were always delighted to see him, as he was extremely affectionate and indulgent to them, and without in any way interfering with their mother's authority, he usually managed to show especial kindness and favour to any one of them upon whom he thought she had been rather severe.

For Maria Carolina resembled her mother in another and less desirable way; although, like her, she loved all her children devotedly, yet she had favourites amongst them.

As Christine had been the most beloved of the daughters of the Empress Maria Theresia, so Maria Carolina adored her eldest daughter, and now that she was separated from her she gave her next preference to Christine, who was a sweet, gentle girl, but not nearly so clever nor so advanced in her studies as Amélie. This vexed the Queen, who also observed that Amélie had a love of admiration and a hasty and impetuous temper, which the Queen might have been expected to understand and make allowances for. She, however, showed too plainly that she did not wish Amélie to surpass her sister, was too ready to find fault with her even in public, and too eager to counteract the tendency to be proud and overbearing which she thought she detected in this young Princess.

The King, on the other hand, seeing that his wife preferred Christine, made a special favourite of Amélie, and was nearly as delighted as the child herself when he could get leave to take her with him on one of his hunting expeditions in the neighbourhood of Caserta or to the marshes of Capua. And all her life Amélie, who loved her father passionately, used to look back upon these excursions with him as some of her happiest times.

The propensity to make favourites amongst children, though very common with parents, is one of the most unfortunate and mischievous possible; and scarcely ever fails to do incalculable harm. It sows dissension in families, destroys the belief in the justice of their parents' rule, which is all important for young people to possess, and is most likely to prevent, or at any rate weaken, the mutual affection of brothers and sisters, making the favoured ones selfish and overbearing and the others jealous and resentful, more especially as the partiality of a father or mother is very seldom bestowed on those most deserving of it.

And though parents cannot of course help in many cases feeling more affection for one child than another who may be less attractive and less lovable, they are not justified in acting upon their inclination by giving one of their children, for no reason but their own preference, more advantages, more money, or more indulgence than another, or treating with severity in one child faults they would excuse or pass over in another.

However, in all other respects the Queen was an excellent mother to all her children, and they all loved her with the deepest affection.

The Empress of Germany and the Grandduchess of Tuscany wrote to her constantly, confided to her their hopes and fears, and told her everything that went on at their courts; her other daughters also grew up with the same habits and the same affectionate attachment to her.

A few weeks after the departure of Nelson the fearful news of the murder of Marie Antoinette arrived at Naples. Everybody was filled with horror and consternation, while the Queen, who had hoped until the last, never being able to believe that the worst would happen, was overwhelmed with grief and despair.

It was in a deeply impressive manner that Queen Carolina made known to her children this lamentable news. Summoning them all into her presence, with her face bathed in tears she led them to the chapel of the palace, where, as they knelt with bowed heads before the altar, there began the solemn tones of the prayers for the dead, in which the young voices of the awe-stricken children followed the trembling accents of their mother, as with tears and sobs she joined in the intercessions for the soul of her murdered sister.

And if the passionate desire for vengeance on her murderers mingled with grief for her sufferings and death, and compassionate anxiety for her helpless, desolate children still in the hands of their persecutors, who can wonder? For in her strong, passionate human nature Maria Carolina did not resemble Marie Antoinette. She would never have said, after a long succession of perils and insults from her own subjects to herself and those dearest to her:

"J'ai tout vu, tout su, et tout pardonné."

The just punishment of atrocious crimes was her earnest wish and continual aim, and for Louis XVI., who had been too weak either to stand by his friends or fight his enemies, and whose conduct she blamed for these deplorable events, she had nothing but contemptuous pity. The following letter, written a short time after this terrible catastrophe, shows how completely Maria Carolina was prostrated by the shock and the grief of it.[1]

"*Le 25 Dec., 1793.*

"Excessivement malade je puis a peine tenir ma plume et ne passe que des momens hors de mon lit, je ne puis donc vous voir mais mes vœux vous accompagneront et j'espère dans des temps plus heureux et prochain de même que votre ami vous voir tranquilement établie *ici*, dites lui bien que je n'abandone pas cet espoir, *et au plutot.* Je vois la tracasserie que l'on a faite, rien ne m'etonne, j'en ai tant vue dans ma vie; et c'est ce qui m'a fait entièrement retirer du monde et vivre à moi seule. Je souhaite à votre digne estimable ami un heureux voyage, un meilleur succes qu'il me conserve son estime, plaigne mes circonstances tourmantantes de toutes façons et qui ont ruiné ma santé, et si je reste *en vie* je me flatte voue encore realiser tous nos projets et le voue avec les *amis parens* tranquille et agreablement a *Naples* cet espoir me rend moins douloureux son present Elorgnement. Adieu."

These terrible scenes left a profound impression upon the children, particularly upon the Princess

[1] From Mr. A. M. Broadley's collection of MSS.

Amélie, whom they appeared deeply to affect. It was about this time that she was to make her first communion, and that solemn event, with the terrible tragedies being enacted around her, seemed to have altered her tastes and disposition. She became graver and quieter, cared less for childish amusements and more for study, and above all for religion, showing, in fact, already the germs of that saintly and exalted character so fully developed in her after-life, and now fostered by the loving care of her governess, Signora Ambrosio.

Into the charge of this excellent woman the Princess Amélie had been given by the Queen, according to the custom of the Neapolitan court, immediately after her birth, and it was soon evident that no better choice could possibly have been made of a guardian upon whom rested the whole care and education of the Princess during infancy, childhood, and girlhood.

Donna Vincenza Rizzi had been the wife of a distinguished Neapolitan lawyer, Don Bernardo Ambrosio, who had left her a widow with twelve children; her wise counsels, good example, and constant kindness had gained the respect and love of her pupil, the future Queen of France, who always spoke of her with the deepest affection and gratitude.

Shortly afterwards there arrived at Naples the Marchesa Solari, an Englishwoman by birth, who had been one of the ladies of Marie Antoinette, and had at the end of 1791 brought letters from her to Maria Carolina.

The Marchesa did not know until she approached

Naples whether the fatal news had yet reached that country, and dreaded to see the Queen in consequence. But Sir William and Lady Hamilton, who knew she was coming, drove out several miles from the city to meet her, and directly she saw them and the deep mourning they wore she understood that the tidings must have become known. On hearing from Sir William Hamilton that the Marchesa had arrived, the Queen desired that she should come to her immediately.

When the Marchesa saw Maria Carolina she was so struck by her likeness to Marie Antoinette that, overcome by her recollections, she hesitated and faltered while the Queen, whose face expressed the agony she was feeling, gave a tremendous shriek, and, as soon as she could find words, exclaimed :

"Good God! did you ever think the French would have treated my sister and her husband in so horrible a way?" Then, as the Marchesa began to reply in French, she continued :

"For God's sake do not, I beseech you, let me hear any more of that murderous language! You speak Italian and German—pray address me for the future in either of those languages."

But after this burst of anguish the Queen became calmer, recovered something of her usual fortitude, and continued the conversation in French, which seemed her habitual language.[1]

The murder of her favourite sister embittered and changed the character of Maria Carolina ; her whole soul was filled with an ardent longing for revenge upon the ruffians who had committed these atro-

[1] "The Queen of Naples and Lord Nelson."

cities, and who were still revelling in bloodshed and threatening others dear to her. In her *cabinet de travail* she caused to be placed a picture of Marie Antoinette, and under it the inscription, " Je poursuiverai ma vengeance jusqu'au tombeau."

CHAPTER XIII

Dark days—Gallant efforts of the Queen—Society at Naples—"Let us eat and drink, for to-morrow we die"—Earthquake and fearful eruption—Trial of the conspirators—Execution of the leaders —Attacks on the Queen—Friendship with Lady Hamilton.

WITH all her natural courage and fortitude, combined with the desperate resolution to resist to the last the torrent of destruction which evidently threatened all Europe, the Queen strained every nerve and used every resource available to help on the efforts being made to stem the revolutionary tide advancing with such appalling swiftness.

In the previous year (1792) she had made strenuous attempts to induce the Italian States to unite in the defence of Italy against the horrors of a French invasion. She wrote in the King's name to the governments of Sardinia and Venice, urging them to take part in a league for the safeguarding of all Italy, pointing out that while the combined Italian armies might successfully resist the invader, division would be fatal to them all. "The hope of escaping singly," she wrote, "has ever been the ruin of Italy."

If these two powers had agreed to the proposition she was certain that the Pope would have been with them, and that the minor Italian states could not have held back. But although the King of Sardinia eagerly accepted the invitation, Venice refused, and with that cowardly and selfish refusal were extinguished all hopes of an Italian federation just before the suddenly threatened bombardment of Naples by Admiral La Touche.

The Queen, however, did not relax her efforts. With feverish anxiety she pushed on warlike preparations of all kinds, with eagerness she watched for news of success or disaster.

During December, 1793, rumours had been heard of some misfortune at Toulon. Nothing was certain. Christmas went by—a gloomy Christmas, full of sorrow for the past and foreboding for the future. Early in January it was reported that some English ships had been heard of from Livorno, and the Queen wrote at once to Lady Hamilton the following letter, which in spelling and composition might be compared with less excuse to the effusions proceeding from the pen of the latter:

"Ayant scue l'arrivee a Livourne de plusieurs batiments Anglois des Iles d'Hieres Je desirois bien vivement savoir si elles ont mandes des nouvelles de Toulon au Chevalier Hamilton par la poste d'aujourdhui mon interet a tout ce qui a rapport a cette Expedition etant infinie Je prie Miledy de vouloir bien m'eclaircir sur des objets aussy interessant ce qui peut satisfaire mon cœur et l'empressement General et de me croire avec bien de l'Amitié,

"Votre devoué,
"CHARLOTTE." [1]

[1] "Having learnt the arrival at Livorno of several English ships from the Hyeres islands, I should very much wish to know if they

There was no good news. Toulon had been taken by Bonaparte, the young Corsican General, whose fame was beginning to rise rapidly. The Neapolitan force came back in a deplorable condition, having lost six hundred men, killed or prisoners, and had all their horses captured, besides an immense loss of tents, arms, standards, provisions, &c., &c., which could be ill afforded at the present crisis.

The festivities of the Carnival were stopped and the churches thronged with people, while prayers were offered and lamentations and forebodings of approaching evil took the place of the songs and revelry with which, even at this time, the lighthearted Southern populace had been engrossed; while, undismayed by this reverse, the Queen busied herself in raising more forces and collecting more money to repair the losses.

With enthusiastic energy she worked, to such considerable effect that she collected and raised twenty battalions of infantry, thirteen squadrons of cavalry, and a train of artillery, and three regiments of cavalry to help the German troops in Lombardy, besides sending more ships, arms, and soldiers to the English.

Thanks to her exertions, past and present, the Neapolitan fleet now consisted of forty gun-boats and forty larger vessels; she had forty-two thousand troops of the line under arms, and a still more

have sent any news by the post from Toulon to the Chevalier Hamilton to-day. My interest in regard to everything which relates to this expedition being infinite, I beg you, my lady, to be good enough to inform me on matters so interesting of what may satisfy my heart and the general eagerness, and to believe me, with much friendship, your devoted Charlotte."

numerous reserve of militia—a force of considerable strength for a kingdom of the size of the Two Sicilies, of which the inhabitants were by no means rich.

The whole city was thrilled with excitement: the shows and entertainments of the Carnival were replaced by manœuvres and sham sea-fights in the bay of Naples, which were witnessed by admiring crowds of spectators.

The camp in the plain of Sessa was another centre of interest; the King, the Queen, and Acton were continually there, inciting the soldiers by their presence, exhortations, and promises.[1]

All this was at first extremely popular, but it very shortly became evident that such preparations, however necessary, could not but entail an enormous expense, which the existing resources were inadequate to meet.

Heavy taxes were imposed, donations or subsidies were asked for and given, the churches, monasteries, and charitable institutions were ordered to bring to the royal mint all the consecrated plate which was not necessary for the performance of the offices of religion; but even this and other expedients, which need not be enumerated in a work of this kind, proved insufficient.

Then the Queen, driven to desperation, resolved upon a measure which it is impossible to justify, and which can only be described as a flagrant breach of trust and of the simplest honesty. Fictitious paper money, in the form of notes on the seven national banks, was issued; the deception went on

[1] Colletta.

for some time without being found out, but at length its discovery caused the panic, loss, ruin, and clamour which were the natural consequences of such proceedings.

"State necessity, the instincts of despotism, the ease with which the money could be obtained, while the theft could be concealed by fabricating fresh paper, and the hope of replacing the missing sum before it could be discovered; finally, the belief entertained by all absolute monarchs that the property as well as the lives of their subjects belongs to them," were, says General Colletta in his history of Naples, the motives and explanation of this indefensible conduct. The people who had suffered by these fraudulent transactions were naturally furious and became the enemies of the Queen, the King, and Acton, whom, in a reaction of feeling which cannot surprise one, especially in that excitable population, they accused of having robbed the banks to enrich themselves.

But through all this time of public and domestic distress and calamity the court and society of Naples had never been more brilliant. Foreigners who stayed there on their travels remarked with wonder the continual round of pleasure that seemed to be unceasing in that bright city and on those sunny shores, where music, dancing, and careless, light-hearted gaiety seemed to occupy the time and thoughts of every one, from prince to peasant.

The birthday of the King of England (June 4th) was celebrated by a large party at the English embassy, on the occasion of which the Queen wrote to Lady Hamilton her compliments to all the company assembled, her longing to join in the song of "*Good* save great George, our King," and her delight in the alliance with the brave, loyal English, who would save Europe from the scourge which threatened it.

To those who saw Maria Carolina at this time—fascinating, charming, surrounded by flatterers, the centre and life of everything that was going on, political, social, artistic, or charitable, sitting in the council, transacting the business of the state, frequenting churches and convents, supervising the pursuits of her children, joining the King's hunting parties, appearing at theatres and balls, her *salon* ever thronged with a brilliant society—it was difficult to realise that, mingling with all this excitement and apparent enjoyment, were the constant harass of financial difficulties, the haunting remembrance of her sister's fate, and the dread of future disasters, which, by the successes of the French armies and the growing disaffection at home, were brought nearer and nearer.

"Let us eat and drink, for to-morrow we die," might well have been the motto of that brilliant company, who shut their eyes alike to the tragedies which had taken place and to the coming events already casting their shadows before, and vied with each other in their luxurious entertainments and trifling pleasures. Not only figuratively, but actually, they were living on a volcano.

A week had passed since the celebration of the King of England's birthday, the gaieties were at their height, crowds were flocking to the opera to hear the famous English cantatrice, Mrs. Billington, when, " on the night of the 12th of June a violent earthquake shook the city, and a hollow and deep rumbling noise indicated an approaching eruption of Vesuvius. The inhabitants of the cities and towns at the foot of the mountain fled from their houses, waiting in the open air for the dawn of day, which broke calmly; but at the summit of the volcano a dense black cloud obscured the azure and glow of the sky, and as the morning advanced the noise increased, as well as the darkness and terror. Thus passed three days. On the night of June 15th–16th there came a report as from a hundred pieces of ordnance, and a fiery column was seen to rise from the side of the mountain, divide, and fall by its own weight, circulating round the declivity; vivid and long flashes of lightning issuing from the volcano vanished in the sky, and balls of fire were hurled to great distances, the rumbling sound bursting out in tones of thunder. Flame rose above flame, for the crater of the volcano continued unchanged, and two streams of lava were formed, which first advanced rapidly and then slowly towards Resina and Torre del Greco. The population of these cities, 32,000 persons, stood gazing at the scene in grief and wonder.

"The town of Resina covers the site of ancient Herculaneum, and Torre del Greco was originally built where the mountain meets the sea. Half was covered by a prior eruption, which had brought down so much matter as to form a promontory upon the ruins of the city. New houses had been built on that elevation, and the two cities, the high and the low, communicated by steep streets formed in steps. The eruption of 1794 completed the work of destruction, leaving only the tops of a few buildings visible in the upper town and covering the lower city entirely . . . even the towers of the churches. Many of the fields around Resina were consumed, the lava only ceasing to flow after it had reached the furthest extremity of the town.

"The first stream from Torre del Greco entered the sea, drove back the waters, and left in their place a mass of basalt of sufficient magnitude to form a mole and roadstead where small vessels could seek shelter from tempests. The two streams, bending with the fall or curvature of the land, sometimes met and sometimes again divided; a convent containing three persons was surrounded, flight became impossible, and they all perished from suffocation caused by the intense heat. The road followed by the greater stream of lava was four miles in length, a distance which it traversed in three hours.

"Thus the night passed away. The morning hour struck, but the light of day had not dawned, for it was concealed by the thick, black shower of ashes which poured down like rain for many miles round the city. The appearance of continual night spread gloom throughout the metropolis, and, as is commonly the case, all turned for consolation to the resources of religion. Men and women of every age and condition, with bare feet, dishevelled hair, and ropes round their necks, walked in processions . . . chanting hymns and prayers. . . . The Cardinal Archbishop of Naples, followed by all the clergy in their robes, bearing the golden statue of San Gennaro, . . . invoked the mercy of God in psalms. . . .

"The people set to work to clear from the roofs and terraces of their houses into the streets below the weight of ashes threatening to crush them.

"Night stole on, only recognised by the sound of the bells, which rung as usual. After some hours the darkness became so intense that the city, which was not then lighted by lamps, was like a close room, and the people, afraid to enter their houses, stood bewailing themselves in the streets and squares.

"On the third day the darkness sensibly diminished, though the light of day could still only be feebly distinguished, the sun appearing, as at its rising, pale and dim; the shower of ashes was less copious, and the fire and thunder from the volcano ceased. . . .

"The inhabitants returned to their houses, worn out with fatigue and terror; but in the middle of the night they were awakened by another earthquake, and while the ground still trembled beneath them they heard a crash as of the fall of many houses. . . .

"At daybreak the cause was discovered; the mountain was seen deprived of its summit, which had been swallowed up in the vortex of the volcano. . . . Vesuvius had before towered above Monte Somma, but they had now changed their relative positions, and the latter soared highest. . . .

"The truncated mountain remained of a conical form . . . the greatest thickness of the lava eleven metres, the land for nearly five hundred acres covered with liquid fire, and the mole, which projected twenty-five metres into the sea, rose six metres above the waves. Thirty-three men and two thousand four hundred animals had perished.

"But soon, while the soil was yet warm, a new city arose upon the ruins, houses upon houses, streets upon streets, churches upon churches." [1]

The royal family and the Prime Minister fled to the camp at Sessa, where they took refuge and waited till those terrible days were over.

The trials of the Jacobin conspirators were now going on, and the first to be tried was a certain Tommaso Amato, a native of Messina, who had forced his way into the church of the Carmine while the service was going on and rushed towards the sanctuary, fighting and overpowering the friar who tried to stop him, and pouring forth the most frightful blasphemies against God and the King.

Horror and consternation spread through the crowds assembled in the church; the man was at length secured and carried off to prison to await his trial, by which he was sentenced to the gallows. When it was too late and the sentence had been carried out, a letter from Messina brought the information that the man was mad, or at any rate subject to fits of insanity, and had escaped from a madhouse, to which, of course, he would have been sent back had these facts been known in time. It was one of those unfortunate miscarriages of justice of which there have been and still are many examples in all countries and in less troubled and perilous times, without the excuse of panic and

[1] Colletta

horror acting upon the minds of men surrounded with danger and conspiracy.

That the Queen should be blamed for this mistake of the judges is only an instance of the iniquitous malice of her enemies. The exaggerated accounts given by the republican and radical writers of the whole proceedings concerning the trial and punishment of the Jacobin conspirators should be read with caution, allowance being made for the unscrupulous bitterness with which they not only maligned every action of the partisans of religion and order, but invented and circulated the most infamous falsehoods in order, for political reasons, to make them appear guilty and to justify the crimes and cruelties committed against them by the Jacobin party.

As to the spies employed by Maria Carolina after her return from Austria in 1791, there exists in England a strong feeling against them, which was undoubtedly confirmed by the disclosures during an unfortunate trial in another country, although it has been questioned whether the existence of this dislike or prejudice has not often been the cause of considerable injury to the nation by whom it is entertained. In consequence of it (as, for instance, before the Boer War) the government is often left in ignorance of matters about which it is essential it should be informed. But such an idea would never have been entertained, nor even understood, at the court of Naples, nor at any other court a hundred years ago. The secret police of Napoleon was looked upon by him as an indispensable instrument of government. Before the establishment of Maria Carolina's system of police at Naples, robberies and murders in the streets had been so frequent that people were afraid to walk about at night. Directly after the new police arrangements all these crimes ceased, many bad characters and dangerous criminals being seized and transported to Lampedusa and Tremiti.

The fifty persons accused were tried between the 16th of September and the 3rd of October, but although General Colletta and others inveigh against the proceedings in their usual manner, the fact remains that of that number ten were liberated, one sentenced to confinement for life, three to the galleys, twenty to a term of imprisonment, and thirteen to lesser punishments. Three only were condemned to death, and although these three were by no means the worst characters amongst the prisoners, they were conspicuous and fanatical leaders in the dangerous attempts to bring the horrors of the Revolution into Naples, and did not attempt to deny the part they had taken in the treasonable proceedings proved against them. They were all students of the University, distinguished by their superior talents and influence, which they had used, in conjunction with the French officers, to spread the doctrines of the Jacobins. They had belonged to secret societies, taken part in the treasonable supper and worn the red cap of the Jacobins, to whose party they belonged. It was a lamentable thing that their lives should have been sacrificed, for they were not like some others, low scoundrels or bad characters, but foolish, misguided young fanatics, like many young Frenchmen at the beginning of the Revolution. These young Neapolitans had, however, less excuse, as they knew perfectly well the results of the principles they were trying to introduce into their country. There was no room, as in the early days of visionary enthusiasm in France, before the new ideas had begun to be acted upon, for any doubt whatever as to where they would lead. All the civilised world was horror-stricken at the crimes and atrocities of the Jacobins, and it cannot be surprising that these young men, whatever their private virtues, had to pay with their lives for the treason of which they were convicted. Colletta himself affirms that "though inflexible to crime, Maria Carolina had no desire to persecute the innocent," but only desired strict justice.

The young men died bravely, one of them, Emanuele di Deo, refusing to earn his pardon by revealing the names of other conspirators. His father brought him this offer from the Queen. Brave and disinterested, though fanatical and misguided, he refused to betray his comrades, while admitting that he knew of a thousand implicated in the conspiracy; and gloried in his treason. He was twenty, and the other two who were executed, nineteen and twenty-two years old.

The friendship between the Queen and Lady Hamilton had meanwhile become more intimate. The deep and affectionate sympathy shown by the latter in her sorrows touched Maria Carolina, as may be seen by a letter sent by her some time before, with the portrait of the unfortunate Louis XVII.

"Ma chere Miledy,—J'ai été bien touché de l'interet que vous prenez a l'execrable catastrofe dont se sont souillés les infames françois. Je vous envois le portrait de cet innocent enfant qui implore Vengeance, Secours ou, s'il est aussy imolé, ces Cendres unis a ceux de ses infortunes Parens, crient avant l'Eternel pour une Eclatante Vengeance. Je compte le plus sur votre Genereuse Nation, pour remplir cet objet et pardonez a mon cœur dechiré ses sentiments.

"Votre attachee amie,
"Charlotte."[1]

The Queen, who was always called Charlotte in her own family, was in the habit of thus signing herself in her German and French letters, using the name of Carolina when she wrote in Italian. It is certainly singular that a woman of her undoubted talents and attainments should never have succeeded in composing, expressing, or spelling correctly her letters in a language which had been familiar to her from childhood, and which she habitually employed. Added to her other trials were now the infamous libels which, set about in Paris, were finding their way to Naples. She

---

[1] "My dear Milady,—I have been greatly touched by the interest you take in the execrable catastrophe with which the infamous French have stained themselves. I send you the portrait of that innocent infant, who implores vengeance, succour, or, if he is also sacrificed, his ashes, united to those of his unfortunate parents, cry before the Eternal for a swift and signal vengeance. I rely most upon your generous nation to accomplish this object, and pardon my torn heart its sentiments.—Your attached friend, Charlotte." (Egerton MSS., British Museum.)

was, of course, an object of hatred to the French revolutionary party, who looked upon her as an active and dangerous enemy. Her powerful influence had incited Germany against them, she had given all her energies to unite the Italian States into a league to protect Italy from their invasion, her ships had joined those of England in victory over a French fleet, her troops had helped the Germans in Lombardy, and her vigilant government and strong hand had for a time extinguished the Jacobin conspiracy in Naples and brought its leaders to justice.

They revenged themselves by the foulest slanders respecting her private life, and Lady Hamilton, in a letter to Mr. Greville, December 18, 1794, says:

"If ever you hear any lyes about her, contradict them, and if you should see a cursed book written by a vile french dog with her character in it, don't believe one word. She lent it me last night, and I have by reading the infamous calumny put myself quite out of humour that so good and *virtus* a princess should be so infamously described."[1]

[1] "The Queen of Naples and Lord Nelson" (Jeaffreson).

CHAPTER XIV

Another conspiracy — Terrible tragedies — State of society in Naples — Prince Caramanico — Attempts to obtain the release of Louis XVII. and Madame Royale — Death of Louis XVII. — Distress of the Queen — The King pays homage to Louis XVIII — Hunting at Carditello — The fish-market — Shrove Tuesday at San Carlo.

THE government of Ferdinando and Carolina, irritated by past dangers and provocations and alarmed for the future, was no longer the paternal despotism of former years.

Heavy but unavoidable taxes weighed down the people, continual anxiety and suspense hung like a cloud over the city, suspicion was in the air, arrests were always liable to take place, every one with the least tendency to liberalism was looked askance upon, watched, and ran the daily risk of a visit from the police, possibly of finding himself in the prisons of St. Elmo. And prisons at that time and in that country were widely different from the well-aired, sanitary, constantly inspected abodes of England in the twentieth century. Those of Naples were probably no worse than others, but no one ever heard of a Neapolitan tramp or beggar breaking a window or committing any slight breach of the law on purpose to get himself sent there, and thus insure being supplied with food and lodging, as occasionally happens under our more lenient system of legislation. No; the most desperate and destitute vagrant that ever lounged on the shores or loitered in the streets of Naples would have preferred want or even starvation outside the walls of the prison to the chance of what he might find within them.

Though one dangerous conspiracy had been discovered and stopped, another one was soon suspected and after a time brought to light, in which were involved more than thirty members of many of the first families in Naples, some of whom were women, and several hundreds of persons of the lower classes. Again panic spread over the city. Liberals, radicals, and Jacobins were in terror of imprisonment and execution, royalists of assassination.

Strict precautions and supervision over the food and drink of the royal family were rigorously enforced. The apartments of the King and Queen were changed from one day to another, arrests were numerous, espionage was universal, nobody was safe.

The fury of party ran higher and higher; families were split up into opposite factions, natural affection turned into enmity, such as one can only realise when one reflects upon what the division meant. It was no ordinary political quarrel, like Whigs and Tories, Conservatives and Liberals. To a young man either besotted with visions of Greek republics and Utopian unrealities, or longing for the reign of atheism, licence, and plunder, his father and brothers were arbitrary, unenlightened bigots and tyrants.

To his father and brothers, believing in God and their religion, loyal to their King, proud of their name, desiring the preservation of order and property and abhorring the Jacobins and all their works, a son or brother who should connect himself with that infamous and bloodstained crew was a disgrace to their house, a stain upon their honour, a curse and injury to the whole family.

Terrible tragedies and unnatural cruelties arose out of this state of things, and frightful stories, many of course exaggerated, but others well authenticated, are told of that time and of both parties.

"Brothers were seen to close their doors on brothers, wives on husbands, fathers on sons. One father, to show his love for the King, betrayed and gave up his son to the infuriated mob, thus purchasing his own safety with the blood of his child," says Botta,[1] writing of the rising of the *lazzaroni* in 1799—a riot attended with massacres and horrors innumerable.

One of the accused was Luigi de' Medici, the head of the police, hitherto a trusted, loyal, and efficient servant of the Queen and government, against whom no proof of guilt could be discovered. The enemies of Acton accuse him of being jealous of Medici

---

[1] "Vidersi fratelli chiuder le porte ai fratelli, spose a sposi, padri a figliuoli. Fuovi un padre il quale per dimostrare il suo amore pel Re scoperse e diè in mano il proprio figliuolo alla furibonda plebe, comprando in tal modo la salute propia co sangue della sua creatura" (Botta, "Storia d'Italia").

and conspiring to effect his destruction. Medici was imprisoned for some time and afterwards released.[1]

But it was easy enough for an innocent man to be suspected and imprisoned when the whole air was so full of terror, suspicion, and secret treachery that evidence of plots was eagerly seized upon, while fear, fury, and excitement were pervading the public mind and influencing those in authority, whose lives were in continual danger, and who, becoming more and more accustomed to the deeds of blood and cruelty which were always going on both in France and Italy during the years of the revolutionary struggle, grew more and more hardened as time went on, and as they felt more keenly that they were fighting for their lives.

It would not be possible in a work of this size and of this nature to describe in detail the plots and counterplots, the trials and punishments, the treaties and alliances, the battles and sieges, the political and military events crowded during these years into the records of the Two Sicilies. Nor would they perhaps be interesting to the general reader. The more serious student of history will find all those important matters exhaustively recounted in the works of the various writers, German, Italian, French, and English, of different political parties,

[1] Acton laid before the King and Queen the evidence brought by the informer, rewarded him, and searched for further evidence ; but there is no proof that he did not believe in his culpability. The statements of the Signora di San Marco, quoted by General Colletta, cannot be relied upon, as she was a person unworthy of credit.

who have devoted so much time, learning, and enthusiasm to the subject.

This book being intended to describe the life and personal history of Maria Carolina, it is necessary to touch lightly upon the numerous struggles, reverses, crimes, and cruelties which took place, and from which material could easily be collected to fill many volumes, and to go on to matters concerning the private life of the Queen.

The friendship and protection she showed Lady Hamilton at this time is attested by a number of existing letters from one to the other, in which the Queen invites Lady Hamilton to take her husband to the royal palace at Caserta for a change after illness, begs her to come to her in the evening to sing and act something to amuse her children, sending on her music by her maid; or inquires with sympathy after her health, and confides to her various domestic anxieties of her own:

"My daughter at Vienna causes me uneasiness. Her disorder does not please me at all, and to lose her would be a fearful blow for my heart, which might not kill me, but would inflict an incurable wound."

More slanders came to distress the Queen at the beginning of 1795, when the Viceroy of Sicily, Prince Caramanico, having died suddenly, it was set about, as if in mediæval times, that he had been poisoned by Acton at the instigation of the Queen. There was not the slightest reason to suppose he was poisoned at all, but in order to

MADAME ÉLISABETH, SISTER OF LOUIS XVI.

conjure up a motive for so outrageous an accusation it was suggested that the Queen had carried on a *liaison* with him many years before, and that Acton was afraid he might some day regain his influence. Other persons, equally resolved to lay the blame of his death upon Acton, said that the Prince had committed suicide for fear of being accused of treason by that minister.

The facts being that Caramanico had always been a trusted and honoured friend of the Queen, who had made him Ambassador to Paris, to London, and finally Viceroy of Sicily, and had never withdrawn her confidence from him. No suspicion of anything but friendship in their intercourse had ever been before suggested.

Next came a dangerous insurrection in Sicily, promptly quelled and severely punished; and at the end of March a new and poignant sorrow was reserved for Maria Carolina in the death of her sister's son, the unfortunate little King Louis XVII., who sank from the effects of the brutal treatment of the revolutionists.

Since the murder of Madame Elisabeth, which had soon followed that of Marie Antoinette, the efforts of all their relations of Bourbon and Habsburg, French, German, Italian, and Spanish, had been concentrated on the rescue of the two helpless children left in the clutches of the tigers. One had been sacrificed, but there still remained a victim who might be rescued. Hitherto the Salic law had saved her, and negotiations had been opened with the Convention before the death of her brother.

Their uncle, the Comte de Provence, had sent a despatch to the Austrian Minister, Thugut, begging that the Emperor would make an official request for the release of both of them, and had written himself to Boissy d'Anglas, who replied that after the country had been delivered from Robespierre his first thought had been for the captive children, whose liberty he had tried to obtain. But that the Convention absolutely refused to give up the young King, though promising that he should *now be only treated as a hostage, not a victim*. As to his sister, the matter was different: "*la loi salique la sauve, alors qu'on a renversé toutes les autres lois de la monarchie; elle peut donc aller où l'on voudra la conduire. L'Espagne peut la réclamer de concert avec l'Autriche, offrir en échange les prisonniers qui sont dans les prisons de l'Empire, et l'on croira ici faire un bon marché. Mais, je vous le répète, si l'on mêle le nom du frère avec celui de la sœur, tout manquera; le parti pris à ce sujet est irrevocable. . . .*"[1]

Having received this letter, the Comte de Provence wrote again to the Emperor. But Franz, cold, selfish, and incapable, could not be induced to move in the matter. He declared it was impossible to compromise his honour by negotiating secretly

---

[1] "The Salic law saves her, when they have destroyed every other law of the monarchy; therefore she may go wherever they wish to take her. Spain and Austria may demand her, offering in exchange the prisoners who are in the dungeons of the Empire; and here it will be considered a good bargain. But I repeat to you, if they mix up the name of the brother with that of the sister all will fail, for their decision arrived at on that subject is irrevocable. . . ." ("Mémoires de Louis XVIII").

Louis XVII.

with the Republic, and he refused to give up his French prisoners.

The Comte de Provence then appealed to the Empress Catherine of Russia, who immediately ordered her ambassador at Vienna to open the negotiation. Austria thereupon agreed to join, but no power could be found willing to make the proposals. Finally, however, Boissy d'Anglas applied to the American legation, which undertook to make the first advance. It was proposed to exchange Madame Royale for various prisoners who had been seized by Austria—amongst others, Drouet, the regicide postmaster who had betrayed the royal family during the flight to Varennes, and so been the cause of their destruction. He had been captured while trying to escape when with the Army of the North; he was not, however, one of those eventually selected.

The young Louis XVII. was now better treated, and placed under the care of humane persons, but it was too late to save him, and even then the republican tyrants had not the common humanity to let the orphan brother and sister be together during the last days of the child's life. Madame Royale had now her *sous-gouvernante*, Mme. de Soucy, with her, and some persons appointed for her service.

The King of Naples sent the Prince di San Nicandro to Verona to present his homage to the Comte de Provence, now Louis XVIII., as head of his family; the Duke of Parma did the same; and the King of Spain paid him a monthly pension of twenty thousand francs, upon which he supported a numerous household and suite.[1]

On the 19th of December, 1795, Madame Royale, then seventeen years old, was released from the prison of the Temple. She did not know of the death of her aunt and brother, and this final blow seemed to render her, at first, indifferent to the fact that she was free. She was conducted as rapidly as she could travel across the frontier of Germany and consigned to the care of her Austrian relations. But this was not what she desired. She was of course received with all honour by her cousins, the Emperor and Empress, and by her Austrian uncles and aunts. Besides the Queen of Naples and Duke of Modena in Italy, there remained in Germany the Archduke Maximilian, Elector of Cologne, a fat, merry, good-natured personage, without much brains, but hospitable to the *émigrés* and generally popular, and the Archduchesses Christine and Elisabeth. But they were all strangers to her, and her heart was with her French relations, whom it was now her one desire to join. Her father had, in a letter, charged her not to marry any one but the Duc d'Angoulême, eldest son of the Comte d'Artois, and heir, after his uncle and father, to the throne of France. She soon discovered, however, that it was intended to marry her to the Archduke Carl, brother of the Emperor, and to claim for her the provinces of Burgundy, Bretagne, Alsace, Lorraine, and Franche Comté; all of which, it was truly said, had come to France through the female line, and of which she was, therefore, the lawful

[1] "Mémoires de Louis XVIII."

MADAME ROYALE.

heiress. It was perfectly true; but there were two obstacles in the way of the plan. First, the French would never entertain the idea of dismembering France; secondly, Madame Royale refused to consent to the proposal. The imperial family tried all means of persuasion, and even prevented the French *emigrés* having access to her; but it was useless. She remained in Austria till 1799, and then, by the interposition of the Emperor Paul of Russia, was given up to her French uncles and married to the Duc d'Angoulême.[1]

In a letter to Lady Hamilton, replying to one of condolence from the latter upon the death of the hapless Louis XVII., the Queen observes that "it has re-opened wounds that will never be healed"; and the withdrawal of the King of Spain from the coalition against France was another blow to her.

Her health, always delicate, was much affected by all the grief, anxiety, and excitement which of late years had been her continual portion, but with courage and fortitude she bore the burdens laid upon her. There was very little rest for her either of mind or body, and one of the fatiguing things she was obliged to do was to accompany the King in his hunting excursions.

Like her mother, Maria Carolina did not like hunting, but, like her, she never allowed her personal liking or disliking to interfere with what she considered advisable for the welfare of her family or the conduct of affairs.

Notwithstanding the absurd assertions of republican writers that Ferdinando hated and loathed his

[1] "Mémoires de Louis XVIII."

wife, he was anxious that she should be with him in his favourite amusement; and, much as she detested the whole thing, ill or well, she would go cheerfully with him to the Casino Reale of Carditello, the farm and chase in which he delighted, where wild boars, stags, and all manner of game abounded.

"Je dois partir pour toute la journée pour Carditello. Ma Sante et ma frele machine n'aiment pas ces longues gite, mais il faut obeir, ..." she writes to Lady Hamilton, weary and ungrammatical, in April, 1795.

It was absolutely necessary, in order to preserve the influence she had over Ferdinando, to enter into his pursuits and diversions, as she had, by her mother's directions, done ever since her first arrival at Naples; and to pretend to take an interest in them.

She would even go to the fish-market to see him sell fish, as he did on certain occasions, dressed up in a white cap and apron, holding up the fish and selling it by auction to the highest bidder, with chaff, slang, and coarse jests in the dialect of the *lazzaroni*, who shouted with delight at his speeches.

The Marchesa Solari describes in her memoirs how she went on Christmas Eve with Sir William Hamilton to see this spectacle.

Another favourite entertainment of Ferdinando was on the night of Shrove Tuesday, when the *lazzaroni* and all the lowest classes in Naples had a right to assemble in the pit of the magnificent theatre of San Carlo without paying anything.

None of the decent, respectable citizens who were accustomed to go to the pit went there on that night, but the boxes were crowded with well-dressed people, and in one of those on an upper tier the King stood, attended by servants carrying huge dishes of hot macaroni dressed with cheese and oil, of which he took handfuls with his bare fingers, directly it was cool enough not to burn him, and flung it down upon the crowds below, who scrambled and fought to get it.

While this was going on the Queen, who did not like to see it, sat at the back of her box, but when the King had changed his clothes and returned, she appeared with him in front of the box and graciously acknowledged the salutations and acclamations of the *lazzaroni*.

As long as they were not poachers the King was extremely kind and generous to the peasants; if they were, his wrath was kindled against them.

All these ways and characteristics of Ferdinando, however undignified and unkingly, endeared him to the *lazzaroni* and the lowest classes of his people—another proof that people's virtues and vices have very little, if anything, to do with their popularity, especially amongst the mob.

Louis XVI. was a man of irreproachable character, without vices, eager for reforms and the good of his people, who cared nothing about him, despised his amusement of making locks and keys, and ended in consenting to his ill-treatment and murder.

Ferdinando, good-natured and good-tempered as a rule, was profligate, despotic, and, if opposed or angered, violent and cruel. But he was adored by the *lazzaroni* and the populace, who would never have allowed him to be put to death publicly in the midst of them like his unfortunate brother-in-law.

Besides the diversions just described, however, he was fond of balls, cards, and music. He played and sang, though not particularly well, and would spend hours over duets with the Queen, Lady Hamilton, or the ladies of the Queen's court and household.

Though Maria Carolina showed such tact and skill in the management of Ferdinando, influencing him to adopt her opinions and making him think they were his own, praising him when he was successful in any project and excusing him if he failed, this did not, as it would with some women, prevent her caring for him. She had never had any illusions about him to be destroyed; from the earliest days of their marriage she had seen exactly what his character was, and it had in fact been a great relief to her to find him no worse. The entire success of her plans for his subjugation, his admiration and deference for herself, his habitual good spirits and good temper, and, later on, their mutual interest and delight in their children, their joint grief over those they lost, and love for those that remained, all combined to draw them together in spite of the intrigues and infidelities of Ferdinando, about which, after a time, she ceased to trouble herself much, unless the objects of them were likely to be dangerous or detrimental, in which case she promptly interfered and he yielded. On one occasion, indeed, a certain Signora Banti, whose conduct and attempts to influence Ferdinando gave some uneasiness to the Queen, found herself arrested one evening, placed in a travelling carriage, and conducted across the frontier, safely removed from the Neapolitan dominions. When the King was ill she nursed him with care and anxiety; whenever she mentioned him in her letters it was in terms of consideration and affection.

"My dear Miledy," she wrote to Lady Hamilton, "I know your heart; I can therefore give you my news from the hospital where I am. Thank God! the King is much better and without fever, the eruption is perfect, and he is in good spirits, at ease, talks, and causes me no anxiety. Mimi, who is covered with it, suffers more, but is in no danger. They have put a blister on her. Amélie already writes for herself, and is free of the affair. For myself, I have a pain under my arm which I must treat and I feel wretched. My dear friend, I dare not see you for fear of giving you our infection. The English courier has arrived this morning; nothing can be fairer or more polite than everything they write to us from London. That would attach me, were I not so already for life. A thousand compliments for the Chevalier. Pity me, my good friend! I need it much, but in what a position do I find myself! Your dear friend for life."

Whether small-pox, measles, or what was the matter with the King and Princesses does not appear, but this and all her letters give the idea of an affectionate family, on good and friendly terms with each other.[1]

The reign of Ferdinando and Carolina of Naples may be divided into two periods, absolutely different in their characteristics. The minority of Ferdinando,

[1] "The Queen of Naples and Lord Nelson" (Jeaffreson).

under the sway of Tanucci, forms another period with which this book has, of course, no concern. The years from 1768 till 1791 were those of a happy and prosperous reign. The King and Queen were popular, powerful, and happy, their government was paternal and beneficent, the people were contented and loyal, reforms and improvements of every description were continually going on, and the kingdom arrived at the height of its splendour and prosperity.

The breaking out of the French Revolution put an end to all this. The murder of Marie Antoinette embittered and changed the character of Maria Carolina and filled her whole soul with a deep, passionate longing for revenge upon the French, and upon the Jacobins of whatever nation. The conspiracies and attacks directed against him aroused in Ferdinando those dark passions of hatred, cruelty, violence, and tyranny which had hitherto been hidden under a genial manner, a careless good-humour, and an easygoing kindliness.

From henceforth their lives and their kingdoms were filled with a succession of calamities, tragedies, and crimes, which made the latter years of their reign as disastrous as the former were fortunate.

CHAPTER XV

The Queen's justice—An Ambassador of the Republic—Marriage of the Duke of Calabria—A patched-up peace—The battle of the Nile—The English fleet at Naples—Declaration of war — Exciting times — Ferdinand enters Rome — Disasters and defeats—Approach of the enemy—Horrors and dangers — Preparations for flight.

THE enormous number of persons arrested, the alarm and confusion everywhere rife, caused such intolerable delay in the trials that the unfortunate and often innocent prisoners languished for months and even for years in their dungeons without being able to be heard. One day two ladies, one a venerable woman of great age, the other just past her youth, both dressed in deep mourning, presented themselves at the palace and asked for an audience. They were the Duchess of Cassano and the Princess Colonna, who, overwhelmed with grief, had come to entreat the Queen to show mercy upon their unfortunate sons, who for four years had languished in prison, saying that they scarcely knew whether they were alive or dead, and conjuring the Queen by her love for her own children and by the mercy of God to listen to them.

On the Queen's asking if they were guilty, the

Duchess and Princess solemnly assured her that they were innocent, and then, overcome by their grief, took their leave.

The Queen was deeply moved and began to doubt whether there might not be innocent and unjustly treated persons detained in the prisons of the State. She gave orders that they were to be brought to fair trial immediately, and that no further delay was to be suffered, in consequence of which, twenty-eight of the accused, many of them nobles or learned men, amongst whom were Colonna, Cassano, and Medici, were acquitted and set at liberty.[1]

The rapid successes of Buonaparte and the defeat of the Austrians at length obliged the King and Queen of Naples to agree to an armistice offered by the victorious general, and terms of peace were arranged. The treaty was a most disadvantageous one for Naples, an indemnity of eight million francs to be paid to the French Republic being one of the stipulations.

However, neither France nor Naples had any intention of observing the treaty a moment longer than it should suit their convenience to do so, and meanwhile both powers looked forward to future vengeance.

"On the 8th of December, 1796, arrived the news of peace for Naples with cursed France," as Lady Hamilton wrote on the back of a letter.

Maria Carolina was in despair; everything looked black around her. The King of Spain had written in the previous September to his brother that he

[1] "Königin Karolina von Neapel und Sicilien" (Helfert), "Storia del Reame di Napoli" (Colletta)

was about to ally himself with France to make war upon England. The Queen sent this letter by Lady Hamilton to Sir William,[1] who at once wrote to warn the English Government. The ambassador at first sent by France to Naples was a man of refined, courtly manners, who was received with politeness and relief by the court and *corps diplomatique*. But he was very soon withdrawn, and replaced by a brutal, ignorant, conceited ruffian named Trouvé, with manners so outrageous that it was impossible to associate with him. He knew nothing, of course, about the customs of a court, and refused to comply with them when they were pointed out to him. He would not kiss the King's hand, he refused to rise when the King and Queen entered the theatre, and was only with difficulty persuaded to do so by the other ambassadors.

His despatches were couched in uncouth, insolent language, he tried to interfere in the affairs of Naples, he was furious at not being called "*citoyen*," and soon he was looked upon with such detestation and loathing that scarcely anybody would salute him or speak to him, and the French government was obliged to recall him.

But they sent in his place another odious person, who, if less violently offensive, was a vain, pompous idiot, troublesome, intolerable, and totally devoid of any knowledge of diplomacy.[2]

[1] In after years Lady Hamilton made the absurd boast that *she* had persuaded the Queen to do so, and that the Queen had " stolen it out of the King's pocket " As the Queen was all-powerful with the King and in the government, this ridiculous statement needs no comment.
[2] A. Bonnefonds.

It will be remembered that in 1790, when the two eldest daughters of the King and Queen of Naples had been married to the Austrian Crown Prince, now Emperor of Germany, and the Grand-duke of Tuscany, the Prince Royal of Naples had been betrothed to the Archduchess Clementine, a younger daughter of the Emperor Leopold.

Owing to the tender age of these children the marriage could not take place at that time, but the Prince Royal being now nineteen and the Archduchess fifteen years old, it was decided that their wedding should be celebrated in June, 1797, at Foggia, where the royal family accordingly awaited the Archduchess, who was to sail from Trieste.

Like Maria Carolina herself nearly thirty years before, the young princess dreaded her marriage, and lamented over her exile from her native Germany.

The Prince Royal, Duke of Calabria, was, in spite of all his mother's efforts and care for his education, stupid and without cultivated tastes, caring for little but sport and outdoor pursuits, and whether Clementine had misgivings about him, through what she might have heard, or through the letters he occasionally wrote, or whether it was only a young girl's natural sorrow and reluctance to leave her own family and country for what she considered a life of exile, Clementine cried bitterly when she saw the Italian ships which had come to Trieste to fetch her, and had to be persuaded to go on board.

She appears, however, to have got on very well

with her young husband, to have been a great favourite with the royal family and the people, especially the *lazzaroni*, and to have held her little court or society merrily and happily.[1]

But it was widely different from the brilliant prospect with which Maria Carolina and Ferdinando had begun their married life. Treachery at home and danger from without clouded the horizon and filled the mind of everyone. There was an atmosphere of suspicion: everyone distrusted everyone else, no one would speak upon any but the most indifferent subjects, arrests were still frequent, people kept disappearing in a mysterious manner, and were supposed to be immured in the prisons of the state.

Buonaparte had seized Malta, Berthier had marched upon Rome, Pius VII. had fled, and in spite of the treaty still subsisting between the two countries the presence of the French troops in Rome caused great uneasiness at Naples, besides the indignation aroused by the treatment of the Pope.

The French fleet, with General Buonaparte, after taking possession of Malta, had proceeded to Egypt. The Queen kept up a secret correspondence with London, and was anxious that the English fleet should be within reach in case of an attempt upon Naples or Sicily. Lady Hamilton wrote for her to Lord St. Vincent, who replied that the Queen was to be of good cheer, as a knight of superior prowess (Sir Horatio Nelson) had already been charged to preserve her from harm. Sir

[1] Helfert.

William Hamilton also received notice that Nelson would soon be on his way to the protection of the Two Sicilies. The celebrated Cornelia Knight, afterwards governess to Charlotte, Princess of Wales, who with her mother, Lady Knight, escaped from Rome when it was occupied by the French troops, and was at this time living in Naples, writes as follows:

"Our conversation by day and our dreams by night had for their sole and only subject the meeting of the hostile fleets.

"The court of Naples had not publicly renounced its neutrality, though its dislike of the common enemy and its wishes for the success of the allies were well-known to all parties. The common people generally agreed with the court, but many of the young nobles were infected with the revolutionary spirit. Endowed with more imagination than judgment, and greatly addicted to dissipation, they were anxious to throw off all inconvenient trammels, or, if led by their genius to nobler pursuits, they were captivated by the false theories of the philosophers then in fashion, and who had been among the first victims to the revolution they had evoked. It must also be borne in mind . . . that there existed two opposite national parties. Although the war of 1745 had placed the Spanish branch of the house of Bourbon on the throne, the Queen herself was an Austrian, and was supposed to be partial to her native country. The Spanish families established in the Two Sicilies [1] and the ad-

[1] Among the Spanish nobles settled at Naples were the four great families of Arragon, Duke of Novino, Marquis of Santo

herents of Spain were secretly if not avowedly her enemies. . . . It is but just, however, to remark that amongst those who were warmly attached to their party there were many who, disgusted by the system of cruelty and irreligion then prevailing in France, felt a natural horror in the presence of the revolutionary agents and heartily wished for their expulsion from the country. The Italians in general were well affected towards the English, and certainly the majority of the inhabitants of Naples anticipated with pleasure the arrival of a British fleet.

"Our telescope was constantly directed towards the entrance of the beautiful bay, the prospect of which we so perfectly enjoyed from our windows."[1]

On May 21st, Nelson had received a letter desiring him to proceed with a powerful squadron "in quest of the armament preparing at Toulon and Genoa, the object whereof appears to be either an attack upon Naples and Sicily, the conveyance of an army to some part of the coast of Spain for the purpose of marching towards Portugal, or to pass through the Straits with a view of proceeding to Ireland," which armament he was directed to "take, sink, burn, or destroy."

The alarm and anxiety of the Queen was therefore very well grounded, and it was no wonder that she waited in suspense for news of Nelson and his fleet.

"May the breeze and the good God bless the

Mario, Counts of Accarra and Avilos. They all walked together in the procession of the Corpus Christi (Swinburne).
[1] Autobiography of Miss Cornelia Knight.

English and accompany them! My vows and prayers follow them, and I long for the moment when all our forces and means will help them, ..." she wrote to Lady Hamilton, and, as Mr. Jeaffreson points out, it could not have been true that Lady Hamilton, as she made Nelson believe, and as in after years she used to boast, *persuaded* the Queen to obtain from the King the order to revictual the English fleet, which they were longing to help, and from which they hoped for their own deliverance.[1]

In full pursuit of the French fleet, Nelson wanted provision for his ships, and sent a message to the Queen through Lady Hamilton, asking permission to revictual at Syracuse. This was, of course, a breach of neutrality, but Maria Carolina did not hesitate. She appealed to the King and obtained from him an order to the Governor of Syracuse to revictual all Nelson's ships, and her doing so enabled him to win the battle of the Nile. But surely no one knowing anything of the character of the Queen of Naples, her vows of vengeance against the murderers of her sister, the desperate position in which she was placed, her courage and indomitable resolution, would believe that she required any

---

[1] In after years Lady Hamilton, in the days of her fallen fortunes, was in the habit of making many false statements to exalt the prestige of her past associations. So absurd were her assertions, and so exaggerated her idea of her own importance and influence, that she used to believe, or at any rate to say, that it was she who had influenced the Queen in favour of England and detached her from Spain, though the Queen had destroyed Spanish influence at Naples and had an English Prime Minister many years before Emma Hart ever set foot in her dominions.

persuasion at all in the matter. She was eager and delighted to do any possible thing to help the cause she loved and punish the enemy she hated; and that she did on this occasion experience the joy of retribution is certain, for Nelson, his ships provisioned by order of the King through her influence, sailed from Syracuse, overtook the French fleet in Aboukir Bay, and destroyed it; leaving the best army of the republic detained in the deserts of Africa.

". The English fleet under my command," wrote Nelson, " would never have been able to return the second time to Egypt if the influence of Lady Hamilton over the Queen of Naples had not obtained letters to be written to the Governor of Syracuse ordering him entirely to revictual. Arriving at Syracuse, we received all provisions. From thence I sailed for Egypt, where I destroyed the French fleet.—NELSON." [1]

Miss Knight describes in simple but graphic language the arrival at Naples of the news of the victory of the Nile: how she was sitting reading to her mother at the window when they discerned a sloop of war in the offing, how they eagerly watched through the telescope as it approached, how they perceived the blue ensign and gold epaulettes, the commotion as the two officers got into a boat and were brought to shore, the gestures

---

[1] Lady Hamilton's absurd boasts in after years as to what she did and induced every one else to do, were addressed to many persons besides Nelson. As time went on, her vainglorious fancies became more and more preposterous; she appeared to believe she had been the ruling power at the court of Naples.

of the sailors, representing the sinking and blowing up of ships, the appearance of Captain Hoste and Captain Capel with despatches from Nelson for Sir William Hamilton and for England.

"The battle of the Nile had been fought and won. Never, perhaps, was a victory more complete ! . . . Old General di Pietra . . . lived in a house adjoining our hotel, and there was a door of communication between them. He had been very attentive to us and we met excellent society at his table, for he delighted in giving dinner-parties. We knew his anxiety to receive the earliest accounts of the meeting of the two fleets, and my mother desired me to give him the first intelligence. I ran to the door, and the servant who opened it, and to whom I delivered my message, uttered exclamations of joy which were heard in the dining-room, where the General was entertaining a large party of officers. The secretary was instantly sent to me, and I was obliged to go in and tell my story. Never shall I forget the shouts, the bursts of applause, the toasts drunk, the glasses broken one after another by the secretary in token of exultation, till the General, laughing heartily, stopped him by saying that he should not have a glass left to drink Nelson's health in on his arrival.

"The first care of Sir William Hamilton was to take Captain Capel to the palace. The King and Queen were at dinner with their children, as was their custom, for they dined very early. As soon as the King heard the good news he started up, embraced the Queen, the Princes, the Princesses, and exclaimed :

E G Y P T
BAY OF BEQUIRE
BATTLE OF THE NILE,
BRITISH SQUADRON.
FRENCH FLEET.

"'Oh, my children, you are now safe!'

"The Cardinal of York was then at Naples, having fled from Rome to avoid falling into the hands of the French. He was told of the news by Sir William Hamilton, who introduced Captain Capel, saying:

"'This gentleman, a brother of Lord Essex, was in the action, and is going home immediately with the despatches.'

"'In that case, sir,' said the Cardinal to Captain Capel, 'when you arrive in England, do me the favour to say that no man rejoices more sincerely than I do in the success of the British navy.'"[1]

When the news of the victory spread, Naples was transported with joy. The city, especially the houses of the English, was illuminated for three days, everywhere was an air of festivity, in every quarter were heard acclamations and cheers for England.

On the 22nd of September the sails of the victorious fleet were descried upon the horizon.

A tumult of excitement filled the city as the stately ships approached, the flag of England floating from their masts and the captive warships of France following in their wake.

Hurriedly the King, the English Ambassador and his wife embarked on ships decorated as if for a gala and went out to meet the conqueror, who received on board his own ship their enthusiastic welcome. The Ambassador thanked him in the name of England, and the King presented him with a splendid sword. The Queen afterwards,

[1] Autobiography of Cornelia Knight.

among other things, gave him a jewel on which was inscribed "To the hero of Aboukir."

All Naples waited to watch the fleet come into the bay and then rushed to the palace to see Nelson.

In the evening there was a grand representation at the San Carlo, which was illuminated as for a national rejoicing. As the King and court entered, accompanied by Nelson, the nobles and ladies wearing ribbons and girdles on which the inscription "Viva Nelson" was set with jewels, the vast crowd that filled the immense theatre burst into frantic shouts and cries, in which mingled cheers for the King and Queen, for Nelson, for England, applause for the victory, and curses on the French.

The few ships which had escaped in a battered condition to Sicily had been plundered or driven away, the fleet with its captives was at anchor in the bay, the city was in a delirium of joy and triumph.

War was again declared with France, against which a new confederation had been formed. England, Germany, Russia, and the Two Sicilies were arming; troops and stores were hastily raised and collected; Naples was filled with the excitement and bustle of warlike preparations.

General Mack arrived from Austria to take command; there were reviews of the troops, councils and consultations in Naples and at Caserta, in which Nelson, Sir William Hamilton and General Mack took part, and in which the Queen, supported by the English, strongly urged the immediate invasion of Rome.

It was a time of intense anxiety and excitement to

Maria Carolina, who was, of course, transported with joy at the new aspect of affairs.

"I am wild with joy, my dear Miledy!" she wrote to Lady Hamilton, when the news came of the Nile. "I embrace my children, my husband. . . .

"My children, all who belong to me, feel all that they owe you and are wild with joy. . . ."

She removed with her court to San Germano, where the troops were encamped, and stayed there for weeks, driving or riding through the lines in a blue riding-habit, with gold fleurs-de-lys at the neck and a general's hat with a white plume.

Nelson had returned from Malta, where he had been, and Miss Knight records in her journal: "November 5, 1798.—Appeared in sight Admiral Nelson in the *Vanguard* . . . the Admiral came on shore in the afternoon and went immediately to Caserta, where he was scarce arrived when the hereditary Princess was brought to bed of a daughter, bells ringing, guns firing, &c."

Nelson, who was there occasionally and appeared now and then at the reviews, watched General Mack with disapprobation, and one day, observing that he had allowed himself to be surrounded by the troops of "the enemy," he exclaimed contemptuously: "That fellow doesn't understand his business!"

It was, of course, only too true. Mack was a pompous fool, utterly incapable, and with neither sympathy for nor influence over his soldiers.

The troops marched to Rome, which the French evacuated for the time, and Ferdinando, taking up his quarters at the Farnesina, wrote to the Pope begging him to return.

But the success was of short duration. Before the middle of December disastrous tidings were sent day after day of lost battles, troops, guns, horses, standards, and stores; and Ferdinando returned to Naples in disguise in the carriage of the Duke d'Ascoli, with whom he had changed clothes.

"If Mack is defeated this country is lost," wrote Nelson to Lord St. Vincent; "for the Emperor has not yet moved his army, and if the Emperor will not march, this country has not the power of resisting the French."

Events very soon proved the truth of his words. The Neapolitan troops fled in all directions; the Jacobins in Naples, filled with joy, sent messengers to the French general, Championnet, who was marching forward, to beg him to hasten and give him all information about the strength and position of their native city, which they were eager to deliver into the hands of the foreigner. This infuriated the *lazzaroni* and the rest of the lowest classes, more loyal and patriotic, but fierce, unruly, and savage. There were continual quarrels and fights between them and the Jacobins, bloodshed and murder went on in the streets, the police lost control and nerve, and very soon the city was a scene of rioting.

Even now, more than a hundred years after the time of these events, the populace of Naples is strangely behind those of more northern cities in the very elements of civilisation.

During the last epidemic of cholera, not much more than twenty years ago, it was reported and believed that the people were being poisoned by the doctors. Others, who did not share this belief, but were scarcely more enlightened, would not take their medicine unless the doctor gave them five francs.

At a small town somewhere in that neighbourhood which was infected by cholera, it was decided not to allow the trains to stop, which so offended and enraged the inhabitants that they collected in groups at the station to throw stones and hoot at the train as it passed. Their cruelty to animals is also only worthy of a savage country.

The horrors of such a mob, excited, enraged, and let loose in furious riots, can hardly be imagined. In their rage against the French invaders and the treachery of the Jacobins they began to attack all the houses whose owners were known to be of the party of the Revolution, or where they thought any Frenchmen might be hidden. They sacked the houses and ill-treated or murdered those whom they suspected. An unfortunate King's messenger, Antonio Ferretti (or Ferresi), who was going from the town to the harbour, carrying despatches to one of the British ships, had the rashness to ask in French for a boat.[1] He was seized by the furious multitude, declared to be a French spy or at least a Jacobin traitor, murdered and dragged through the streets under the very windows of the palace, where Ferdinando, hearing the tumult and going out into the balcony to see what was the matter, recognised with horror the dead or dying man, but was unable to make the least impression upon the maddened, raving multitude.

[1] Helfert.

Championnet was on his march towards Naples, which the Jacobin party were waiting to deliver into his hands. The fate of Marie Antoinette and the French royal family threatened Maria Carolina, her husband, and children, and foreseeing this, the Queen had for the last few days been preparing for flight.

Her most trustworthy servants had, under her supervision, packed up clothes and valuables, which in the darkness of night had been taken down to the docks or to the British Embassy, where they were consigned to the care of Lady Hamilton to be passed on to Lord Nelson.

The Hamiltons and Mrs. Cadogan were packing up all Sir William's most valuable antiquities and artistic treasures, which were sent to London.[1]

"My Dear Miledy," wrote the Queen. "Behold three more portmanteaus and a little box. In the first three there is a little linen for all my children, for use on board, and in the box some petticoats. I trust I am not imprudent in sending them to you. The remainder of what can go shall go by a Sicilian vessel, as I do not wish to inconvenience you. Believe me to be for life your grateful and faithful friend. I hope to see you to-morrow evening with our dear and precious Admiral" (December 18, 1798).

And on the following day these two letters and more boxes:

"My Dear Miledy,—I abuse your goodness and our brave Admiral's goodness. Let the great boxes be thrown in the hold and the little ones

[1] "The Queen of Naples and Lord Nelson" (Jeaffreson.)

be near at hand. It is so because I have unfortunately an immense family. I am in the despair of desolation and my tears flow incessantly. The blow, its suddenness have bewildered me, and I do not think I shall ever recover from it. . . . My son has returned from Capua and tells horrors of the flying troops. . . . I would commit myself to the Divine Providence . . . but the moment is deadly. . . ."

"MY DEAR MILEDY,—The dangers increase. Aquila is taken with six hundred men, to the everlasting shame of our country. Mack writes in despair. The weather seems favourable, and therefore the King is urgent. I am in bewilderment and despair, as this changes entirely our estate—being life and position—everything that shaped my ideas and those of my family for life. I do not know where my head is. This evening I will send some other boxes and clothes for my numerous family and myself, for it is for life. Tell me frankly whether I may send our trunks this evening by a trusty man, Lalo or Saresio. . . ."

In a third letter written on the following day the Queen says:

"The popular tumults (attended with) the slaughter of people are a sure indication of more mischief to come. That will grow daily, and I tremble at the atrocities that will be perpetrated by a people who do not defend themselves against the enemy, but will allow themselves all the horrors of the most unbridled licence."[1]

[1] These letters, given by Mr. Jeaffreson in his book on "The Queen of Naples and Lord Nelson," show, as he points out, the

Upon the envelope of this last letter is written in Lady Hamilton's handwriting :

"December 21, 1798.—God protect us this night."

absurdity of Lady Hamilton's boast, many years afterwards, that it was she who persuaded and helped the Queen and royal family to escape, she who packed up all their things—she, in fact, who did everything and directed everybody.

CHAPTER XVI

Alarming state of things—Escape of the royal family—Terrible storm—Death of Prince Carlo Alberto—Arrival at Palermo—Adventures of Lady Knight and her daughter—Perils and hardships—Palermo—Lovely scenery—Loyal Sicily—Death of the Archduchess Christine—The Parthenopeian Republic—Departure of Caracciolo—The King's warning.

AS they possessed another country and another capital in which they could take refuge, and as, if Naples was full of traitors and rebels, Palermo was loyal, it was there that the King and Queen naturally intended to go.

"From the 18th," wrote Nelson to Lord St. Vincent (December 28th), "various plans were formed for the removal of the royal family from the palace to the waterside. On the 19th I received a note from General Acton, saying that the King approved of my plan for their embarkation. This day, the 20th-21st, very large assemblies of people were in commotion, and several people killed, and one dragged by his legs to the palace. The mob by the 20th were very unruly, and insisted the royal family should not leave Naples. However, they were pacified by the King and Queen speaking to them."[1]

[1] "The Queen of Naples and Lord Nelson" (Jeaffreson).

It is difficult to see any justice or reason in the abuse poured by various writers upon the King and Queen for " deserting " the capital, where their position was a terrible one.

The Neapolitan troops, beaten and scattered, had just proved their inability to defend themselves against the victorious armies of France, now advancing upon them.

Naples was a prey to violent factions—the *lazzaroni* and lowest class of the populace, loyal to the King but savage and ungovernable, and the Jacobins, steeped in treachery, and eagerly waiting to deliver their city into the hands of the French.

That Maria Carolina should have dreaded the fate of her sister and brother-in-law for her husband and herself, and that of the unfortunate Dauphin for her children, cannot be surprising. She remembered perfectly well how Louis XVI. had refused to fly when he could have saved himself and his family, and waited until it was too late. She felt convinced that if they stayed they would fall into the hands of her sister's murderers. Nelson urged their departure.

Like most sanguine, impetuous people, Maria Carolina was subject to reaction and depression, and she believed that she was leaving Naples for ever.

Ferdinando, on the contrary, never thought any such thing, but declared that he should soon come back again with a large army, which, in his opinion, he could organise much better in loyal Sicily, where he would be safe and free, than in Naples, honeycombed with treachery and overrun by a powerful enemy.

Another grievance against Ferdinando and Maria Carolina is that they took away with them all the property which could be removed, not only from their palaces at Naples and Caserta, but the treasures of the State, gold from the Mint and banks, objects of art and antiquity from the Museum—everything, in fact, which they could bestow on board the ships—English, Portuguese, and Neapolitan—then at anchor in the bay.

Ought they then to have fled penniless into exile, without means to carry on the government and court, or provide for the defence of their new capital? Ought they to have left their works of art to be carried to Paris, and their treasures or those of the State to fall into the hands of the French?

Twenty vessels, merchantmen and transport, were loaded with treasure and thronged with members of the court, society, and adherents of the King. At nine o'clock on the evening of December 21st the royal family secretly went on board Nelson's ship, the *Vanguard*, which, with two Neapolitan warships, one of which was commanded by Admiral Caracciolo, was to form the escort.

For two days and nights they waited about in the bay of Naples while the convoy was preparing for the voyage. At last, all being ready, the *Vanguard* first, and afterwards the rest of the long procession of ships, set sail for Sicily. But the wind, hitherto favourable, now changed: the ships were scattered, some taking refuge at Malta, others in Calabria.

A violent blast struck the *Vanguard*, tearing her sails to pieces. The courtiers in terror crowded into the state cabin occupied by the royal party. Nearly everybody was dreadfully seasick, except Lady Hamilton, who, being an excellent sailor, was invaluable in helping the Queen, whose attendants were all prostrate, and especially in looking after the royal children, who were very fond of her, and whom she nursed and comforted as well as she could. They were all very ill, and the youngest, Prince Carlo Alberto, a delicate child of seven, died from exhaustion the night before they arrived at their destination.

The bay of Palermo is by many pronounced to be more beautiful than that of Naples, and the approach to the lovely shores is eagerly watched by those who, on a bright summer morning or an evening golden and crimson with the sunset, or brilliant under the light of the southern moon, glide over its waters. But in the darkness of a winter morning before dawn, ill, miserable, and exhausted, no such consolation awaited the fugitives. Thankful to have arrived, however, the Queen and her children lost no time in landing in their new home, and before five o'clock a.m. they went on shore under the escort of Nelson, and entered the royal palace.

Exhausted by all she had gone through, to which the death of her child had added another blow, the Queen retired to bed with a violent headache and cold on the chest, and sent for the doctors, who bled and physicked her until it was a wonder she got well at all.

The Hamiltons had taken a house, to which Maria Carolina sent a letter begging that certain boxes of clothes might be sent her at once, as on Sunday they would have to receive many people.

Ferdinando, on the contrary, was perfectly self-possessed. He was too affectionate a father not to have grieved for the loss of his boy; but as regards other matters he declared they would come right again, and that their stay in the island would not be a long one. Meanwhile, the country was excellent for sporting purposes, and he had taken care that among the passengers from Caserta and Naples were his favourite dogs.

In order that they might not fall into the hands of the enemy, all the warships left at Naples, and some that had returned from Sicily, were set on fire, and an immense quantity of gunpowder and other stores thrown into the sea.

This terrible destruction of the splendid fleet which had been the pride of the Queen's heart was a fearful blow. Nothing but disaster seemed to surround them, though they had been received with joy and loyalty by the Sicilians, high and low.

Rabid and violent assailants of Maria Carolina declare that on the voyage to Sicily Ferdinando cursed and swore, and accused the Queen of being the cause of all these misfortunes by her ambition and mistaken policy. This, however, is not corroborated by less violent and bitter enemies. General Colletta merely says that the King looked at her with indignant glances amidst his prayers and vows to San Gennaro and San Francesco.

Miss Knight and her mother were among those who fled from Naples. The following is the account she gives of their experiences at the time:

"Like a dark cloud announcing a tremendous storm, the enemy kept gradually approaching. . . . The populace of Naples, and many of the higher orders, indeed, stoutly affirmed that they would never suffer their King and his family to fall into the hands of the enemy; but still it was thought more prudent to make preparations for departure. Unfortunately there was no English ship of war then in the bay except that which bore the flag of Lord Nelson and a frigate with a Turkish ambassador on board, attended by a numerous suite. A Portuguese squadron, however, was lying there, and also a fine Neapolitan man-of-war, commanded by Prince Caracciolo, and likewise another ship of the line; but it was the opinion of the court that although the *bailli* himself was trustworthy, the same reliance could not be placed in his crew. It was therefore resolved that the royal family should go with Lord Nelson.

"How far these suspicions were well founded I cannot say, but I have no doubt that this step hastened the desertion of Prince Caracciolo.[1]

"We met him about this time at General di Pietra's,

---

[1] In an earlier passage in her book Miss Knight says of Caracciolo. "That unfortunate man had . . conceived a jealous resentment against the hero of the Nile. . He told me that . in the engagement off Corsica . . Nelson had passed before him contrary to the directions previously issued This he thought very unfair, as British officers had frequent opportunities of distinguishing themselves, which was not the case with his own service"

and I never saw a man look so utterly miserable. He scarcely uttered a word, ate nothing, and did not even unfold his napkin. However, he took the ships safe to Messina, where they were laid up in ordinary. . . .

"We were informed of it [the intended departure of the King and Queen] by Sir William Hamilton, but with injunctions of strict secrecy. . . . We packed up everything as quietly as possible. We dared not venture out, as we knew not at what time we might be sent for to embark, and we were equally ignorant of the destination of our voyage.

"The populace had become very riotous, crowding about the King's palace and beseeching him not to leave them. It was unsafe for strangers to be in the streets unless well known, for all foreigners were liable to be mistaken for Frenchmen. Day after day passed away in anxious expectation, until one evening, just as we were retiring to rest, an officer from Lord Nelson's ship, attended by some seamen, made his appearance, and told us that a boat was waiting to take us on board. We hastily paid our bill, and sent an ambiguous message to our Roman friends which would put them on their guard. We then accompanied the officer to the shore. Both he and his men were armed.

"The night was cold, for we were in December (21st), and it was between twelve and one before we were in the boat. There were several people in it already, and an English child fell into the water, but was taken out unhurt. We had a long way to go, for the ships had cast anchor at a great distance from the city, to be beyond the range of the forts in the event of treachery or surprise. When we came alongside the Admiral's ship, the captain, Sir Thomas Hardy, stepped into the boat, and told my mother that the ship was so full there was no room for us. In vain we entreated to be taken on board. The thing was impossible. We must take our passage in a Portuguese man-of-war, commanded by an Englishman, who had been a master in our navy, but had now the rank of commodore.

"There was no alternative, but we were some time before we reached the ship to which we had been consigned. The young midshipman who conducted us was constantly jumping about in the boat to keep himself from falling asleep, for during the last forty-eight hours he had been unceasingly engaged in getting the baggage and numerous attendants of the royal family on board.

"We reached our destination about two in the morning, and were ushered into the chief cabin, where we found many ladies of different countries. Only one, a Russian lady of high rank and great wealth, had a bed to sleep on, the others being obliged to content themselves with mattresses on the floor. We now learned that we were bound for Palermo, and it was a great satisfaction to us to receive this confirmation of our previous hopes.

"The manners of the commodore were by no means prepossessing, but he was apparently annoyed at having his ship so crowded with helpless passengers. All the ships of the Portuguese squadron were commanded by Englishmen except, the flagship, the captain of which was a French emigrant nobleman. . . .

"After an uncomfortable night we rose to witness so violent a storm that no communication could take place between the ships. We obtained, however, a small cabin for our exclusive use, which was an unspeakable comfort.

"On the following morning, the weather being more calm, we perceived on Lord Nelson's ship the signal for sailing, but on none of the others. Our feeling of desertion is not to be described. . . . Presently we perceived a barge making towards us. It was that of Captain Hardy, whom Lord Nelson had sent with a message to my mother expressive of his concern that he could not take us on board his own ship, and informing us that the *Culloden*, Captain Troubridge, was shortly expected from Leghorn, and would, if we wished it, convey us to Palermo. Captain Hardy then returned to his ship, and soon after we saw the anchor weighed, and Lord Nelson, with the King and Queen and royal family of Naples, sailed out of the bay. It is impossible for any one who has not been in similar circumstances to imagine the feeling of helpless abandonment which I then experienced. Accustomed to look up to our squadron as our sole protection, having no confidence in the persons with whom we were left, and hearing of nothing but revolutionary horrors, I was really miserable."

From the discomforts and miseries of the Portuguese ship Lady Knight, her daughter, and two Cardinals with whom they had made friends on board were rescued by Captain Wilmot, of the

Alliance, who came in from a cruise on the 24th—Christmas Eve—and offered to take them in his ship to Palermo next day.

On the morning of Christmas Day, accordingly, they went on board, but another tremendous storm arose before they had proceeded far on their voyage, which forced them to return to their old moorings. Next morning the Portuguese Admiral who was commander-in-chief at that station, hearing of their return, sent for Captain Wilmot to help in the work that was being pressed on of saving whatever stores in the dockyard had not been yet sent to Sicily, but could still be removed. Everything that could not was destroyed to prevent its falling into the hands of the French. Lord Nelson's chaplain, who had been accidentally left behind, came on board, and at last they got off, and, as Miss Knight continues:

"After a voyage of thirty hours arrived in sight of Palermo. Accustomed as I had been to the lovely and magnificent scenery of Italy, I was not less surprised than delighted at the picturesque beauty of the Sicilian coast. Then, when the prospect of the city opened upon us, with the regal elegance of its marble palaces and the fanciful singularity of its remaining specimens of Saracenic architecture, it was like a fairy scene. . . .

"On our arrival we heard sad accounts of Lord Nelson's voyage. Exposed to all the fury of the storm we had escaped, the flagship had been in the greatest danger and had suffered considerably in her masts and rigging. Prince Albert, the King's youngest son, had died of sea-sickness, and his funeral was the first welcome this noble island could give to the royal personages who now took refuge on its shores. . . .

"We were in all about two thousand persons who left Naples at this time. The French entered the city about a fortnight after the King's departure and took possession of the castles, but they seldom ventured into the streets except in large parties, as the *lazzaroni* were greatly irritated against them. The environs, too, swarmed with armed peasants under the command of Cardinal Ruffo, a man of singular ability and decision of character and endowed with every advantage of mind and body that is sought for in a military leader. Though a cardinal, he had never taken holy orders, and before his elevation had been treasurer to the Pope.

"We took apartments on the Marina, a magnificent promenade of considerable length. It consisted of a row of good houses, some of them really handsome buildings, a wide road for carriages, and along the seashore a terrace for foot passengers with statues of the Kings of Sicily at regular intervals. The Marina led to a beautiful garden, called the Flora Reale . . . and in the summer-time a band of music used to play there for the amusement of the company. The garden belonged to the King, and near it was a very pretty villa which Sir William Hamilton occupied until he removed to a larger one near the Mole. . . . It was wonderful to see the improvements and resources which started up in Palermo after the arrival of so many strangers. . . . It was delightful to hear the Sicilian music on fine moonlight nights from the vessels and boats that entered or crossed the bay."[1]

During the year 1798, now closing, and which had been so full of turmoil and calamity for Maria Carolina, she had experienced another loss in her own family, that of her sister, the Archduchess Christine, Duchess of Saxe-Teschen and Governess of the Netherlands.

It seems strange that not one of the children of Maria Theresia lived to really old age.

The loyalty and affection with which the royal family were received in Sicily could not but touch their hearts. Welcomed with transports of enthusiastic devotion by all ranks of their subjects, they soon, after they had recovered from the fatigues, hardships, and sorrows of their flight, settled into their usual life in their new home.

The two eldest Princesses, Christine and Amélie, who had been accompanied by their beloved Signora di Ambrosio, pursued their studies and spent a great deal of their time in devotion and charity. In after years Queen Amélie would often recall to her mind the enthusiastic rapture of devotion she used to feel when she knelt in the chapel royal of Palermo.[2]

The King and Queen waited in suspense for news from Naples, considering meanwhile the best means of reconquering that country and putting Sicily into a proper state of defence. The news was bad enough when it did come. The "Parthenopeian Republic," as the Jacobins had christened the

[1] Autobiography of Cornelia Knight
[2] "Vie de Marie Amélie, Reine des Français" (A. Trognon).

MARIA CAROLINA, QUEEN OF NAPLES.
From a print in the possession of Mr. Hardy Manfield.
Picture given by the Queen to Lady Hamilton.

kingdom of Naples, had been declared and received with acclamation by the Jacobin party, whose delight, however, was soon considerably diminished when they found their property seized and their pockets emptied by Championnet with the first detachment of their new friends, and what was left taken from them by the next arrivals under Faypoult.

Court gaieties went on at Palermo as at Naples, but the Queen was melancholy and depressed, and in spite of the loyalty and devotion of their Sicilian subjects and the enchanting beauty of her second capital she began to wish that she had taken refuge instead with her eldest daughter at her beloved Vienna.

"No news from my dear Naples," she writes to Lady Hamilton, January 1, 1799. " My compliments to our excellent Admiral. I much wish to have a quiet conversation with him about the defence of this island, for everything I see, hear, and understand deprives me of all tranquillity. I am neither consulted nor even listened to, and am excessively unhappy. I regret that I did not go elsewhere with my children, and shelter myself with my family from events which must inevitably occur from the line of conduct pursued; but one must submit to fate and die. I grieve only for my children." [1]

That Ferdinando did blame the Queen for the plight they were in is evident. Her plans had certainly not prospered lately, and the defeat of Mack had shaken the King's confidence in Maria

[1] "The Queen of Naples and Lord Nelson" (Jeaffreson).

Carolina, whose countryman Mack was, and by whose nephew he had been sent to Naples; though it was certainly not the fault of the Queen that Mack was a bad general, and that a good one could not be found in the Neapolitan army.

However, Ferdinando when he arrived at Palermo showed a determination to take the reins of government himself, and a disregard of the Queen's opinion which he had never yet displayed during the thirty years of their married life.

After they had been a few weeks in Sicily, Admiral Caracciolo came to the King one day and asked for leave of absence.

This permission he granted, but remarked in a warning manner, as he did so: "Beware of meddling with French politics, and avoid the snares of the republicans. I know I shall recover the kingdom of Naples."[1]

Caracciolo left Palermo apparently a loyal and devoted subject of the King whose uniform he wore and whose commission he still held, and joined the Jacobins who betrayed Naples to the French.

The *lazzaroni* were anxious to defend their city, which, however, the Jacobins treacherously surrendered, proclaiming their own dishonour by boasting that the city had not yielded to assault or conquest but to their willing betrayal. General Manthoné, who made this declaration to Championnet, suffered the due reward of his treason a few months later.

[1] In her "Naples in 1799" Signora Giglioni says that this interview and warning were given by Acton, not Ferdinando.

CHAPTER XVII

Preparations for the reconquest of Naples—Ruffo—Calabria—A fearful war—State of Sicily—Travellers in the olden times—The brigands of Sicily—An escort.

THE royal family and court had exchanged one beautiful capital for another, were delivered from immediate danger, and surrounded by loyal subjects instead of traitors, but there was little rest or breathing time for any one.

The reconquest of Naples filled their thoughts, and the constant messages received by the King and Queen from their loyal subjects all over the kingdom encouraged their hopes and hastened their preparations.

The mass of the people hated the Jacobins and the French, and were everywhere rising for the King; from Calabria especially came urgent entreaties for arms, money, and somebody to lead them against the detested foreigners.

Calabria was certainly not a district in which republican or any new doctrines were likely to spread. To this day it and its inhabitants differ widely from the rest of Italy and the Italians. It is more difficult to see, and more strange and picturesque, than any other district of that country.[1]

In its great forests of chestnut and ilex hotels and modern conveniences of travelling do not exist, or, at any rate, did not a very few years ago.

The manners, customs, and ideas of its inhabitants are wilder and less civilised than in other parts of the country, and this applies not only to the peasantry but to the nobles, whose castles are buried in these lonely regions, and whose lives are regulated by the tastes and notions of bygone days.

Those who have heard the accounts and descriptions given by northern Italians, Roman, Florentine, Milanese, &c., of the experiences they have passed through during visits they have paid to some of these castles, will not have failed to be struck by the strange mediæval character and tone which pervades every detail and incident.

The extraordinary seclusion of the women; their monotonous lives; the large hunting parties, from which they are excluded; the great banquets occasionally given in the castle hall, in which only the men of the family take part, their mothers, wives, and sisters watching the arrival of the guests from some upper window in the castle; the young men, who, even if they have been, as now and then happens, educated at some foreign

[1] Brydone, writing of Calabria in 1770, says it is "pretty much in the same state as the wilds of America that are just beginning to be cultivated—little spots in the woods cleared . . . a wild and barren wilderness overgrown with thickets and forests, &c. . . . retaining in the ferocity of its inhabitants more of Gothic barbarity than . . . anywhere else. Some of these forests are of vast extent and almost impenetrable" ("A Tour through Sicily and Malta").

university, falling back on their return to their fathers' estates into the old ways, passing their days in galloping after cattle, hunting in the forests [1]—all this belongs to another age and to another system of life.

That a hundred years ago this state of things existed to a much greater degree and far more extensively need scarcely be said, and though General Colletta remarks that there were more republicans in Calabria than in Naples, it is exceedingly difficult to believe in anything so unlikely. At any rate, Cardinal Ruffo, whom Ferdinando sent to take command there, found the inhabitants eager to join him, and burning to sweep the French and the Jacobins from the country and revenge upon them the wrongs suffered by the King and the Church.

And the vengeance they took was terrible; though not at all worse than the cruelties and murders of those who were proclaiming the "rights of man" and the reign of universal happiness.

It is usual for republican writers to describe Ruffo's army as composed entirely or chiefly of brigands and convicts.[2] It is one of the usual exaggerations which recall the well-known words of a great poet:

"A lie that is all a lie can be met and fought with outright,
But a lie that is half the truth is a harder matter to fight."[3]

The King's army was composed in great part of

[1] All this I have not myself seen, but it has been told me by an Italian friend who took part in it. (Note by author.)
[2] He says that in Calabria they were about one per cent.
[3] Tennyson.

honest peasants who fought for the Church and the monarchy, and of soldiers already enlisted in his service.

But it is equally true that besides these were released prisoners and brigand chiefs with their bands, whose deeds of horror gave a fearful character to the war which soon raged over that unhappy country.

Fra Diavolo and other well-known and atrocious brigand chiefs were employed by Ruffo with the consent and approbation of the King and Queen, whose one desire and resolution was to recover the kingdom which had been wrested from them.

It must not, however, be supposed that the cruelties practised were worse on one side than the other, or that there was the least difference in their readiness to employ any and every body who could be found able and willing to fight for them.

The generals, officers, and soldiers of Joseph Buonaparte and Murat were just as cruel and remorseless as those of Ferdinando, with this difference, that the royalist troops were fighting for their King, their religion, their homes, their families, and their country, while the French were simply foreign invaders joined by a small portion of the Neapolitan people. General Macdonald, by no means a cruel specimen of the officers of the Republic or of Napoleon, gave and published the following orders :

"Every town or city in rebellion against the Republic shall be burnt and levelled with the ground.

" Cardinals, bishops, abbés, curés, and all ministers of divine worship shall be held responsible for acts of rebellion in the places where they reside, and shall be liable to the punishment of death.

" Every rebel shall be liable to the punishment of death, and every accomplice, whether lay or spiritual, shall be treated as a rebel.

" None are permitted to ring a double peal, and, wherever heard, the ecclesiastic of that parish shall be punished with death.

" Whoever shall spread news adverse to the French or to the Parthenopeian Republic shall be declared a rebel and shall suffer death.

" The loss of life shall be accompanied with loss of property."[1]

It must be remembered that what the Jacobins meant by *rebels* were people fighting for their lawful King and their own country against a foreign tyranny. For this, or for giving shelter, food, or help to their own father, husband, or child who opposed the Jacobin tyrants overrunning their country, women, old men, even children, were put to death without mercy.

But directly the case was reversed and the King got possession of Naples again, there arose an outcry of indignation because those who had rebelled against him, driven him from his kingdom, and given up their capital into the hands of a foreign invader, were punished as traitors. It is not, however, my intention to enter into the details of the terrible war that now and later raged in this unfortunate kingdom, nor to relate the vicissitudes,

[1] Colletta, &c.

crimes, and atrocities, which are given at full length by various historians of the time, which would only horrify my readers and which do not belong to a book of this kind.

The news which reached Palermo very soon became more encouraging. Ruffo was in Calabria in February, his army ever increasing as the royalists flocked to his standard. In March the Austrians had gained two victories in the north of Italy, invested Mantua, and were threatening Milan. The Russians and Turks had taken possession of the Ionian Islands and landed thirty-two thousand men on the coast of Italy.

Macdonald had retired from Naples with the greater part of his troops, leaving only enough soldiers to garrison Gaeta, Capua, St. Elmo, and the other forts. The Neapolitan Jacobins, first plundered and then deserted by their new friends, looked uneasily across the sea in the direction of Sicily.

In Naples itself various conspiracies had been formed for the recovery of the city by the royalists, of which the most formidable was one organised by a certain Baccher, who had lived for many years in Naples and whose sympathies and principles were strongly royalist.

This Baccher was a banker, and of Swiss nationality; he had four sons, of whom one, Gerardo, was an officer in the Neapolitan cavalry.

Some historians have asserted that they were English and that their name was in reality Baker, but, however that may be, they had between them arranged a conspiracy for the restoration of the

King, the execution of which, after having been delayed for some unknown reason, was instead of the 5th of April, as originally intended, decided to be carried out upon the 8th of that month.

All was carefully settled respecting the details of the plan to be followed, which would very likely have proved successful had it not been for the infatuation of Captain Baccher for a certain Luigia di Sanfelice, a woman of noble blood but loose morals, with whom he was in love.

The brothers Baccher and their friends had found means of communicating with the Sicilian and English fleets, and it had been agreed that upon a *festa*, when everyone would be amusing themselves and off their guard, some shells should be thrown from the ships into the town. The soldiers would then rush to the forts, leaving the city unprotected, a tumult would be raised, the houses of the Jacobins attacked and set on fire, the rebels put to death, and the city restored to the King.

But it was necessary that there should be no mistakes between friends and enemies, in order to prevent which houses were secretly marked by the conspirators upon the doors or walls, indicating whether their inhabitants were to be destroyed or protected. In most of the houses certainly many families lived, but this difficulty could be met by marking the doors which opened upon the public staircase. There were, however, many persons living together, or even of the same family, belonging to the opposite factions, and to distinguish them from each other papers were secretly given by which their safety would be assured. It was this measure which caused the ruin of the enterprise and the destruction of its authors.

Captain Baccher knew that Luigia di Sanfelice was a rabid republican, but his anxiety for her safety caused him to betray the trust placed in him by his companions, and not only to give her one of the papers in question, but to disclose to her the plan in contemplation. This act of folly and treachery cost not only his own life, which of course he had a right to risk or throw away if he chose, but the lives of his companions who had trusted him, besides causing the failure of the project. One cannot but think that he might have found some other means of saving the life of this woman, who did not care for him but was in love with a certain Lieutenant Ferri, a violent republican, to whom she gave the paper and revealed the whole matter.[1]

Ferri naturally went at once to the republican officials, showed them the paper and told the history of it. They sent for Luigia, who gave them all the information in her power, affecting to refuse to disclose the name of the man who had saved her, in which she was supported by the revolutionary authorities, who made a parade of their

[1] A republican authoress of the present day (Constance Giglioli) writes in rapturous admiration of the party who, in 1798-99, gave their country into the hands of the foreign invader, quotes from the most virulent Jacobin writers their raving abuse of the Queen, but does not show the slightest sympathy with her grief at the murder of her sister and the ruin of her family. She says that the name of the man to whom Luigia betrayed Captain Baccher and his companions was Coco, and that he was a solicitor. Colletta, however, and other writers state that his name was Ferri and that he was a lieutenant in the service of the "Parthenopeian Republic," and that he was either killed in the war or fled to France.

virtue in not insisting upon, and her heroism in not telling, the name, which, as she could not help being aware, they knew perfectly well. Even if the handwriting on the paper were not recognised, she had already betrayed Captain Baccher by revealing his name to her other lover, Ferri.

The conspiracy was crushed, the conspirators arrested and shot, Captain Baccher and one of his brothers of course amongst them, while Luigia di Sanfelice was flattered and called the saviour of the Republic and mother of her country. To this day in the writings of the revolutionary authors this woman is exalted as a heroine, an angel, and a martyr.

After the battle of the Nile Nelson received a peerage from King George III., and the King of Naples gave him the estate of Bronte, with the title of Duke which it bears.

The sword presented to him by Ferdinando was set with diamonds and had belonged to his father, the King of Spain.

The little Prince Leopold, now youngest son of the King, on hearing his mother say that she desired to have a portrait of Nelson painted for herself, said that he should get a copy and stand before it, saying "Dear Nelson, teach me to become like you."[1]

"We are now arrived at the great capital of Sicily, which in our opinion in beauty and elegance is greatly superior to Naples," writes the learned traveller, Mr. Brydone, a few years earlier,[2] at the beginning of Ferdinando's reign.

[1] Autobiography of Miss Cornelia Knight.
[2] "A Tour through Sicily and Malta, in a series of letters to William Beckford, Esq., of Somerby, in Suffolk, from P. Brydone, Esq., F.R.S." (1770).

"The two great streets intersect each other in the centre of the city, where they form a handsome square, called the Ottangolo. From the centre of the square you see the whole of these noble streets, and the four great gates of the city which terminate them, the symmetry and beauty of which produce a fine effect. . . . The Porta Felice, much the handsomest of these gates, opens to the Marino, a delightful walk, which constitutes one of the great pleasures of the nobility of Palermo. It is bounded on one side by the wall of the city and on the other by the sea, from whence, even in this scorching season, there is always a refreshing seabreeze. In the centre of the Marino they have lately erected an elegant kind of temple, which during the summer months is made use of as an orchestra for music; and as in this season they are obliged to convert the night into day, the concert does not begin until the clock strikes midnight, which is the signal for the symphony to strike up: at that time the walk is crowded with carriages and people on foot; and the better to favour pleasure and intrigue, there is an order that no person of whatever quality shall presume to carry a light with him. The flambeaux are extinguished at the Porta Felice, where the servants wait for the return of the carriages; and the company generally continue an hour or two together in utter darkness, except when the intruding moon with her horns and her chastity comes to disturb them. . . .

"Their other amusements consist chiefly in their *conversazioni*, of which they have a variety every night. Here the people really come to converse, whereas in Italy they only go to play cards and eat ices. I have observed that seldom or never one half of the company is engaged in play, nor do they either play long or deep. There are a number of apartments . . . illuminated with wax lights and kept exceedingly cool and agreeable; and it is indeed altogether one of the most sensible and comfortable institutions I have seen. . . . The Sicilians are much fonder of study than their neighbours on the Continent, and their education is much more attended to. We were a good deal surprised that, instead of that frivolity and nothingness which so often constitute the conversation of the Italian nobility, here their delight was to talk on subjects of literature, of history, of politics, but chiefly of poetry. . . . We were astonished on our first arrival at Palermo to hear ourselves addressed in English by some of the young nobility, but still more so to find them intimately acquainted with many of our celebrated poets and philosophers. Milton, Shakespeare, Dryden, Pope, Bacon, Bolingbroke, we found in several libraries, not in the translation, but in the best editions of the originals."

Changes were slow in those days, and the state of things in Sicily was very little, if at all, altered from these descriptions given between twenty and thirty years earlier.

Besides making many friends amongst the Sicilian nobles, Brydone travelled all over the island, and gives the following amongst other details of his journey:

"We are just returned from the Prince's. He offered us the use of his carriages, as there are none to be hired, and in the usual style desired to know in what he could be of service to us. We told him . . . that we were obliged to set off tomorrow and begged his protection on our journey. He replied that he would give orders for his guards to attend us; that they should be answerable for everything; that we need give ourselves no further trouble; that whatever number of mules we had occasion for should be ready at the door of the inn at any hour we should think proper to appoint. He added that we might entirely rely on those guards, who were people of the most approved fidelity as well as the most determined resolution, and would not fail to chastise on the spot any person who should presume to impose upon us.

"Now, who do you think these trusty guards are composed of? Why, of the most daring and most hardened villains perhaps that are to be met with upon earth, who in any other country would have been broken upon the wheel or hung in chains, but are here publicly protected and universally feared and respected. It was this part of the police of Sicily that I was afraid to give you an account of, but I have now conversed with the Prince's people upon the subject, and they have confirmed every circumstance Mr. M. made me acquainted with.

"He told me that in this east part of the island, called Val Demonio from the devils that are supposed to inhabit Mount Etna, it has ever been found impracticable to extirpate the banditti, there being numberless caverns and subterraneous passages in that mountain where no troops could possibly pursue them; that besides, as they are known to be perfectly determined and resolute, never failing to take a dreadful revenge on all who have offended them, the Prince of Villa Franca has embraced it, not only as the safest, but likewise as the wisest and most political scheme to become their declared patron and protector. And such of them as think proper to leave their mountains and forests, though perhaps only for a time, are sure to meet with good encouragement and security in his service; they enjoy the most unbounded confidence, which in no instance they have ever yet been found to make an improper or a dishonest use of. They are clothed in the Prince's livery, yellow and green, with silver lace, and wear likewise a badge of their honourable order, which entitles them to universal fear and respect from the people.

"I have just been interrupted by an upper servant of the Prince's, who, both by his looks and language, seems to be of the same worthy fraternity. He tells us that he has ordered our muleteers at their peril to be ready by daybreak, but that we need not go till we think proper, for it is their business to attend on *nostri eccellenzi*. He says he has likewise ordered two of the most desperate fellows in the whole island to accompany us; adding in a sort of whisper, that we need be under no apprehension, for if any person should presume to impose upon us to the value of a single *baioce*, they would certainly put them to death. I gave him an ounce,[1] which I knew was what he expected; on which he redoubled his bows and *eccellenzi*,

[1] About eleven shillings.

and declared we were the most *honorabili signori* he had ever met with, and that if we pleased he himself would have the honour of attending us and would chastise any person who should dare to take the wall of us, or injure us in the smallest trifle. We thanked him for his zeal, showing him that we had swords of our own, on which, bowing respectfully, he retired.

"I can now, with more assurance, give you some account of the conversation I had with Signor M., who, as I said, appears to be a very intelligent man, and has resided here for many years.

"He says that in some circumstances these banditti are the most respectable people of the island, and have by much the highest and most romantic ideas of what they call their point of honour; that, however criminal they may be with regard to society in general, yet with respect to one another, and to every person to whom they have once professed it, they have ever maintained the most unshaken fidelity. The magistrates have often been obliged to protect them, and even pay them court, as they are known to be perfectly determined and desperate, and so extremely vindictive that they will certainly put any person to death who has ever given them just cause of provocation. On the other hand, it never was known that any person who had put himself under their protection and showed that he had confidence in them had cause to repent it, or was injured by any of them in the most minute trifle; but on the contrary, they will protect him from impositions of every kind, and scorn to go halves with the landlord, like most other conductors and travelling servants, and will defend them with their lives if there is occasion. That those of their number who have enlisted themselves in the service of society are known and respected by the other banditti all over the island, and the persons of those they accompany are ever held sacred. For these reasons most travellers chuse to hire a couple of them from town to town, and may thus travel over the whole island in safety. . . .

"They have a practice of borrowing money from the country people, who never dare refuse them; and if they promise to pay it they have ever been found punctual and exact, both as to the time and the sum, and would much rather rob and murder an innocent person than fail of payment at the day appointed; and this they have often been obliged to do, only in order, as they say, to fulfil their engagements and to save their honour. It happened within this fortnight that one of these heroic banditti, having occasion for money and not knowing how to procure it, determined to make use of his brother's name and authority, an artifice which he thought could not easily be discovered; accordingly, he went to a country priest and told him his brother had occasion for twenty ducats, which he desired he would immediately lend him. The priest assured him he had not then so large a sum, but that if he would return in a few days it should be ready for him. The other replied that he was afraid to return to his brother with this answer, and desired that he would by all means take care to keep out of his way, at least till such time as he had pacified him; otherwise he would not be answerable for the consequences. As bad fortune would have it, the very next day the priest and the robber met in a narrow road; the former fell a-trembling as the latter approached, and at last dropped down on his knees to beg for mercy. The robber, astonished at his behaviour, desired to know the cause of it. The trembling priest answered, 'Il denaro! il denaro!'[1] but send your brother to-morrow and you shall have it.'

"The haughty robber assured him that he disdained taking money from a poor parish priest, adding that if any of his brothers had been low enough to make such a demand, he himself was ready to advance the sum. The priest then acquainted him with the visit he had received the preceding night from his brother, by his order, assuring him that if he had been master of the sum he should have immediately supplied it.

"'Well,' says the robber, 'I will now convince you whether my brother or I are most to be believed; you shall go with me to his house, which is but a few miles distant.'

"On their arrival before the door the robber called on his brother, who, never suspecting the discovery, immediately came to the balcony; but on perceiving the priest he began to make excuses for his conduct. The robber told him there was no excuse to be made, that he only desired to know the fact, whether he had gone to borrow money of that priest in his name or not. On his owning that he had, the robber with deliberate coolness

[1] "The money! the money!"

raised his blunderbuss to his shoulder and shot him dead, and turning to the astonished priest, 'You will now be persuaded,' said he, 'that I had no intention of robbing you, at least.' . . .

"GIARDINI, NEAR TAUROMINUM, *May 22nd.*

"We have had a delightful journey. . . . We left Messina early this morning, with six mules for ourselves and servants and two for our baggage. This train, I assure you, makes no contemptible appearance; particularly when you call to mind our front and rear guard, by much the most conspicuous part of it. These are two great drawcansir (*sic*) figures, armed *cap-à-pie*, with a broad hanger, two enormous pistols, and a long arquebuse. This they kept cocked and ready for action in all suspicious places, where they recounted abundance of wonderful stories of robberies and murders; some of them with such very minute circumstances that I am fully persuaded they themselves were the principal actors. However, I look upon our situation as perfectly secure; they pay us great respect and take the utmost pains we shall not be imposed upon. Indeed, I think they impose upon everybody except us; for they tax the bills according to their pleasure, and such cheap ones I never paid before. To-day's dinner for eleven men, our three muleteers included, and feeding for ten mules and horses, did not amount to half a guinea. And although we pay them high, an ounce a day each, yet I am persuaded they save us at least half of it upon our bills. They entertained us with some of their feats, and made no scruple of owning having put several people to death, but added, 'Ma tutti, tutti honorabilmente,' that is to say, they did not do it in a dastardly manner, nor without provocation.

"The sea-coast of Sicily is very rich; the sides of some of the mountains are highly cultivated, and present the most agreeable aspect that can be imagined—corn, wine, oil, and silk, all mixed together and in the greatest abundance. However, the cultivated part is but small in proportion to what is lying waste. The sides of the road are covered with a variety of flowers and of flowering shrubs, some of them exceedingly beautiful. The inclosures are many of them fenced with hedges of the Indian fig, or prickly pear, as in Spain and Portugal, and our guides assure us that in many of the parched ravines round Etna there are plenty of trees which produce both cinnamon and pepper; not so strong, they allow, as those of the Spice Islands, but which are sold to the merchants at a low price by a set of banditti who dress themselves like hermits. These spices are mixed with the true pepper and cinnamon from the Indies and sent all over Europe."[1]

I have given these extracts from the long-forgotten writings of a learned traveller of nearly a century and a half ago in order to convey an idea of the state of things which prevailed in Sicily and Calabria during the reign of Ferdinando and Maria Carolina. These letters, which bring before us the incidents of daily life and the perils and picturesqueness of travelling, were written two years after their marriage, and the conditions, social and political,

[1] "Sicily and Malta" (Brydone).

were unchanged at the time of their retirement to their island kingdom.

It will be seen by any one who can at all realise the conditions of life, customs, opinion, and tone of thought at that time and in those countries, that the brigands inhabiting the mountains and forests of Sicily and Calabria formed a numerous and powerful portion of the population, recognised and frequently, one may say constantly, employed by high and low, and that in the desperate war of defence and reconquest of their own country, their enlistment in the army of Ferdinando and Ruffo was a matter of course.

It should also be constantly borne in mind that the ideas and principles prevalent in all countries a hundred and fifty years ago differed considerably from those now generally accepted, and it may fairly be asked whether the brigand bands who fought for Ferdinando were better or worse than the tribes of Indian savages, with their tomahawks and scalping knives, who swept the country during the wars in America, murdering and torturing men, women, and children, in the employment of both England and France.

CHAPTER XVIII

The King's country house—End of the Parthenopeian Republic—Recovery of Naples—The treaty annulled—Attitude of the Queen—The King returns to Naples—Miss Knight and Lady Hamilton—Capture of the *Généreux*.

ONE of the most important things, in the opinion of Ferdinando, was to arrange a place for himself where he could hunt and fish. This he soon secured. And having established himself in his new country house near Palermo, he amused himself very well in his usual manner, notwithstanding the dangers and calamities by which his kingdom was beset.

The Queen wrote in January to the Empress of Germany:

"Your dear father, whether from religion or resignation, keeps well and is content; he has taken a pretty little country house, builds and gardens, in the evenings goes to the theatre or the masquerade, is cheerful, and I admire him. Naples, to him, is like the Hottentots: he does not think about it."[1]

On June 4, 1799, a grand dinner was given at the English Embassy in honour of the birthday of King George, and was followed by a court ball, soon

[1] Helfert.

LORD NELSON.
An Italian portrait painted at Naples, and given by Queen Maria Carolina to Sir Thomas Hardy.
From the original now in the possession of Mr. Hardy Manfield, of Portesham.

after which most of the English ships left for Naples. Deserted by their French friends, the Jacobins of the Parthenopeian Republic looked out in vain for the sails of the fleets of France and Spain to appear on the horizon for their deliverance. The warships of England had retaken all the islands, and now the victorious army of Ruffo took possession of the city, and the forts, which were garrisoned by the remaining French troops and a Neapolitan force, capitulated to Cardinal Ruffo upon an agreement as favourable as if it had been between two foreign Powers at war with each other, instead of a king and his rebellious subjects.

So thought the King, the Queen, Sir William Hamilton, and Nelson ; and it was resolved that the treaty, which it was declared Cardinal Ruffo had no authority to make, and to which by the law of nations[1] the King, not having consented, could not be bound, should therefore be annulled.

The terms of the capitulation, with the Queen's indignant comments upon them, are still preserved. It was natural enough that she and those belonging to her should feel disgusted at the immunity of their disloyal subjects, who were not only to enjoy freedom and security, but "the honours of war." But at the same time, and whatever might be the technical right or wrong of the case, it appears to many persons not radical that the annulling of this agreement was a lamentable thing, and that it would have been a thousand times better that any number of persons should escape the punishment they so

[1] Jeaffreson.

richly deserved than that the rebel garrison should have been thus entrapped.

However, the King's word, not having been given, was in consequence not broken, and his position, that he was not bound to treat with rebellious subjects, cannot be denied; but still, the consequences that followed were so terrible that it is impossible not to deeply deplore what took place.

The agreement was signed by the commandants of the two castles (Castel dell' Ovo and Castel Nuovo), by Cardinal Ruffo and the Russian and Turkish plenipotentiaries, and sent to Captain Foote, who returned it, signed, on the 23rd of June.

Micheroux, who was a loyal subject in the King's service and as merciful as he was loyal, was very anxious that this or some treaty of the kind should be arranged, and had desired that a herald should be sent to Naples and terms of surrender agreed on before Ruffo's troops should arrive.

Ruffo knew very well that he was not authorised to promise any such terms, and told Micheroux so, but finally agreed to the plan, thinking that it might put an end to the terrible state of things then existing, and hoping and believing that the treaty would be observed.

But the day after the signing of the agreement (June 24th) the *Foudroyant* appeared in the bay of Naples with Nelson and Sir William Hamilton on board, and when Captain Foote presented them with a copy of the capitulation they both declared it to be illegal and refused to acknowledge it.[1]

[1] One of the inventions circulated by the Jacobins and believed by many persons was that the Queen heard of the capitulation of

Ruffo, in consternation, went on board the *Foudroyant* to explain matters, and assured Nelson that it was too late to object, as the treaty was already in force. It was of no avail. Nelson and Hamilton scouted the idea, saying that kings do not treat with their rebel subjects, and after long and stormy discussions, which went on for a day or two, Nelson gave the Cardinal his written opinion as follows: "Rear-Admiral Lord Nelson, who arrived in the Bay of Naples on the 24th of June with the British fleet, found a treaty entered into with the Rebels which he is of opinion ought not to be carried into execution without the approbation of his Sicilian Majesty."

The details of the discussions and disputes concerning this deplorable affair do not belong to a book of this kind, and cannot be entered into at length.

Ruffo protested in vain—threatened to restore the rebels to the position in which they were before the treaty; in fact, did all he could—but it was useless. The capitulation was annulled, the castles taken possession of, and the leaders of the revolt, with many others concerned in it, seized and imprisoned to await their trial.

A republican writer,[1] who represents the repub-

the castles *at Palermo* after Nelson had sailed, and sent Lady Hamilton after him in a swift sailing vessel to persuade him to annul the treaty, and that Lady Hamilton gave herself to Nelson *as a reward!* But the treaty was signed June 23rd. Nelson was at Naples June 24th, and on June 25th the Queen wrote to Lady Hamilton that the Cardinal had written, but only to the General, and said "little of the treaty, nothing of the operations."

[1] Constance Giglioni (*née* Stocker), "Naples in 1799." To give an example, Ettore Carafa, one of the Jacobin leaders, whom this author describes as a faultless hero, but whose ambition and cruelty are denounced even by republican writers. Signora Giglioni

licans and Jacobins of Naples to have been like saints and angels, accuses Nelson of ferocity because he annulled the treaty,[2] and of intolerance and quotes the French General Macdonald, who praised him on one occasion for his conciliatory methods of dealing with the *revolted* populations. (N.B.—The "*revolted* populations" means the loyal subjects who refused to submit to the French invaders.) The other proof brought forward is that Carafa, according to the document quoted, having *himself* led a troop of Jacobins and foreign invaders to attack a loyal city which was the property of his family, his own birthplace, the home of his childhood, and that of the faithful friends and retainers of his family, tried in the first place to persuade the city to surrender, and when the indignant people fired upon him as an unnatural traitor, and the place was stormed by his troops under his own directions, he tried to persuade the French General he had enabled to seize the hapless city not to burn it to the ground, and himself, perhaps touched with horror and remorse, interfered to prevent some of the worst outrages of his new associates upon his old retainers and friends! And then this author proceeds to extol his humanity, proved, she asserts, by these documents! But Colletta, who was himself in the war, who fought for the Jacobins and afterwards served Murat, who knew the officers and chief Jacobins, and was strongly prejudiced for the republicans and against the loyalists, must have known perfectly well what he was saying. "Ettore Carafa, valiant in war but cruel in council," he writes. And the deeds of Carafa speak for themselves. He was imprisoned in St. Elmo for his treasonable share in the Jacobin conspiracy, but managed to escape to Milan, and returned with the French invaders of his country, whom he led against the faithful city of Andria, which every tie of nature and decency ought to have made sacred to him. Andria made a gallant but unavailing defence, and its "humane," "patriotic" assailant writes to his employers: "The city was all in flames, and the dead may be as many as four thousand." He next, with his associates, took and sacked Trani, which, Colletta says, "was reduced to heaps of corpses and ruins! Ceglie and Carbonara shared the same fate, and it must be remembered that the only fault of these unfortunate cities was loyalty to their King and country and hatred of the foreign invader. And this traitor ought not, according to the republican author, to have suffered in his turn for all this treason and bloodshed.

[2] "Entering the bay just in time to annul the treaty, in precise accordance with the law of nations" (Jeaffreson).

narrow-mindedness because he hated the French and the Jacobins. Considering that a short time previously these worthies perpetrated the September massacres, made France one scene of bloodshed and slaughter, and amongst other notable performances had tied young girls and men together and thrown them into the Loire, and had collected five hundred little children together and mown them down with grape shot, his dislike to them is not inexplicable, and was at any rate shared by a very considerable number of people all over Europe.

To an ordinary mind it might seem that the "ferocity" was on the other side.

But whether Nelson was a ferocious character or not can safely be left to the judgment of history.

Charged by the English Government to fight the French wherever he could find them, Nelson had been searching in vain for the French fleet. He had started for Naples first on the 13th with the Prince Royal on board, but had returned to Palermo with him.

One of the atrocious sentiments for which the Queen is abused by her republican enemies, is:

"It would appear . . . that a second squadron has entered the Mediterranean. May it please God that they [*i.e.*, Nelson's and the other English squadron] should unite and meet with the infamous republicans [the Brest squadron] and destroy them."

Are not republicans, then, in the habit of wishing for the success of their armies and navies? Ought not England to have rejoiced at the victory of the Nile and the destruction of the French fleet? Or France at Marengo and Austerlitz?

The Queen had greatly hoped that Naples might be recovered without much bloodshed, and wrote to Lord Nelson : " Notwithstanding I have been so misunderstood there, I still regard the ungrateful city, and solicit your forbearance. I hope that the imposing force by sea and their being surrounded on all sides will be enough without shedding blood to make them return to their allegiance.

" Je désire que cela ne coûte point de sang, celui de mes ennemis même n'étant précieux."

Another expression of the Queen's has been made into a specimen of her atrocious cruelty :

" I urge Lord Nelson to deal with Naples as if it were a rebel city in Ireland, behaving in like manner."

The Government of King George III. was not, however, looked upon as particularly cruel or bloodthirsty, and it is difficult to see in what consists the iniquity of wishing that Naples might be dealt with as the English King would have dealt, through his officers, with a rebellion in his dominions. It would have been, indeed, a good thing for Naples if this wish could have been realised.

But the spite of the revolutionary writers against the Queen, their bitter opponent, turns into evil her every thought, word, and action, however harmless or even praiseworthy.

"The King," says Miss Knight, "went with Lord Nelson to take once more possession of his capital, where he established a council of regency, and afterwards returned to Palermo, where the Queen and the royal family had remained. It was during the absence of our fleet and of Sir William and

Lady Hamilton, who had accompanied the King, that my mother's lengthened sufferings came to an end. . . . When Sir William Hamilton and Lord Nelson came to take leave of her before their departure for Naples, she had particularly commended me to their care, and, previous to their embarkation, Sir William and Lady Hamilton had left directions with Mrs. Cadogan that, in case I should lose my mother before their return, she was to take me to their house. That lady came for me, and I went with her to our Minister's, knowing that it was my mother's wish that I should be under his protection; and I must say that there was certainly at that time no impropriety in living under Lady Hamilton's roof. *Her house was the resort of the best company of all nations,*[1] and the attentions paid to Lord Nelson appeared perfectly natural. He himself always spoke of his wife with the greatest affection and respect; and I remember that, shortly after the battle of the Nile, when my mother said to him that no doubt he considered the day of that victory as the happiest in his life, he answered, 'No; the

[1] The italics are mine. I give these extracts because the Queen's friendship with Lady Hamilton has been brought as another crime against Maria Carolina by her assailants, one of whom accounts for the fact of Lady Hamilton's being received by everyone at Naples by saying that the court was so corrupt that it was not surprising But Lady Knight and her daughter were persons of the strictest propriety—the latter afterwards companion to Charlotte, Princess of Wales—and their testimony shows that at that time Lady Hamilton was received not only by Neapolitans but by "the best company of all nations." The friendship for her, therefore, of the Queen, who was attracted by her beauty and musical talents, and by the sympathy and affection she showed for herself in her troubles, seems less surprising and not unaccountable. (Note by the author.)

happiest was that on which I married Lady Nelson.'

"It is painful to reflect on the scenes that passed at Naples; and no one can have a greater dislike than myself to political executions, because, however legally just they may be, they are revolting to humanity, and do no good to the cause which they are meant to uphold. On the contrary, they create a feeling of exasperation, and excite compassion in favour of the guilty. But it is only right to say that Caracciolo was taken in arms against the forces of his Sovereign, that he was tried by a court-martial of Neapolitan officers, and executed on board a Neapolitan ship. I grieve for his fate, and still more for his defection, but many strange misrepresentations have been circulated upon this subject.

"The Queen, who has been accused of so much vindictive cruelty, was, to my certain knowledge, the cause of many pardons being granted. And there was one lady in particular whom she saved, who was her declared enemy and at the head of a revolutionary association."

The *Généreux*, a French ship of the line which had escaped from the battle of the Nile and taken refuge in the port of La Valetta in Malta, was captured by our cruisers while endeavouring to gain Toulon. When Lord Nelson heard the good news he exclaimed:

"Ah! she knew that she belonged to us, and her conscience would not let her stay away any longer."

Miss Knight was called by the officers of the fleet Nelson's "charming poet-laureate." She wrote various stanzas in his praise, more patriotic than poetical, which were sung with the National Anthem. After the battle of the Nile:

> "Join we great Nelson's name,
> First on the roll of fame,
>   Him let us sing.
> Spread we his fame around,
> Honour of British ground,
>   God save our King."

After the capture of the *Guillaume Tell*:

> "While thus we chant his praise,
> See what new fires blaze,
>   New laurels spring.
> Nelson! thy task's complete;
> All their Egyptian fleet
> Bows at thy conqu'ring feet
>   To George, our King!"

After the capture of the *Généreux*:

> "Lord, Thou hast heard our vows!
> Fresh laurels deck the brows
>   Of him we sing.
> Nelson has laid full low
> Once more the Gallic foe;
> Come, let our bumpers flow
>   To George, our King."

The Order of St. Ferdinand was instituted by the King for the recovery of his Italian States, and crosses were given to the English officers, Neapolitan Ministers, and others attached to the court who had followed the royal family to Palermo. A Neapolitan one day remarked that this order had not been given to a single Sicilian, upon which a Sicilian gentleman who was present replied:

"His Majesty is perfectly right to give his new order to the few Neapolitans who have remained faithful. If he had given it to us, it must have been to every inhabitant of the island, for all have been true to him."

The loyalty of the Sicilians was certainly beyond doubt, and they were delighted to have the King, royal family, and court at Palermo.

They also hated the French with an undying detestation, and would speak with pride and satisfaction of the Sicilian Vespers, which they would have been glad enough to repeat if occasion offered. Nor was there any love between them and Naples. In the time, more especially, when that kingdom was under the domination of Spain, Sicily was oppressed, her commerce injured, and the export of corn either forbidden or enormously taxed. The Queen did not accompany the King on his triumphant return to Naples. On the 2nd of July she wrote to Lady Hamilton:

"This [Nelson's letter] has decided the King to start to-morrow evening, which has already cost and will cost me many tears. The King does not think it well that I should go with him for the little time he expects to remain there. In brief, he starts to-morrow evening ... I shall remain in great sadness, making my prayers to Heaven that everything may succeed, for glory and for real good. But I am deeply moved, and think much of what I desire, and in the future ought to be...."[1]

On July 7th she wrote again to Lady Hamilton:

[1] "The Queen of Naples and Lord Nelson" (Jeaffreson).

"My Dear Miledy,—I owe you thousands and thousands of thanks for your two letters, which I received last evening, much after time. I note in them everything you tell me with so much friendship. At the time I am writing this, I think the King will have arrived at Naples, because, thank God! the vessel which left on the 5th of this month met him forty miles from Capri. That has consoled and quieted me. My attachment to his person, my zeal for his good, I dare say even my enthusiasm, made me intensely desire to go to Naples. I was not able to obtain permission to do so, and my reason makes me feel it is for the best. Alas! they would, albeit with injustice, have attributed everything to me, from malice and a spirit of vengeance. . . . In short, my dear Milédy, I have the misfortune to know thoroughly the Neapolitan nobility and all the classes, and I will always say the same: only the *bourgeoisie*, the artizans, and the most humble people are faithful and attached. The latter sometimes surrender themselves to licence, but their sentiments are good. This conviction causes me to have no commission to give you, for I am determined, on returning to Naples, to live entirely isolated from the whole world, the experience of thirty-one years during which I have lived to oblige everyone and find myself deserted, having made an impression that will never be effaced. I am ready to return to Naples the moment the King shall wish it. We go daily to [sing] a *Te Deum*, to pray and carry in procession the Holy Sacrament, to bless the sea and to pray for the King and Naples. . . . Poor Belmonte has received from another quarter intelligence of his brother's arrest; he is greatly afflicted, more for seeing him guilty than all the rest. One sees only the unhappy, and that makes one miserable.

"CHARLOTTE."[1]

The Queen had heard of the treason of this man before the knowledge of it had come to the King's ears, and, touched with compassion for his brother's grief, she did all she could to save him, by means of Lady Hamilton. However, Ferdinando was told and the Count arrested. The Queen, whose paramount influence over the King was gone, still did her best to help the culprit. She pretended to leave him to his fate, as in his present humour any interference would only have irritated Ferdinando against him; but she gave private instructions to Lady Hamilton, pointing out that, although guilty in serving the Republic, he had not fought against the King, and, in consequence, he was placed on the *Culloden* under the supervision of Nelson. For this the Queen wrote heartfelt thanks to Lady Hamilton, describing the terrible state of grief and anxiety in which Prince Belmonte had been, and his joy and gratitude at his brother's being saved.

The Signora di San Marco, of whom the Abbé Galiani expressed so strong an opinion, after having been a favourite and confidant of Maria Carolina, who was extremely incautious and injudicious with any one to whom she took a fancy, had deserted her and gone over to the French and Jacobin party. Now that the royalists had the upper hand she wrote to try and ingratiate herself again

[1] "The Queen of Naples and Lord Nelson" (Jeaffreson).

with the Queen, who remarked that she should answer the letter one of these days, but that she had been deeply pained by the conduct for which Mme. di San Marco could not justify herself.

The first trial which took place was that of Caracciolo, who had fled from the victorious troops of the Sovereign he had deserted, but whose hiding-place had been discovered or betrayed. His execution is violently inveighed against by all the revolutionary and republican writers as a crime, but they have no reason to give for their assertions. Why was it a crime? Is it, or is it not, the universal rule that a soldier or sailor deserting to the enemy in time of war is, if taken, put to death? And if for a poor sailor or soldier death is the penalty of desertion, dare they say that an officer is to be differently judged, even if he be general or admiral? The excuses and extenuations of his apologists and admirers show the feebleness of their case. There can, of course, be no pretence of denying that Caracciolo was a traitor and deserter, seeing that while he was still holding the King's commission as admiral of his fleet, he left him and joined the enemy.

The palliation offered by one is that he enjoyed the respect and affection of his fellow-citizens, that he did not at first intend to desert, but was over-persuaded. Is a man tried for desertion at a court-martial acquitted because he is popular, or because he was over-persuaded, or because his crime was not premeditated?

Others, ignoring the simple fact that he was a deserter and traitor, declare that he was put to death because Nelson had always been jealous of him; but this can need no comment. Nelson jealous of Caracciolo!

Of the vileness, the infamy, the ferocity, the "*vilta*" of Nelson, his puny assailants may rave to their hearts' content; his fame, his glory, and his honour are far beyond the reach of their calumnies.[1]

But that, instead of being shot according to his petition, Caracciolo was hanged from the mast of the *Minerva*, many persons will always deplore. It is true that the fate of André at the hands of Washington has not, as far as one knows, caused that eminent republican to be called a tyrant or murderer by radical writers, although André was not, like Caracciolo, a traitor, but a loyal soldier and stainless gentleman, who died for his King and country, and whose only crime was that he obeyed the orders given him. It is asserted by some of the writers against the Queen, and by others who have accepted their false statements without examination, that she was present on board the ship and witnessed

---

[1] Mr. Jeaffreson remarks: "No English historian of Nelson's conduct in the Bay of Naples is likely to repeat Southey's deplorable mistakes touching the traitor's trial and the capitulation of the castles But let it not be inferred that I claim credit for putting those transactions for the first time in a true light. The credit of that great literary service is wholly due to two other writers—first, and in by far the greatest degree, to Commander Jeaffreson Miles; secondly, and in a less degree, to Sir Harris Nicolas. Thanks are due to Mr John Paget for popularising the facts and arguments of these two writers, but he neither strengthened the arguments nor made a single addition to the facts of their perfect vindication of the Admiral's honour in respect to this passage of his glorious career."

the execution. Also that, Ferdinando being too tender-hearted to carry on or behold the trials and punishments of the rebels, he returned to his country house in Sicily and left the Queen to execute justice at Naples in his place![1]

The facts, however, are that Maria Carolina, at the time she is asserted by these persons to have been at Naples, torturing and killing her subjects, was, during the first months of this terrible time, at Palermo, where she had just then so very little influence with the King and government that, in order to obtain the pardons of the many persons she helped and saved, she was obliged to resort to subterfuge, to get Lady Hamilton or some other person to intercede for them, and to prevent the King, whose ambition it now was to be considered independent, from supposing she took any interest in those she wished to protect. The last year and a half, during which took place a trial for which she has been especially reviled,[2] she was not in Italy at all, but in Austria, and at the time of that trial she had not seen her husband for three months.

Ferdinando, on the other hand, was not hunting at his country place near Palermo, unable to bear the sight of the sufferings in Naples, but was carrying out his vengeance there in a manner which, notwithstanding the provocations and injuries he had received, can only be called horrible.

"Pour peu qu'on y gratte on trouve un Tartare," was the well-known remark of Napoleon con-

[1] Sir Archibald Alison.
[2] That of Luigia Sanfelice.

cerning Russians; and the observation is so far applicable to Ferdinando that, although in his case a Tartar would not have been found, a savage certainly would. He was a thorough Neapolitan, and his nature resembled that of his favourite companions, the *lazzaroni*. Good-natured, easygoing, pleasant, even kindly, in daily life, cheerful and apparently patient in adversity, there lay hidden under all this fair surface a violent, cruel, remorseless nature, always ready to break forth if his passions were aroused, just as the rich gardens and sunny vineyards on Etna and Vesuvius are at any moment liable to disappear, swept away by a torrent of liquid fire from the depths of the volcano.

The injury and the offences to be punished were very great. The Parthenopeian Republic had been forced upon the vast majority of an unwilling people by a small but violent faction, supported by the troops of a foreign invader. In order to carry out their plans they had given their country over to fire and sword, had betrayed their capital and fortresses into the hands of foreigners, and slaughtered many thousands of their own countrymen. And, having wrought all this destruction, misery and bloodshed, when the collapse in which it ended arrived, their partisans claim not only that they should have been allowed to go unpunished, but to remain, a constant danger, in the State and city upon which they had brought such calamity.

Such was not the opinion of Nelson or of the Queen, neither of whom doubted that the leaders of the revolt and those most guilty must be executed, and that others concerned in it should receive various proportions of punishment according to the degree of their culpability. And in those days, in any country in Europe, an amnesty after such a rebellion would have been a thing utterly unheard of.

But between the stern and just retribution necessary to restore order and punish crimes and the state of things Ferdinando established at Naples there can be no comparison whatever.

The opinion of Clarke and McArthur,[1] which they derived from an examination of Nelson's papers relating to that time, was that the number of persons executed, having been tried and convicted, was about seventy. The various republican writers declare that they were more numerous, and Gagnière, one of the most rabid, asserts that they amounted to a hundred and one, from which women were not excluded. Eleanora Pimentel, a beautiful woman of noble family and stainless morality, but a partisan and instigator of the Jacobin rebellion, was one of the sufferers; and so were various other persons of good character, profound learning, utopian, fanatical ideas, and distinguished talents, which they had applied to the overthrow of the government of their country or to the service of the rebel faction and the foreign invaders. Pagano, Cirillo, and other of the Queen's friends of the days of her liberal associations were among the number.

Many others were condemned to imprisonment, some for life, others for shorter terms; many more were exiled. But what lent horror to the state of things during this time was the ferocious mob, furious against the Jacobins, the French, and everybody whom they at all suspected of sympathising with them, who plundered, sacked, murdered, and committed deeds too horrible to relate.

The last execution was that of the miserable Luigia di Sanfelice, and it was one of those which inspired more horror and compassion than most of the others. Not that the character of the "saviour and mother of the Parthenopeian Republic" called forth much admiration from those who did not belong to that body. Luigia, or Luisa, had been married at seventeen to her cousin, a boy a year older than herself, and apparently equally worthless. They lived a disreputable life, plunged into debt, till at last their friends interfered, took away their three children, placed them in convents, and shut up Luigia and her husband also in separate convents, from which they escaped and returned to Naples, where they led the same scandalous, licentious lives as before.

But although her betrayal of the man who loved and saved her cost his life and many others, it is obvious that she was placed in a terrible position. If she revealed the plot she sacrificed the man who was risking his life for hers; if she kept the secret she sacrificed the other man whom just then she loved; and if her sympathies were with the republicans, she also sacrificed the party to which she belonged. She was arrested, reprieved, then condemned, and in order to save her life declared herself to be *enceinte*, in consequence of which she was shut up with some other ladies in the prison of the Vicaria. After some time it became evident that this was not the case; but months passed, and it was hoped that now, as the year 1800 wore on, she would be pardoned, for a general amnesty was announced, to which there were to be, however, some exceptions.

But she had a bitter enemy in the father of the man she had betrayed, Vincenzo Baccher, the old banker, who owed to her the death of two out of his four sons, and who, with the surviving members of his family, was naturally in great favour with the King; and through his representations Ferdinando, who would probably have allowed Luigia to escape, was again inflamed with fury against her, and gave orders that she should be executed.

Now, it is the most iniquitous falsehood to pretend, as many of the republican writers do, that the Queen had anything to do with this sentence, which excited general indignation and pity. In the first place, Maria Carolina had at this time no influence over Ferdinando or Acton; in the second place, as she was not in Italy, but at Vienna, where she had gone with her children months before the final sentence and execution, she had not, and could not possibly have had, anything to do with the matter; and in the third place, both she and Lady Hamilton had, at an early part of the proceedings, wished to save Luigia Sanfelice.

But it is just one of the cases in which the mingled vanity, folly, and ferocity of Ferdinando so conspicuously appear. Two days before the date fixed for the execution the Princess Clementina, wife of the Prince Royal, gave birth to a son and heir. It was the custom in the Neapolitan court that on the birth of an heir to the throne the mother should have the right to ask of the King three favours, all of which he was expected to grant. The Princess, thinking to make more certain of her request being granted, only asked for one thing, the pardon of Luigia Sanfelice. This she wrote with fervent entreaties in a note which she put on the cradle of the child, ready for the King, whose visit she expected.

Presently Ferdinando arrived, delighted with his grandson, whom he took in his arms and began to admire, when his eyes fell upon the letter.

"What is that?" he asked.

"It is a favour which I ask," said the Princess, trying to raise herself from the pillows which supported her. "Only one favour instead of three, so much do I desire to move the kind heart of your Majesty."

"For whom do you plead?" inquired the King, smiling, as he took up the letter.

"For the unhappy Luigia Sanfelice," replied the Princess Clementina, and she was going on to add more entreaties when her father-in-law's face changed.

"Anything but that!" he exclaimed with a look of fury; and dropping the baby on to the pillows, he turned on his heel and left the room.

Luigia Sanfelice was accordingly put to death, and her fate lent a darker shade to Ferdinando's cruel policy. It was a useless barbarity, for Luigia was powerless to do any further mischief, and although, considering that she had betrayed and defeated a royalist movement, and caused the death of several loyal subjects, she could not have been pronounced anything else than guilty, the reprieve, the re-arrest, the long suspense and imprisonment, and the final refusal of his daughter-in-law's petition, which he was bound to grant, and which would have been an excellent opportunity of exercising the prerogative of mercy—all these augmented the hardship and cruelty of the case, and cast a deeper stain upon the reputation of Ferdinando. If Nelson or the Hamiltons had been there it would have almost certainly been prevented, but it took place after they had left.

CHAPTER XIX

Triumphant return of the King—Honours to the Hamiltons—Pardons obtained by the Queen—Her generosity and charities—Depression of the Queen—Sir William Hamilton recalled—Scene with the King—Visits Naples—Leaves Palermo with Nelson—Perilous voyage to Livorno—The battle of Marengo—Dangerous journey to Vienna—Anxiety of the King.

AS the events recorded at the end of the last chapter happened many months later, it is time to return to Palermo and the events which took place there immediately after the collapse of the Parthenopeian Republic and the recovery of the kingdom of Naples.

On the 8th of August, 1799, the *Foudroyant* appeared in the Bay of Palermo, and the Queen and her children, attended by vast crowds, stood by the water's edge to receive the King, who landed, accompanied by Sir William and Lady Hamilton, amidst the shouts and acclamations of the multitude.

Naples was again their own, the French troops were swept out of the kingdom, and a few weeks later (September 28th) Rome also fell into the hands of the Neapolitans and Austrians. The standard of Naples floated from the walls of S. Angelo, the royal seal of Naples was upon the gates of the Vatican. Maria Carolina felt her spirits rise. Surely the old days of prosperity were coming back again.

During the King's absence she had corresponded continually with Lady Hamilton, through whom she was trying to get the pardon of Pignatelli and Migliano, two of the Neapolitan nobles implicated. Maria Carolina had a violent temper, and when she was angry did not care what she said; but, although she wrote about "that fool Migliano," and called his wife "a viper with an infernal tongue," she busied herself in saving his life, and, in spite of all her indignation and wrath against Naples, she kept sending Lady Hamilton money to distribute among those in want. Six hundred ducats on the 20th of July, for instance; three thousand ducats ten days after, and so on.

"There is that Luciana, who calls herself Fortunata, and another big common woman called Piete del Pesce, near the statue of San Janaro in the Strada Nuova," she writes in one of her letters of charitable directions.

One of the unfortunate characteristics of Maria Carolina was that she had no discrimination of character in choosing her friends, and no reserve or caution when she had chosen them. She confided to them all sorts of things they ought never to have been told, loaded them with kindness and favours, and then after a while found out that they were totally unworthy.

Of Mme. San Marco she had made an intimate friend and confidant, and had found her entirely ungrateful. She refused to go with her to Palermo, and remained behind at Naples, where she associated herself with the revolutionists and spread slanders against the Queen.

Yet when Mme. San Marco found herself in difficulty and danger she wrote to the Queen she had deserted and calumniated, who, in writing of her to Lady Hamilton, remarks: "Should Mme. San Marco be in need of money she can rely on me to help her during all her life, but all the ties of interest and friendship between us have been broken by her conduct." Always generous, even to prodigality, the Queen lavished costly presents upon the Hamiltons when they returned from Naples. She embraced Lady Hamilton, putting round her neck a gold chain with her portrait set in jewels; that of Ferdinando, also set in jewels, she gave to Sir William; and a day or two after their arrival at Palermo she sent the former two coach-loads of costly dresses to replace those she had left behind when she left Naples in December. It was said that the presents given to the Hamiltons in a few days amounted to six thousand pounds.

But republican writers who bring this as a reproach against her do not think it necessary to mention the sums she gave in charity; whereas Lord Nelson, on the 31st of October, 1799, in a letter to the Emperor of Russia (Paul I.), says:

"The laborious task of keeping the Maltese quiet in Malta, through difficulties which your Majesty will perfectly understand, has been principally brought about by the goodness of her Majesty the Queen of Naples, who at one moment of distress sent seven thousand pounds belonging absolutely to herself and children, by the exertions of Lady Hamilton . . . and by the bravery and conciliating manners of Captain Ball."

Like all excitable, emotional people, Maria Carolina had at first been overjoyed and elated at the present success and prosperity of affairs, but soon began to find that all was not so much to her satisfaction as she had hoped and believed, and consequently fell into a state of depression which affected her health.

She found that she could not by any means regain her ascendancy over either the King or Acton, whose confidence in her judgment and capacity had been shattered by the disastrous result of Mack's campaign in the Papal States during the autumn. If only she had not been so impatient, if she had taken the advice of her son-in-law, the Emperor, and waited till the spring instead of forcing on matters before they were ready, all this would not have happened. It was likely enough that Ferdinando declared, and that she herself partly believed, that the loss of the capital for several months, the destruction of the fleet, the flight, and the death of her boy, besides all that was now going on in Naples, need not have happened. At any rate, he would not listen to her now in any political questions, and the loss of the power and influence she had enjoyed for more than thirty years was a bitter trial to her, besides which, she knew that she was unpopular, and was unjustly blamed for all sorts of things with which she had nothing to do, and which she had no power to prevent, that there was no end to the calumnious stories spread against her by her enemies, and that from many persons to whom she had shown the greatest kindness she met with nothing but ingratitude.

She became ill and feverish, thought she was going to die, or said that she wished to retire into a convent, and that only the care of her daughters prevented her from embracing the life of the cloister, than which one cannot imagine anything more unsuitable for her.

Another day her spirits and health would improve, and she would then desire to return to Naples, at any rate for a time.

She did, in fact, go there for a few days in the autumn, when she wrote to Lady Hamilton her intention to stay one night at Caserta and three days in Naples.

It must have been a melancholy glimpse of the scenes of former happiness, and she was glad to return to Palermo and to turn her thoughts to another project she had made—a journey to Austria and Tuscany.

A great sorrow to her just now was the recall of Sir William Hamilton, who was to be replaced as English Ambassador by Sir Arthur Paget.

Sir William Hamilton had been Ambassador at Naples for more than thirty years, and was very popular. It was said of him that he had never injured any one, but always used his influence for good.

The Queen was in despair, for besides her devoted friendship for Lady Hamilton, she was extremely

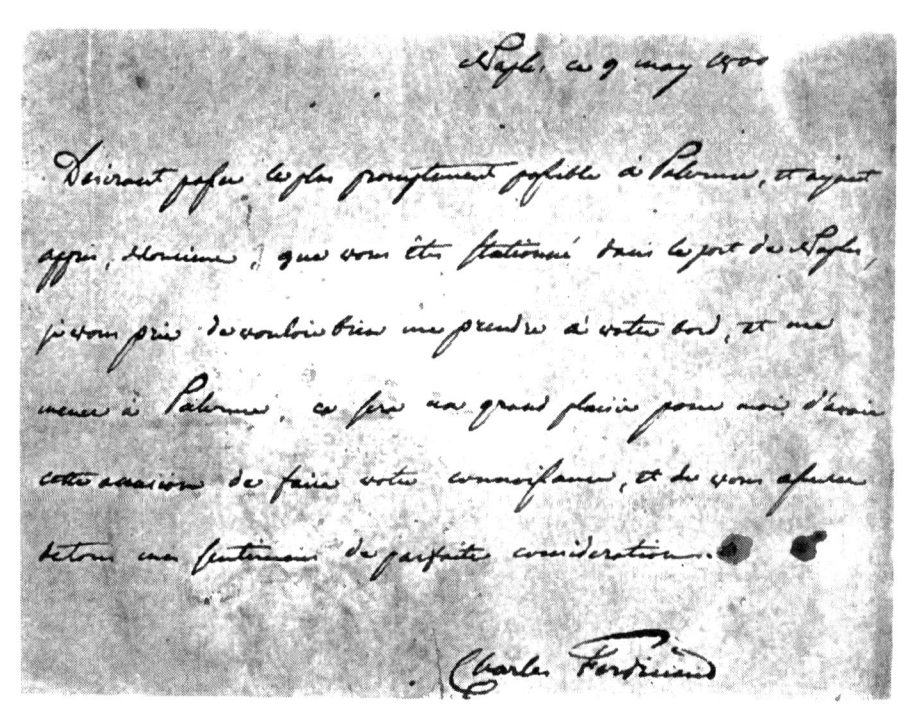

AUTOGRAPH LETTER OF KING FERDINAND OF NAPLES TO AN ENGLISH ADMIRAL,
NAPLES, MAY 9, 1800.
From Mr. A. M. Broadley's collection of MSS.

fond of Sir William, who had been a good and faithful friend to her from the first moment of her arrival at Naples.

She tried to persuade the King to write to England and prevent his being removed, but for some reason or other Ferdinando refused. They had a stormy interview, of which the Queen speaks in one of her frequent letters to Lady Hamilton:

"MY DEAR MILEDY,—I received yester-evening your obliging letter and the papers. I will take care that justice is done to this interesting Duchess Sorentino, and to mitigate her cruel fate. . . . Yesterday on your departure I endured a scene of madness—cries, yellings, threats to kill you, throw you out of the window, to send for your husband to complain that you turned your back. . . . I am extremely unhappy, I have so many troubles. . . . The accursed Paget is at Vienna . . . everything afflicts and desolates me. . . ."

Ferdinando was at Naples during the spring, presiding over the trials and executions by which he made himself such an evil name, but returned early in May, 1800, as will be seen by the letter,[1] asking to be conveyed from thence to Palermo on board an English man-of-war.

Shortly afterwards Ludovica, Grand-duchess of Tuscany, second daughter of the King and Queen, having lost her son, a child of six years old, wrote in great distress entreating her mother to come and see her.

This was sufficient to decide Maria Carolina, who saw that for the present it would be better for her to

[1] From the collection of MSS. of Mr. A. F. Broadley.

leave Ferdinando to himself, and besides her longing to see both her elder daughters, the Empress and the Grand-duchess of Tuscany, and her various grandchildren, was also anxious for political reasons to meet her son-in-law the Emperor, and yearning to be again in her own country.

Therefore she arranged to leave Palermo early in June with her four younger children, the Princesses Christine, Amélie, and Antoinette, and Prince Leopold.

Nelson had gone with the *Foudroyant*, on which they were to sail, on a voyage of pleasure to Malta and Syracuse, having on board the Hamiltons, Miss Knight, and two or three other friends. It was on this voyage, declares Mr. Jeaffreson, that the violent flirtation which had for some time gone on between Lord Nelson and Lady Hamilton developed into the *liaison* which lasted until the death of the great Admiral.

On their return the royal party went on board, accompanied by the Hamiltons, the Prince of Castelcicala, and Miss Knight, a numerous retinue of officers and servants attending them on other vessels, also under Lord Nelson's convoy.

The Duc de Berri had been staying at Palermo, and wanted to marry the Princess Christine, but the present deplorable state of the French royal family did not incline the King and Queen of Naples to accept him as a son-in-law. He came down to the ship to take leave of the Princess and the rest of the royal family, shedding tears as he did so.

The King, too, came on board to take leave of his family; his four children knelt down while he gave them his blessing, and as he returned to land the *Foudroyant* weighed anchor and the shores of Sicily soon disappeared from the eyes that looked longingly backward, for some of those on board—the Hamiltons, for instance, and Miss Knight—felt deeply leaving the country in which they had spent so many happy years.

The Queen was delighted to get away; she was longing to see her daughters, and her spirits rose higher as the stately ship, sailing swiftly with a favourable wind, passed out of the bay of Palermo into the open sea.

During the voyage they were overtaken by a violent storm, which recalled only too vividly their voyage to Palermo eighteen months before; but on June 14th they arrived safely at Livorno, having left Palermo on the 9th.

The Queen exclaimed, "Livorno! Livorno!" in a transport of delight, as they dropped anchor at the Tuscan port, and on landing her joy was a thousandfold increased by the enthusiastic welcome she received and by the arrival of a messenger from General Melas on the evening of the 16th announcing that the Austrians had won the battle of Marengo.

It was five o'clock when she received this news, and *Te Deums* were at once sung in the churches and public rejoicings proclaimed in the streets.

The despatch ran as follows:

"After a long and sanguinary battle on the plains of Marengo, the arms of his Majesty the Emperor have completely beaten the French army conducted into Italy and commanded by General Buonaparte.

The details of the battle will be given in another despatch, as well as the fruits of the victory, which the Lieutenants-General Ott and Zach are gathering on the field. Dated Alessandria, 14th June, 1800."

It was true enough that when General Melas left the field to write this despatch the Germans were victorious; but Napoleon had not recalled his troops nor allowed a retreat to be sounded, as he had just heard that Desaix was coming to his assistance with nine thousand soldiers.

Desaix arrived at four o'clock, the tide of victory turned, the battle was won by Napoleon at the cost of the life of Desaix. In after years he said that Desaix was the greatest genius of all his generals; at any rate he was the only one against whom he was never heard to utter a reproach.

Maria Carolina retired to bed with her heart full of joy, triumph, and thankfulness, giving orders that she should be awakened when the next despatch arrived, no matter at what hour of the night.

Soon after midnight the despatch came, and was carried at once to the Queen's room.

Awakened by one of her ladies, she hastily tore open the paper, exclaiming:

"Let us read the end of the presumptuous army of Buonaparte!"

The despatch ran thus:

"Towards the decline of day the enemy were reinforced by a fresh army, and fighting on the field of Marengo the greater part of the night, have beaten our army, the conquerors of the preceding day. Encamped beneath the walls of this fortress, we are now collecting the miserable remnants of the lost battle, and are consulting on the best course to pursue under present circumstances and in face of the enemy. Dated Alessandria, midnight, 14–15th June."

The Queen read these fatal lines twice over, and then sank fainting into the arms of the lady who had awakened her.[1]

As soon as she recovered her self-possession she caused inquiries to be made as to whether the road to Venice and Trieste was open and safe, and waited in uncertainty for nearly a month before it could be determined which way they should travel; it seemed even doubtful whether they would not be obliged to go back to Sicily.

Meanwhile she enjoyed the protection and hospitality of the Grand-duke Ferdinand, her nephew and son-in-law, whose dominions, however, were then being invaded by the French. Ferdinand resembled his father the Emperor Leopold in his good qualities, and was adored in Tuscany; but his subjects were powerless against the French.

Rumours of the approach of the French army kept circulating in the town, which was filled with terror and agitation.

One night the Queen was so much alarmed that she took refuge with her children on board an English man-of-war,[2] but being more reassured the next day, returned to her quarters on shore.

[1] "Storia del Reame di Napoli" (Colletta).
[2] The *Alexander*, to which Nelson had removed his flag on June 28th.

Lord Keith, the English Commander-in-chief, arrived at Livorno on June 24th, and thinking Lord Nelson too much disposed to employ the ships of his Majesty King George in the service of the Queen of Naples, ordered the *Foudroyant* to be sent to Minorca to be refitted.[1] What was to be done? A Neapolitan frigate was at anchor in the port of Livorno, and it was proposed that the Queen and her family should go in that to Trieste. With much reluctance she consented, but when she went to look at the ship the aspect of it was so unsatisfactory that she declared nothing should induce her to make the voyage in it.

At last it was settled that they should travel by land to Ancona and there embark for Trieste, much to the terror of some of the party, for it was very dangerous, as the French troops were spreading all over the country. Miss Knight, who accompanied them, thus describes the journey to Sir E. Berry:

"*July 16th.*—It is at length decided that we go by land, and I feel all the dangers and difficulties to which we shall be exposed. Think of our embarking on small Austrian vessels at Ancona for Trieste, as part of a land journey! to avoid the danger of being on board an English man-of-war, where everything is commodious and well-arranged for defence and comfort; but the die is cast, and go we must. Lord Nelson is going on an expedition he disapproves and against his own convictions, because he has promised the Queen and that others advise her. I pity the Queen. Prince Belmonte directs the march, and Lady Hamilton, though she

[1] Autobiography of Cornelia Knight.

does not like him, seconds his proposals because she hates the sea and wishes to visit the different courts of Germany. Sir William says he shall die by the way, and he looks so ill that I should not be surprised if he did. I am astonished that the Queen, who is a sensible woman, should consent to run so great a risk, but I can assure you that neither she nor the Princesses forget their great obligations to you. If I am not detained in a French prison, or do not die upon the road, you shall hear from me again."

"*Ancona, July* 24, 1800.— As I find delays succeed each other and England still recedes from us, I will not omit at least informing you of our adventures. We left Leghorn the day after I wrote to you by Mr. Tyson, and, owing more to good-fortune than to prudence, arrived in twenty-six hours at Florence, after passing within *two miles* of the French advanced posts. After a short stay we proceeded on our way to this place. At Castel San Giovanni the coach in which were Lord Nelson and Sir William and Lady Hamilton was overturned; Sir William and Lady Hamilton were hurt, but not dangerously. The wheel was repaired, but broke again at Arezzo—the Queen[1] two days' journey before them and news of the French army advancing rapidly, it was therefore decided that they should proceed, and Mrs. Cadogan and I remained with the broken carriage, as it was of less consequence we should be left behind or taken than they. We were obliged to stay three days to

[1] The Queen had an escort sent by the Grand-duke of Tuscany as far as the frontier of his dominions.

get the coach repaired, and providentially Arezzo
was the place, as it is the most loyal city in
Tuscany, and every care, attention, and kindness
that humanity can dictate, and cordiality and good
manners practise, were employed in our favour.
... Just as we were going to set off, we received
accounts of the French being very near the road
where we had to pass, and of its being also infested
with Neapolitan deserters, but at the same moment
arrived a party of Austrians, and the officers gave
us two soldiers as a guard. We travelled night and
day; the roads are almost destroyed, and the
misery of the inhabitants is beyond description.
At length, however, we arrived at Ancona, and
found that the Queen had given up the idea of
going in the *Bellona*, an Austrian frigate, fitted up
with silk hangings, carpets, and eighty beds for her
reception, and now meant to go with a Russian
squadron of three frigates and a brig. I believe she
judged rightly, for there had been a mutiny on
board the *Bellona*, and for the sake of accommoda-
tion she had reduced her guns to twenty-four, while
the French, in possession of the coast, arm *trabaccoli*
and other light vessels that could easily surround
and take her. I fancy we shall sail to-morrow night
or the next morning. Mrs Cadogan and I are to
be on board one of the frigates, commanded by an
old man named Messer, a native of England, who
once served under Lord Howe and has an excellent
reputation. The rest of our party go with the
Queen, and say they shall be very uncomfortable.
Lord Nelson talks often of the *Foudroyant*, whatever
is done to turn off the conversation, and last night

he was talking with Captain Messer of the manœuvres he intended to make in case he accepted of another command. In short, I perceive that his thoughts turn towards England, and I hope and believe he will be happy there. The Queen and her daughters have been very kind to me, especially when I was ill.... The Queen speaks of you often, and always with the highest esteem.... Lord Nelson has been received with acclamations in all the towns of the Pope's States.... Our cots are ready and the carriages on board. ...

"*Trieste, August 9th,* 1800.—... I told you we were become humble enough to rejoice at a Russian squadron conveying us across the Adriatic; but had we sailed as was first intended, in the imperial frigate, we should have been taken by eight *trabaccoli*, which the French armed on purpose at Pisaro. Sir William and Lady Hamilton and Lord Nelson give a miserable account of their sufferings on board the Commodore's ship (Count Voinovitch). He was ill in his cot, but his first lieutenant, a Neapolitan named Capaci, was, it seems, the most ignorant and insolent of beings. Think what Lord Nelson must have felt! He says a gale of wind would have sunk the ship. ... I hope we shall be able to set off to-morrow night for Vienna. The Queen and thirty-four of her *suite* have had fevers; you can have no idea of the *helplessness* of the party. How we shall proceed on our long journey is to me a problem, but we shall certainly get on as fast as we can, for the very precarious state of Sir William's health has convinced everybody that it is necessary he should arrange his affairs. ... Poor

Lord Nelson, whose only comfort was in talking of ships and harbours with Captain Messer, has had a bad cold, but is almost well, and, I think, anxious to be in England. He is followed by thousands whenever he goes out, and for the illumination that is to take place this evening there are many "*Viva Nelsons*" prepared. He seems affected whenever he speaks of you, and often sighs out, 'Where is the *Foudroyant?*' "[1]

At last the wearisome, perilous journey came to an end, and the immense party arrived safely at Vienna. In spite of the coolness which had been between him and the Queen, King Ferdinando had been exceedingly anxious all this time about the safety of his wife and family.

"The King had, perhaps, never in his life written so many letters to his imperial daughter in Vienna as at this time, when he had no certain news of the fate of the travellers, and every line makes it evident that the stalwart Nimrod had not one peaceful hour until he knew that 'mamma and the children' were out of danger."[2]

[1] Autobiography of Cornelia Knight
[2] "Der König hat vielleicht in seinem Leben nicht so viel Briefe an seine Kaiserliche Tochter in Wien geschrieben als in dieser Zeit da er nichts sicheres uber das Schicksal der Reisenden wusste, und jede Zeile spricht dafur dasz der gewaltige Nimrod nicht eine ruhige Stunde hatte, so lang er nicht 'Mamma und die Kinder' ausser aller Gefahr wuszte "—"Maria Karolina von Oesterreich" (Helfert).

CHAPTER XX

Arrival at Vienna—Departure of Lord Nelson and the Hamiltons—The two surviving daughters of Maria Theresia—The imperial family circle—Life at Vienna and Schönbrunn—The Prime Minister Thugut—The war—Flight of the Grand-duke and Grand-duchess of Tuscany—Treaty of Luneville—Naples threatened—Paul, Emperor of Russia—Naples, saved by the Queen—A dramatic concert—The Archduke Anton and Princess Amélie—The Spanish proposals—Terror of Amélie—The Prince of the Asturias chooses Antoinette—A melancholy parting.

AFTER so long, so perilous and so harassing a journey, it was not surprising that the Queen was worn out and ill for several days. However, she was now safe, and once again in her own country, among her own people, with the daughter she idolised. "We will go and see the dear mother and all her darling children," she had exclaimed when talking of her proposed departure from Palermo; but the desire to see her relations and revisit her old home had not been the only reason for her journey.

The plan had been made and begun to be carried out in the full height of her confidence in the continuation of the success which was just then attending the arms of the allied Powers, and Maria Carolina, in the joy and triumph of her heart, not only felt secure in the possession of the Two Sicilies, but desired that the dominions of Ferdinando should be further extended as a reward for the great assistance they had undoubtedly rendered to the cause.

It was about this that she wished to speak to the Emperor, and also to strengthen his resolution and confirm his animosity against the French. But the disaster of Marengo and the calamities which followed put an end to all projects of gaining any additional territory; the question now was whether they would be able to keep what they already had; only the Queen was still just as resolved to exert her influence over her son-in-law in order to prevent his relaxing in his efforts.

The Queen's influence over the Emperor was exactly what the Austrian Prime Minister Thugut foresaw and dreaded. He heard with consternation of her coming, and even tried to persuade the Emperor to send a messenger to put her off.

It was, however, decided that this was impossible. To decline the visit of the aunt of the Emperor and mother of the Empress, herself a reigning Sovereign, was out of the question; no steps were therefore taken to dissuade her; she was welcomed with all the honour due to the daughter of Maria Theresia, while the progress of Nelson from Trieste to Vienna was one long triumph.

Lady Hamilton was presented at the court of Vienna by Lady Minto, wife of the English Ambassador, and all, Neapolitan and English, were magnificently entertained by the great Austrian nobles as well as by the imperial family.

FRANCIS I. EMPEROR OF AUSTRIA.
After the painting by Leopold Kupelwieser, in the Imperial Château of Laxenburg, Austria

At Eisenstadt, the castle of Prince Esterhazy, where they spent four days, they were always served at dinner by a hundred grenadiers, the shortest of whom was six feet high, who stood round the table.

Towards the end of September the Queen took leave of the Hamiltons, who were returning to England with Lord Nelson. It was a final farewell; Sir William, who had been the tried friend of more than two-thirds of her lifetime, was failing in health and lamenting his departure from Italy, which he did not long survive. Lady Hamilton, still ardent in her professions of love and devotion to the Queen and gratitude for her constant kindness and generosity, she never met again.

One sister still remained to Maria Carolina, the Archduchess Elisabeth, Abbess of Innsbruck, who, in spite of the great disappointment of her life, that no husband had been found for her, and that, as she feared, she had been obliged to stay at home with the Emperor, was as lively and popular as ever. All of us, when youth has passed, know the melancholy feeling which mingles with the pleasure of family reunions in the old home, especially after any considerable time of absence, and the meeting of Elisabeth and Maria Carolina must have been deeply affecting to them both.

The young Princes and Princesses on both sides were delighted with each other and were always together, much to the uneasiness of Thugut,[1] who saw with disapproval and perturbation the intimacy and affection between the cousins, which daily

---

[1] A. Bonnefonds, Helfert.

increased in the *vie de famille* at Vienna and Schönbrunn.

The meeting with their two eldest sisters was a great happiness to the Neapolitan Princesses, and they found themselves warmly welcomed in the very large circle of their relations of the imperial family.

Like François de Lorraine and Maria Theresia, Leopold and Luisa of Spain had had sixteen sons and daughters, of whom fourteen survived them; and the merry children and young people who pervaded the imperial palaces and gardens must have vividly recalled the olden times to the two surviving daughters of the great Empress.

Albert of Saxe-Teschen, the widowed husband of the Archduchess Christine, was also at Vienna, and showed much interest and affection for the young nieces of the wife to whose memory he was ever constant.[1]

M. Trognon in his life of Marie Amélie, Queen of France, speaks of the affection shown at this time to that Princess by her uncle the Duke of Saxe-Teschen and her brother-in-law, Ferdinand, Grand-duke of Tuscany.

After the stormy, troubled life of the last two or three years at Naples and Palermo, the peace and shelter of the Austrian home, the comfort and cheerfulness of their daily life, and the simple amusements and *fêtes de famille*, the only ones permissible just then, were enchanting to the Neapolitan royal family.

The court during the first few months of their stay could not be very gay, owing to the disaster of

[1] He was the last Governor of the Austrian Netherlands.

Marengo and the number of families thrown into mourning by the results of that battle and of Hohenlinden, which took place a little later. Much anxiety was also prevalent as the progress of the French armies grew more and more rapid and alarming.

After the battle of Marengo Napoleon wrote to the Emperor offering terms of peace very favourable to Austria. The Emperor hesitated, but the Queen of Naples threw all her influence into the opposite scale, in which she was supported by Lord Minto, and by the all-powerful Minister, Thugut, who hated France much more than he disliked the Queen.

"She is curiosity and tactlessness personified," he wrote of her in 1795 to Colloredo; "in political affairs she mixes herself up in everything, great and small . . ." and he went on to complain of her readiness to listen to gossip and her incautious way of repeating things, declaring she might do more harm to the affairs of the Emperor than the loss of a battle.[1] She now offered the Emperor a Neapolitan army to join the Germans in Tuscany and the Papal States, and although matters were so far advanced that the Emperor had written an autograph letter to Napoleon, promising to ratify whatever his ambassador, Count de St. Julien, should decide, negotiations were already going on, and Duroc had started for Vienna, he was persuaded to cut short the preliminaries of peace and recall St. Julien.

[1] "Königin Karolina von Neapel und Sicilien im Kampfegegen die franzosische Weltherschaft" (Freiherr v Helfert).

The war began again, and Napoleon, attributing it in great part to the influence of the Queen of Naples, was all the more infuriated against her.

The progress of events, however, soon became so alarming that the Austrian government made fresh overtures for peace, an armistice was proclaimed at Hohenlinden, and finally the treaty of Luneville was concluded, putting the French in possession of nearly the whole of Italy north of Naples.

The grand-duchy of Tuscany was seized and given to the Duke of Parma, that State having been taken and united to what was called the "Cisalpine Republic," to the grief of the Tuscans, who were devoted to their own Prince and his family.

To Ferdinand, instead of the province he and his father had ruled so admirably, was given later on a deplorable substitute, the grand-duchy of Wurzburg.

But fourteen years afterwards the fall of Buonaparte and the victory of the allied Powers replaced him in his own dominions. Meanwhile he took refuge with his wife and children at Vienna.

By the treaty of Luneville peace was concluded with every country except England. The unparalleled success of the French arms had plundered, diminished, or confiscated various States in Italy and Germany; but in spite of all this there was a general sense of relief from the terrors and sufferings lately prevailing, the exceptions to the rejoicings being the Neapolitan family, whose son-in-law and second daughter had lost Tuscany, and who were themselves excluded from the treaty. The King of Naples had suddenly sent three legions to attack the French in Tuscany during the armistice, and whether they were aware of the armistice or not, this movement did no good but only infinite mischief, for the Neapolitans were defeated, and Napoleon, in a fury, ordered Murat with a powerful army to invade Naples.

Maria Carolina, in despair, sent ambassadors from Vienna to the Emperor of Russia with an urgent letter entreating him to save them by using his powerful influence on their behalf with the First Consul of the French Republic.

Her appeal was not in vain. Paul at once sent Count Lawacheff to Paris to plead in his name the cause of the Queen of Naples, and desired him to stop and see her as he passed through Vienna, where he was completely fascinated by her and by the fortitude and courage which she displayed. His admiration and sympathy made him a strenuous partisan of her interests, and in consequence of his representations the First Consul agreed to a treaty of peace, which, although it consisted of hard conditions, including a heavy indemnity, the loss of the principality of Piombino and other disadvantageous terms, had two great advantages for Maria Carolina. In the first place it saved the crown of Naples, and in the second it restored to her in a great measure the esteem and consideration of Ferdinando, who saw perfectly well that she had saved his kingdom.

For nearly two years the Queen and her children remained in Austria, where Maria Carolina was always overjoyed to be, and where her children were supremely happy.

In February, 1801, after the signing of the peace of Luneville, the court of Vienna awoke to the pleasures and festivities of the Carnival, which was unusually brilliant that year by way of contrast to the troubles and gloom of the last months. Balls, masquerades, concerts, parties of all kinds followed in rapid succession, the capital was crowded with distinguished visitors of all nations, eager to take advantage of the opportunity of travelling in safety.

The Princess Amélie, afterwards Queen of the French, speaks in her journal of the happiness of her life in Austria and of her enjoyment of all these amusements. Being also extremely fond of music, she thoroughly appreciated the opportunities so constantly presented at Vienna for its study and enjoyment. Haydn was then in the height of his fame; Miss Cornelia Knight speaks as follows of a concert given before she left Vienna:

"He was staying at the time with Prince Esterhazy, and presided over the famous concerts given by that nobleman at his magnificent palace in Hungary. At one time the Prince had an intention of giving up these concerts, and told Haydn that the next one would be the last. It was a very fine one. Towards the conclusion Haydn composed a finale so melancholy, so touching, that it drew tears from many of the audience, and he had given orders that while it was playing the lights should be gradually extinguished. All of which made such an impression upon the mind of the Prince that he abandoned his intention of discontinuing these concerts."

With the *vie de famille*, the simple pleasures and

outdoor amusements of the German imperial family was mingled, especially on state occasions, much of the usage and ceremonial of ancient times.

Amongst other great functions attended by the young Neapolitans were the reception of their cousin, the Archduke Charles, as Knight of the Teutonic Order, with all the religious pomp and solemnity of the days of chivalry.

Also the opening of the Diet of Presburg, a magnificent spectacle, to which the wild, picturesque figures of the Hungarian nobles, their strange customs and the extraordinary splendour and richness of their costumes lent an almost Oriental atmosphere.

They made a pilgrimage also to Maria Zell, in Styria, the scene of the death of their grandfather, the Emperor François de Lorraine, to which their mother had performed the same journey before her marriage. They travelled for two days through wild and beautiful scenery to the lovely, solitary place amongst the mountains, which, with its imposing church, so impressed the Princess Amélie that she said that if she were to be established in Germany she would often go and spend ten days or a fortnight there.

Why the Queen, amongst so many princes and archdukes, did not find a suitable *parti* for at least one of her daughters seems rather strange, more especially as she was extremely anxious about their establishment.

Leopold, Prince of Salerno, was only nine years old when he came to Vienna ; but Christine, Amélie, and Antoinette were seventeen, nineteen, and two-and-twenty.

One of the young archdukes, at any rate, fell in love with Amélie, and paid her devoted attentions both in public and private. He would loiter about under her windows, looking up anxiously for a glimpse of her; and the Queen, observing this and other incidents, but knowing that the Archduke Anton was destined to be Prince-Bishop of Bamberg, one of the greatest ecclesiastical *seigneuries* of the Empire, spoke to her daughter and offered, if she wished to marry him, to appeal to the Emperor and take measures to get the vows he had already made annulled. It is likely enough that Maria Carolina would not have objected to marrying another of her daughters to a third Archduke, but Amélie did not wish for the marriage, and as there was no strong political reason for it, the matter dropped.

But another husband, who would have been far more distasteful to her, was proposed for Amélie, in the shape of the Prince of the Asturias, and the very idea of this marriage filled her with dread. She knew well enough that about such an alliance she would not be allowed any choice; it was far too splendid and too politically important; it was no more possible for her to refuse the Prince of the Asturias than it had been for her mother and aunt to refuse the King of Naples and Duke of Parma. Only a lucky chance could save her, as it did by the Prince of the Asturias expressing a wish to marry her younger sister, Antoinette. It was, of course, all the same to the royal families of

Princess Amélie,
Wife of Louis Philippe, King of France.

Spain and Naples which of the two it should be, so Antoinette was substituted for Amélie, and the dark future from which the elder sister had recoiled with such gloomy forebodings was transferred from her to the younger one.

It was not until the end of May, 1802, that the Queen and her children returned to Naples. The parting from so many who were so dear to them, and with whom, during nearly two years, they had been living in the most affectionate intimacy, was a very sorrowful one, and would have been still more so had they known that the dearest amongst all those who separated so reluctantly amidst tears and lamentations would meet no more on earth.

CHAPTER XXI

Return to Naples—Death of Clementine, Princess Royal—Renewal of influence with the King—Death of the Grandduchess of Tuscany—More conspiracies—Two Spanish marriages—Isabel, Princess Royal—Threatened dangers—Nelson—The ninety dogs of the King—Unhappy fate of Antoinette, Princess of the Asturias—The King of Spain and the violinist—The Queen of Naples and her daughter-in-law—A dangerous breakfast—Lady Hamilton—Her extravagance and greed for money—Infatuation of Lord Nelson.

IT was with a heavy heart that Maria Carolina once more set out on her journey to Naples, turning away from her beloved Austria, where for the last two years she had led a life so sheltered, honoured, and dignified, so surrounded with affection and security, and so comparatively peaceful that it contrasted only too strongly with the experiences which had gone before and those still to come.

Here, in her native Austria, she felt happy and at home, received and reverenced by her countrymen as an Austrian Princess, daughter and sister of their own Emperors, mother of their present Empress, familiar to them all from her earliest childhood ; here she was amongst civilised and reliable people, unlike, indeed, to the fierce and fickle Neapolitans, who regarded her with jealousy as a foreigner, repaid her benefits with ingratitude and her friendship with treachery, listened to the infamous slanders of the French and Jacobins against her character, laid upon her the blame of all the evil deeds of Ferdinando, and gave him the credit of all her good ones.

In spite of the attempts of Thugut to sow distrust and suspicion between her and the Emperor, which had made the position of the young Empress between her husband and her mother at times rather embarrassing, Maria Carolina had still a great deal of influence over the mind of her vacillating son-in-law, at all events when she was with him; how it would be after her departure she could not foresee. But there was no apparent prospect of the peace in which everybody was rejoicing being broken for the present; the King had gone back to Naples, where he was now holding his court, and where it was now necessary that the Queen and royal family should also return.

During her absence at Vienna another grief had come to Maria Carolina in the death of her little grandson, the son of the Prince Royal, quickly followed by that of her Austrian daughter-in-law, the Princess Clementine, to whom she was much attached.[1] The little granddaughter who survived

[1] On December 6, 1801, the Queen wrote to Lady Hamilton from Vienna: "You have, of course, shared in the grievous misfortune I have experienced in losing my dear and good daughter-in-law. It destroyed the single happiness that remained to me in a perfect union and domestic attachment. This dear and good Princess died like a saint, and her husband is in the deepest despair. My dear children do nothing but mourn for their sister-

was an object of deepest affection to her, and, like her own children, she had secured an Austrian nurse or governess for her.

They stopped at Mariazell on their journey to perform their devotions, and proceeded to Trieste, where a Neapolitan frigate was waiting to take them to Italy. Between Foggia and Naples they were met by the King, and on the 17th August the royal family and their numerous suite entered the capital, which the young Prince of Salerno and his sisters had not seen since their flight from it four years before. To be once again at Caserta, Portici, Capo di Monte, and all the enchanting, well-remembered places, went far to console the Princesses for their leaving Vienna; but for their mother, cares, troubles, and anxieties soon began to accumulate.

A still more severe grief fell upon the King and Queen not many weeks after the return of the latter to Naples, in the death of their second daughter, the Grand-duchess of Tuscany, leaving a son and three daughters.

The Queen had been coldly received by the Neapolitans, who, in spite of the cruelties of Ferdinando, had welcomed him back with acclamations of delight. The calumnies, however preposterous, which had been industriously circulated about Maria Carolina had borne their

m-law, who was a tender sister to them, and would at my death (which by reason of my troubles and griefs cannot be distant) have been a mother to them.... You write now so rarely to me that I believe myself half forgotten by you.... a thousand painful circumstances harder me from establishing my two daughters, whom I must take back to Naples, probably to remain there for life."—"The Queen of Naples," "L'd N's n" (Jeaffreson) fruit, as her enemies foresaw, and were believed, or at any rate asserted, by the Jacobins and their friends. For, as one of the clauses in the treaty with Napoleon had insisted upon an entire amnesty for the Neapolitan Jacobins, they had returned in great numbers to Naples and had recommenced their plots against the government, animated by a fiercer hatred than before of the Queen, whom they regarded as their chief enemy.

Maria Carolina met their conspiracies by renewed vigilance of the police; spies were at work again, and after a short time the King announced his intention of taking energetic measures to defend himself and his kingdom against traitors at home and abroad; following which proclamation came suspicions, arrests of guilty and sometimes of innocent people, trials before the Junta of the State, punishments of various degrees, and all the deplorable atmosphere of alarm and irritation which was the inevitable consequence.

Before this proclamation, however, the marriage took place of the Princess Antoinette with the Prince of the Asturias; also of the Prince Royal, who had been a widower less than a year, with the Infanta Isabel, daughter of the King of Spain.

The Neapolitans, in spite of the little love they now bore the Queen, rejoiced at her return, as, in the first place, they had no longer to support the numerous retinue with which, with her usual extravagance, Maria had held her court at Vienna, and secondly, they welcomed the renewal of the festivities which would of course attend the presence of the Queen and her daughters in the capital.

The marriages of the Prince Royal and his youngest sister were extremely popular for these reasons, and also because it was hoped and supposed that these Spanish alliances would unite the royal families of Spain and Naples as closely as the former ones had done those of Austria and Naples—a hope which proved altogether delusive.

The King had at first thought of conducting his children to Spain himself, but he relinquished the idea and sent Acton instead.

The Princess Antoinette was married to the Prince of the Asturias by proxy at Naples in October, 1802, amidst rejoicings that must have seemed a mockery to the young girl who was thus sacrificed, and to her sisters, who were heartbroken at the parting. In M. Trognon's life of Queen Amélie he describes the bitter grief of that Princess on this occasion. She had hated and dreaded this marriage for herself; she hated and dreaded it for her sister; and when the Spanish warship which came to fetch Antoinette was signalled on entering the bay of Naples her heart sank. For although there was in one way more similarity between Italy and Spain, both Southern countries, their royal families nearly related to each other, still their Spanish and Austrian cousins were regarded in a widely different manner by the children of Maria Carolina, by whom they had been brought up to look upon Austria as a second home, and who loved their Austrian relations with an affectionate familiarity increased by their long sojourn amongst them, and by the superior and amiable characters most of them possessed.

With their Spanish relations it was very different.

Carlos IV. was a weak, miserable prince, under the sway of the Queen, a woman of odious disposition, herself governed by her disreputable favourite, Manuel Godoï. Of the Prince of the Asturias they probably knew little or nothing.

Amidst ringing of bells, firing of guns, illuminations, and shouting crowds, the Spanish and Neapolitan warships left the Bay of Naples conveying the brother and sister—the one to return shortly with a Spanish bride, the other leaving for ever the home of her childhood and all she loved.

The Princess of the Asturias, without being pretty, had a charming, attractive personality. The Duchesse d'Abrantès, who saw her soon afterwards, says of her that no one would have supposed she could have been of Neapolitan blood. She had the blue eyes and fair hair of her Austrian mother and the Habsburg lip. She had the Bourbon nose, but not pronounced enough to be ugly. Though not tall she was extremely dignified, and when she smiled all her face seemed to light up; and though reserved and rather silent, her face was exceedingly expressive and interesting. She was an excellent musician, spoke seven or eight languages, was passionately fond of poetry and painting, and amused herself almost entirely in various artistic and intellectual pursuits.

Spain at that time had altered very little from what it had been for the last hundred or hundred and fifty years.

The Duchesse d'Abrantès, when she passed some

time there with her husband on her way to Portugal, where he was the French Ambassador, says of Spain:

"Nothing can be compared to this first sight of a country so strangely opposed to our own in manners, customs, and language. England, separated from us by the Straits, is much less different from our country than is Spain from the last village of France situated on the banks of the Bidassoa. . . . Spain, with its truly local colour; its usages, singular, but well adapted to the country; the customs suited to the character of its inhabitants; everything, even to the costume which foreign women are obliged to wear to avoid being insulted if they go out without having put it on, it all pleased and attracted me."[1]

After a few days the Prince Royal returned with his young wife, the Infanta Isabel, a young girl by no means calculated either in appearance, manners, or disposition to fill the place in any way of either the Archduchess Clementine, her predecessor, or the Princess Antoinette, for whom she had just been exchanged.

She was only fourteen years old and looked younger, a mere child, stupid, not half educated, plain, and undeveloped. "Little, and as round as a ball," remarks her sister-in-law, Princess Amélie, with disapprobation in her journal.

That the King and Prince Royal, neither of whom was[2] likely to be very exacting with regard to in-

[1] "Mémoires de la Duchesse d'Abrantès."
[2] As another specimen of the want of education of the King: during a discussion in which some remark was made about the

tellectual attainments, regarded her with perplexed consternation is evident from the fact that they both entreated the Princess Amélie to educate and look after her, which that excellent person attempted to do, but soon gave up in despair ; finding, as might be expected, that it was better not to interfere with a married sister-in-law and Princess Royal, even if she were only fourteen years old.

The Queen was by no means pleased with her new daughter-in-law; and the losses she had sustained made her cling all the more closely to the two daughters who remained to her, and who were always with her. They had now a German lady-in-waiting to take the place of their dear and faithful Signora Ambrosio, who, having become blind, could no longer hold that post, though she continued to live in the palace and to pass much of her time with them.

Sir William Hamilton died in April, 1803. In him the Queen lost a firm and valuable friend, whose help and fidelity she could ill spare.

The treaty of Amiens between France, Great Britain, Holland, and Spain was another blow to her ; but that the English Government had not much faith in the intentions of Napoleon, and was mindful of the interests of its Neapolitan friends, is evident by the instructions given from the Admiralty to Lord Nelson, as follows :

"Your lordship is to be very attentive in observing if the French have any design of

power of the Turks and the extent of their dominion, he replied that it was no wonder, for before the birth of Christ all the world was Turkish attacking the kingdom of Naples or Sicily, and your lordship is to exert yourself to counteract it, and to take, sink, burn, or destroy any ships or vessels which may be so employed, and to afford to his Sicilian Majesty and his subjects all the protection and assistance which may be in your power consistently with a due attention to the other important objects entrusted to your care."

The Queen wrote to Lord Nelson expressing her "eternal gratitude" for a protection which was so likely to be required, for the French army in Italy was being steadily increased. The French garrisons, forced by the treaty to be allowed in Neapolitan territory, amounted to thirteen thousand men, and Nelson wrote to the British Government urging them to send troops enough to defend Sicily, garrison Gaeta and the castles of Naples, and send a force into Calabria to support the warlike peasants in case the French became too imperious in their demands.

In a letter to Lady Hamilton he wrote in July, 1803:

"I have made up my mind that it is a part of the plan of that Corsican scoundrel to conquer the kingdom of Naples. He has marched thirteen thousand men into the kingdom on the Adriatic side, and he will take possession, with as much shadow of right, of Gaeta and Naples, and if the poor King remonstrates or allows us to secure Sicily, he will call it war, and declare a conquest."[1]

[1] Jeaffreson.

Meanwhile the King and Queen had not the power to protect themselves, as they were short of money and soldiers, and nearly the whole of their splendid fleet had been destroyed at the time of their flight to Sicily.

An English man-of-war was kept stationed in the Bay of Naples in case of the necessity arising for another flight to Sicily.

On her return from Vienna the Queen found that all authority in every branch of State affairs was in the hands of Acton, who, during her long absence, had acquired a great deal more power and more influence over the King than she was disposed to allow.[1] Maria Carolina was not likely to submit to the dictation of the man whose career she herself had made, and who, having now rendered himself necessary to the King, was disposed to set himself in opposition to her. This state of things she was resolved not to stand, but it was requisite to proceed with caution, as Acton appeared to be all-powerful with Ferdinando, dreaded and flattered by everyone. When he went to Spain with the Prince Royal and Princess of the Asturias he was received with extraordinary honours by Carlos IV., who even bestowed on him the order of the Golden Fleece, while everyone tried to flatter and propitiate him, as he was supposed to be hostile to the friendship and alliance of Spain and Naples.

The influence of the Queen, however, now that, after her interposition had saved the crown of Naples, she had returned there to resume her

[1] A. Bonnefonds.

position and authority, had soon returned. Ferdinando's love for her was now changed into the sort of friendship which long association, community of interests, their mutual affection for their children, and the habit of looking to her for guidance and help, had cemented, notwithstanding the outbursts of violence of temper and excitement which now, as ever, were so serious a fault in her character.

In the spring of 1803 the King, who liked Sicily much better than she did, was anxious to spend some time there. The Archbishop of Palermo, president of the Council, had died, and Ferdinando, on pretext of affairs of business of the State, proposed to go there, and, as a preliminary, sent over ninety sporting dogs. The plan, however, was vehemently opposed by the Queen, who wrote to her daughter, the Empress:

"12 February, 1803. Your dear father is very anxious to return there (to Sicily) which is scarcely possible, seeing that to leave this country would cause the revolution to break out again."[1]

The ninety dogs were accordingly brought back later on under the protection of the Austrian flag.

The French Ambassadors of Napoleon, though as a rule not persons remarkable for their polish or courtly manners, were at all events not the brutal ruffians sent by the Jacobins and their immediate successors, and the one now at Naples was anxious to make himself agreeable to the

[1] "12 Février, 1803. Votre cher père désire virement d'y retourner, ce qui n'est guère possible, vu que de laisser ce pays ci ferait la révolution de nouveau. . ." (Helfert).

Queen, whom he rather admired. Not, one must suppose, for her beauty, which was now a thing of the past, for she was nearly fifty years old, her hair was white, and her face already marked with the deep lines caused perhaps more by care and sorrow than by age. But he was fascinated by her conversation and personality, strange, original, and cultivated,[1] but voluble and imprudent. Talented and full of decision, she was unmethodical, and so incautious that she would let out important secrets without consideration, and so much of impulse was mingled with her diplomacy as to call forth later on the celebrated remark of Napoleon :

"Is your Majesty's mind, so distinguished amongst women, so unable to divest itself of the prejudices of your sex that you must treat affairs of state as if they were affairs of the heart?"

To the revolutionist Ambassador, M. Alquier, it was also flattering to associate with and receive the confidences of the singular and gifted woman who was not only a Queen, but a daughter and sister of Emperors.

With her hostility to Napoleon was mingled a certain admiration of his genius, and just at this time he hoped by flattery and menaces to overcome her opposition to his supremacy. He is even said to have entertained a vague idea of marrying his stepson, Eugène de Beauharnais, to the Princess Amélie, an alliance to which the Queen would never have given her consent.

The oppressive tyranny and interference of Napoleon became more and more insupportable.

[1] A. Bonnefonds.

He insisted upon the retirement of Acton, on the plea that, being an Englishman, he was necessarily hostile to French interests. Powerless to resist, the King yielded, and Acton retired to Palermo with his wife and child.

"He carries with him esteem and confidence," wrote the King to Lord Nelson. "I shall write to him whenever anything happens, and I shall profit by his advice, which I have always found wise, firm, and useful."[1]

The marriage of her youngest daughter had brought fresh sorrow to the Queen.

For Antoinette, or "Toto" as she called her, was very unhappy in Spain. When first she arrived there she found her husband, the Prince of the Asturias, cold and indifferent, but her father and mother-in-law, kind, attentive, and pleased with her.

Very soon, however, all this was changed. The Prince of the Asturias fell violently in love with her. The Queen became jealous, and, the King being a nonentity, her life was made miserable by her mother-in-law and her infamous favourite.

The love of her husband, which she returned, was her only consolation, but both he and she were surrounded by spies and informers and were exposed to the hostility of the Queen and Godoï. Melancholy and sad in the strange, uncongenial surroundings, she thought sadly of the old life at Vienna, Naples, or Palermo, and wished

---

[1] This was a little later. The Queen had also an idea that Jérôme Buonaparte was the husband thought of for one of the Neapolitan Princesses, and observed that she could not bring herself to allow such a *mésalliance*.

she could return to her mother, to whom she wrote that she could not imagine how her sisters could wish to marry, when all she longed for was to go back to her home, where she had been so free and happy.

The Queen's grief and anxiety for her daughter can be easily understood, and appears in many letters of hers at this time:

"My dear, good, and beloved Toto . . . is in every way unhappy. . . . If God strengthens her I hope she will be an honour to us, if only she does not succumb . . ."

"Her husband is everything to her, but her mother-in-law is a wretch. I fear *all*, as she has neither religion, morals, nor any right principles whatever. No one would believe the . . . disorders and infamy of that house, of which my daughter writes to me, and of which I hear from everyone who comes from there. . . ."

"The horrid Queen has dismissed the two faithful Ochiers, sent away la St. Teodoro with her children, and ordered the Duke, Ambassador, not to come any more to the palace but to leave immediately, and all that because they will not repeat to her all that my daughter and her husband do in their own apartments."

The position of the unfortunate young princess was made worse by her having no children. Twice there had been hopes of an heir, but each time they were doomed to disappointment.

Maria Carolina would have gladly received her daughter and son-in-law at Naples, but she was unable to accomplish their removal from Madrid, or in fact to do anything to help the Princess of the Asturias, or to lessen her own anxiety and fear, not only for her happiness, but for her safety.

Her dislike of the French Republic placed her in opposition to Godoi and the Queen. The French Revolution and its government had been the terror and abhorrence of her childhood and youth, which they had filled with dreadful associations and intolerable annoyances. The French Ambassadors, one more vulgar and insolent than another, who had represented the Republic at her father's court, had been absolutely different from those of any other power, and were universally shunned and looked upon with disgust. Stories of their ignorance, their ill-breeding, their absurd vanity and overbearing coarseness, had been repeated and discussed at court and in society. An interview with one of them was looked upon with repugnance.

"Your mamma has had a most indecent scene with the French Ambassador," wrote Ferdinando on one occasion to his daughter, the Empress. "Mamma nearly burst with anger.[1] She will write to you herself about it later."

The murder of her aunt and cousin, the horrible accounts continually arriving of the deeds of the Jacobins in France, the attempts to put Naples into their hands, the plots and conspiracies against her parents, the dangers, flight, and exile she had suffered with her family, were not likely to have disposed Antoinette in favour of those to whom she owed all this misery. She made no secret of

[1] "Mammà ha mancata di crepare."

her feelings, in which she was supported by her husband, and the party in favour of the French alliance, headed by Godoï, abused and calumniated her in consequence.

Junot, afterwards Duc d'Abrantès, one of the generals Napoleon had raised from the ranks and made Ambassador, and afterwards Duke, was, on his arrival at Madrid, completely taken in by Manuel Godoï. Vain and credulous, he believed all he told him, and repeated it to his wife, a clever woman of the world, brought up in the *salon* of her mother, who belonged by birth, principles, and connections to the *ancien régime*.[1]

"The court was at Aranjuez when we arrived at Madrid," writes the Duchesse d'Abrantès. ". . . The *Prince-king* (Godoï) wishing to please the Emperor, was extremely courteous during the interview, and Junot returned quite captivated with him. . . . 'He does not like the Prince and Princess of the Asturias,' said Junot, 'and he warned me that we should be very badly received by them. He told me that France has no greater enemy than the Prince Royal. . . .' He added that it was his wife, the daughter of the King of Naples, who embittered him against us. 'Ah! Monsieur l'Ambassadeur!' he cried, 'Spain will some day have a King who will make her very miserable! . . . This double alliance with the house of Naples forms a link which is connected with Austria, who has married another daughter of the King of Naples. . . . All those women unite in attacking France. Her

[1] "A Leader of Society at Napoleon's Court" (Bearne).

new glory still attends them, and you would hardly believe that this league is formed and directed by the Queen of Naples herself. Our gracious Queen, whom may God protect, combats this evil influence with her son, with all the strength of her mind and her maternal love.'

"'I am astonished at what you tell me,' replied I to Junot, 'I have often heard my uncle Demetrius[1] speak of the Princess of Naples, who is now Princess of the Asturias. He knew her at Naples when he was sent on a mission there by the Comte de Provence. She is charming, according to what he told me, pretty, and the perfection not only of a princess, but of a woman of the world . . . in fact, she is a most accomplished person.'

"'I had a great wish to know the Princess of the Asturias. Having sent to inquire at what hour I could be presented to her, I was told that three o'clock would be the most convenient time for the Princess, who was always occupied, and did not waste her time in sleeping, like the inhabitants of Aranjuez. For reasons known to myself I desired to see the Princess. I had known her for a long time, though I had never seen her. Her misfortunes made her interesting, her reputation was European. One is always grateful to a princess who is above other women, and this one was indeed superior to them. The Queen of Spain ..... from the first took a dislike, which later became hatred, to this charming daughter-in-law, who in the court circle spoke to every Ambassador in his own language. Oh! there is something

[1] Prince Demetrius Comnenus

horrible in the result of hatred produced by a woman's envy. . . . What a destiny was that of the Princess of the Asturias ! I knew from different persons of her household how unhappy she was. Whether he had really been offended by the Prince of the Asturias or by the Princess, the conduct of the Prince de la Paix (Manuel Godoï) towards them both was such that it was impossible the heir to the throne should support it without a determined resolution to revenge himself. . . . He loved the Princess with the deep and true love one feels at twenty ; she returned it with sincerity and fervour, and I knew before that the attachment of these unfortunate young people was the only alleviation they found in a life of constant troubles and annoyances. . . . The Princess . . . was standing by a table, upon which she leant ; a sofa was behind her. The Prince was in an adjoining room. He came immediately and leaned, like his wife, on the same table. Always, I observed, when they were together the Prince followed with his eyes those of the Princess, that he might be guided in what he was to do. . . . She was dressed in white; her gown, made in the simplest manner, was one of those pretty embroidered English muslins, then so much worn, upon which the only contrast was the violet and white ribbon of Maria Luisa ; her beautiful fair hair was only raised with care, and formed in its masses a coiffure nearly as large as that worn by women a year ago. The comb which held them was set with magnificent pearls mingled with diamonds. . . . I came from my audience enchanted and conquered. The Princess had an art, or rather a natural manner, for the word *art* with her is unsuitable; she had, I say, a manner of attracting and conquering which I have never seen in any one else but Napoleon; it was the same expression, first grave, then softening, then becoming altogether charming. The Princess was not pretty; some people even maintain that she was plain; it is possible. I did not trouble myself about it; to me she appeared pretty and graceful, and I found her so because she desired it." [1]

Maria Luisa, Queen of Spain, according to Mme. d'Abrantès, had the remains of beauty; she was very dark; her daughters, although they resembled her, were all ugly.[2]

She conversed well and was a good musician. As to the weak, miserable Carlos IV., his chief delight was in hunting and music. When one of his children was dying he went out hunting all the same, merely remarking that he could do nothing to be of any use.[3] As to his music, it was the scourge of the unfortunate musicians who were obliged to play with him. Every day when he came home from hunting he had a private concert, at which the first violinists in Spain were obliged to accompany him. One of these unlucky

---

[1] "Mémoires de la Duchesse d'Abrantès."
[2] The Queen of Portugal, the Queen of Etruria, the Princess Royal of Naples.
[3] It is a singular thing, but Ferdinando of Naples acted in precisely the same way when, many years later, Carlos IV., having abdicated and settled at Naples, was dying. He wished to see Ferdinando, but he had gone out hunting, saying he could not arrive in time to see his brother.

individuals one day, after an unusually deplorable fiasco, ventured to explain to his Majesty that it had been caused by his beginning at the wrong place, instead of waiting three bars, according to the notes. The King looked at him with amazement, and, taking up his violin again, remarked, as he replaced it under his chin, "Kings never wait."

The unfortunate marriage of her youngest daughter did not make the Queen of Naples any the less anxious nor less ambitious for the establishment of the others. Carlo Felice, Duke of Genoa, youngest brother of the King of Sardinia, came to Naples and fell in love with the Princess Christine in the autumn of 1803. He was eight-and-thirty, but Christine, who was five-and-twenty, and, like her aunt, the Archduchess Elisabeth, did not wish to be "the one to stay at home," said she much preferred him to the Duc de Berri, who had been proposed for her some time earlier, and was willing to marry him. The Queen, however, refused to consent, as the Duke's property was small, therefore the matter was at an end for the present.

She would have liked to marry Christine to her brother-in-law, the Grand-duke Ferdinand, who had made such an excellent husband to her sister; though his German domain was a deplorable substitute for Tuscany. This project, however, could not be realised, as Ferdinand married someone else.

Maria Carolina seems to have had the habit, so irritating to many persons, which prevails in some families, of calling her children, whose real names were pretty, harmonious, and distinguished, by hideous and idiotic nicknames, perhaps originating in some inarticulate, senseless sound made by them in infancy. At any rate, it was by "Mimi" and "Toto" that she used frequently to designate her daughters Christine and Antoinette when she wrote about them to their eldest sister, whom, in spite of her absorbing affection for her, she reproached with considerable vehemence when on one occasion she had not heard from her on her *fête*-day, and when nearly two months had passed without the usual letters, as the Emperor and Empress were travelling in Bohemia.

But notwithstanding her hasty, irritable temper, so regrettable in the Queen, her anger quickly passed away, and her children were all deeply attached to her.

"The mutual behaviour of the children towards the mother and the mother towards the children, which I have had the opportunity to witness, is so affectionate, so unconstrained, and so simple that it cannot but most favourably impress the most casual observer," says a German writer who had been admitted to the society of the royal family of Naples[1]; and Maria Carolina, while entering ardently into all the joys and sorrows of her children, whether at home or far distant, married or single, was anxious to preserve also their affection for each other. On one occasion she points out to the Empress Theresia that she has been a long time without writing to "Toto" in Madrid,

[1] Gerning, "Reise durch Italien," i. S. 262, 266; Kotzebue, "Erinnerungen," ii. S. 174 s. (Helfert).

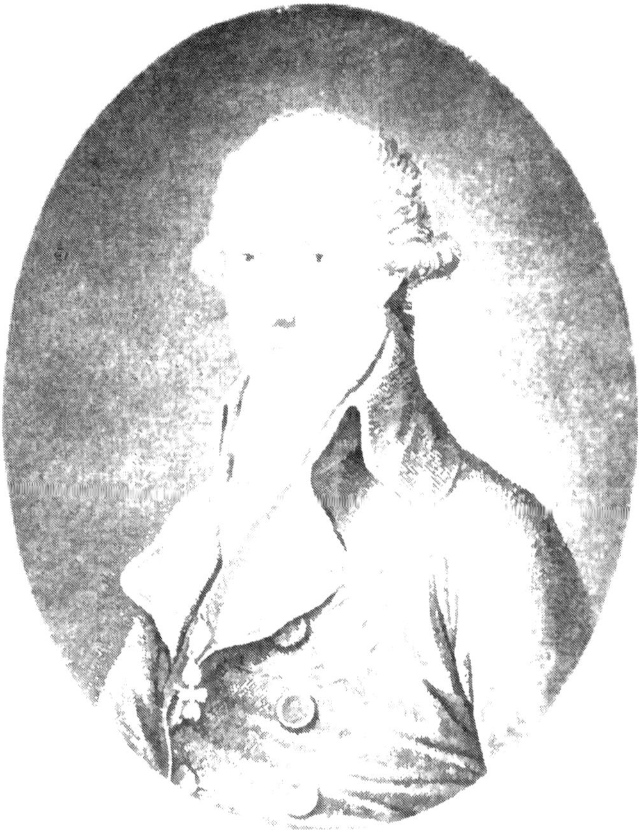

who is longing to hear from her, and that she ought not to forget or neglect the sister who is so much less happy and fortunate than herself.

On the 12th of April, 1803, she writes to the Empress:

"Le jour de Pâques tout en faisant mes dévotions je vous ai, avec le cher Empereur, indignement recommandé à Dieu, puis au déjeuner de Pâques j'ai pris votre portion et celle de la chère Antoinette, et au moins en idée me suis réunie avec vous. Je suis comme sont les vieilles femmes tenant infiniment à toutes les usages, choses; mais tout cela est affaire du cœur et d'un cœur tendrement attaché à ses enfants."

And later:

"J'ai mis de vos cheveux et de ceux d'Antoinette pour vous avoir tous auprès de moi."

Her Spanish daughter-in-law she did not approve of or understand. There was not, as she remarked, either much harm or good in her. In all respects opposed to her own excitable, emotional, passionate disposition, Isabel appeared to be incapable of any deep feeling or interest whatever. She got on very well with her husband, with whom she led the life he liked, farming, riding, and also going into society, but the household of her eldest son was too much in accordance with the tastes of his father to commend it to the ambitious mind and political interests of the Queen.

That Francesco, at such a time as this and with such interests at stake, should be chiefly occupied with his cows and the cultivation of his fields was incomprehensible to her; that Isabel should ride half the day and dance half the night, enjoying herself, in her cool, apathetic sort of way, without a thought or care for anything but trifling pleasures, was provoking; but what most irritated and perplexed her was the attitude of her daughter-in-law when it became evident that there was a chance of an heir to the throne. Of the children of the Queen's beloved Clementine the son had died, and the little daughter was being brought up, under her grandmother's care, by an Austrian governess.

To the King, the Queen, and the State the birth of an heir to the crown was an event of the greatest importance; but Isabel, who was only fifteen, did not like children, was terribly frightened, and considered the prospect as a dreadful calamity. To the Queen, who was passionately fond of her children, whose only regret during her first years of married life had been that she was without them, who had been delighted when she at length had the hope of an heir, and who had welcomed and adored sons and daughters with the same love and satisfaction, Isabel's attitude was altogether inexplicable.

"I should like to know what their household will be like when she is twenty or thirty years older!" the Queen would exclaim; and to the Empress she wrote:

"What I am most anxious to know is whether she will care anything about her child, for at present she has not the slightest indication of any such feeling."[1]

As the time for the birth of the child drew near the terror of the young girl, scarcely more than a

[1] Helfert.

child, increased to such a degree that the Queen assured the Empress that never in all her life had she seen anything like it, and that she and everybody were almost driven out of their senses. She could not, however, have been otherwise than kind to her daughter-in-law, as for some days before her confinement she refused to have any one else with her; and Maria Carolina, though ill herself and overwhelmed with anxieties and troubles, stayed patiently and looked after her until all was over. The child after all was not the hoped-for heir, but a girl, "*das ein schönes kind ist,*"[1] concludes the Queen in her letter to the Empress, to whom, as usual, she poured out all her joys and sorrows.

Since their return from Vienna Maria Carolina had lived rather a retired life with her children. With the King and Acton she was on good terms, as was shown by both Ferdinando and herself being godfather and godmother to a child of Acton's in the spring of 1803.

But the King was generally away hunting, shooting, and fishing; about which he was far more interested than in the most weighty affairs of the state.

Often when some important matter had to be settled in council it was necessary to send messengers and letters after the King, whose whereabouts was probably uncertain. He might be fishing at some place on the Adriatic, or at Persano, on the Bay of Salerno, near the oyster fisheries of Fusaro; but his favourite resort was the Belvedere, while the Queen and her three

[1] "Which is a beautiful child" (Helfert).

younger children were generally either at the Favorita, near Portici, or else at the place they loved best of all, Caserta, near which was the country house, with its farm, of the Prince Royal.

The horrors and commotions of the "Parthenopeian Republic" had given them a dislike to the *palazzo reale* at Naples, which had been sacked and made the scene of many crimes and outrages. The Queen seldom stayed there if she could help it; one of her letters to her daughter, the Empress, is a specimen of her aversion to it:

"Je me trouve à Naples toute isolée, votre père allant à droit et à gauche je suis fine seule dans ce vilain palais que je n'aime point. . . . J'ai arrangé ma bibliothèque, il y a trois chambres, cela a été un grand amusement pour moi, et je la regarde comme une ressource et une distraction dans les malheurs."

And in another letter:

"J'avoue, le séjour dans ce palais dépouillé, où chaque place fait resouvenir d'une abomination me fait frémir."[1]

The enemy without and the Jacobins within the kingdom were a continual threat and danger. One morning the coffee brought for the Queen and her children was found to be full of little needles; this was, however, discovered before any harm had been done, but to the Queen and royal family Naples was becoming like a volcano—at any moment some catastrophe seemed liable to happen.

However, the amnesty was proclaimed, and at a grand ball given by the King at the Favorita the

[1] Helfert.

Queen complained of the restraint and burden of being obliged to go through it under circumstances so uncongenial, and to receive with ceremony and compliments, pretending not to recognise them, many persons whom she knew only too well.

Although the Queen's gratitude to and friendship for England still continued, there began before long to be a coolness in the admiration and liking with which she had hitherto been regarded by Nelson, for the following reason :

When Sir William Hamilton died he did not leave his widow nearly so well off as she expected, or at any rate desired. Eight hundred a year, eight hundred pounds at her bankers', and personal property to the amount of five thousand pounds, although a large portion for the daughter of the Cheshire blacksmith, or the nursemaid and model, Amy Lyon or Emma Harte, was certainly no magnificent provision for the widow of the English Ambassador at Naples. Her income was of course considerably augmented by Lord Nelson, her connection with whom was now well known ; but he was not a rich man, and Emma was a woman like most of her class, through whose hands money ran like water through a sieve.[1] There was no limit to her greediness, extravagance, and absurd ostentation ; and what both she and Lord Nelson now expected was that the Queen of Naples should make

---

[1] After Lord Nelson's death, though complaining of poverty, she ran deeply into debt with milliners, dressmakers, &c., gave extravagant parties, had horses, carriages, and many servants, while even her petticoats were trimmed with lace which cost five guineas a yard.

good Sir William Hamilton's shortcomings and Nelson's want of fortune by herself pensioning this woman, the wife of one and mistress of both of the men who had certainly been good friends to her.

If Maria Carolina had been in the position she held when first Emma Harte appeared at the court of Naples, it is likely enough she would have done so, for no one could question her generosity and kindness, so constantly displayed and so ill requited. But times had changed since those days of prosperity. The Queen had hardly enough money to provide for her children, carry on the routine of her now retired life and diminished court functions, and help the numerous friends and faithful servants who were in pressing need of assistance. The future was so dark, threatening, and uncertain that she had already been trying to collect certain sums of money belonging to her children and transfer them to a safer country, observing that for herself she had little or nothing, and would be obliged to borrow in order to ensure herself the means of subsistence in a foreign land in case of trouble.

In such a position, therefore, to be expected to pay a pension to provide luxuries for a foreign woman, who had already enough to live upon with much greater comfort than her earlier circumstances or her subsequent conduct gave her any right to expect, was preposterous, and to consider it a grievance that the Queen declined to petition the English Government to pension this person as a favour to herself was surely most unreasonable. She had given her magnificent presents repeatedly when she had the power to do so ; she had loaded her with jewels, money, and costly gifts of every description, and she could do no more, except that she reluctantly consented after much importunity to write a letter to the Neapolitan Ambassador in London, which should be shown to the authorities, expressing her hope that Lady Hamilton's request might be granted. More than this she neither would nor could do, but Lord Nelson, besotted with that passion for Lady Hamilton which was the blot upon his glorious career, could not listen to reason where she was concerned.[1]

[1] It has been the fashion to commiserate Lady Hamilton for her extreme poverty, but besides the fortune left her by Sir William Hamilton, Lord Nelson left her a house at Merton with seventy acres of land, an annuity of £600, and between £25,000 and £30,000 in money. She had, therefore, altogether a house, seventy acres of land, an income of £1,400 a year, and money and property in addition to the amount of more than £30,000. And yet she whined about poverty, and because the Queen did not give her a pension besides, which she could not afford and which was not required, except to indulge extravagant folly, she forgot all the former kindness and generosity of Maria Carolina, and with the base ingratitude of a vain, spiteful, ungovernable woman of her kind, revenged her disappointment by inventing atrocious libels against her benefactress. It was, of course, only after the death of Nelson that she did so In a letter from him after his coolness towards the Queen, in which he finds fault with her, he ends by saying, "Do not believe a syllable the newspapers say, or what you hear. Mankind seems fond of telling lies" (Jeaffreson).

CHAPTER XXII

Threatened dangers—The court of Naples—A fearful earthquake—Le Roi s'amuse—The allied fleet—Surrender of Mack—Trafalgar—Departure of the French Ambassador—Austerlitz—Alarm and perplexity at Naples—Flight of Ferdinando—The Queen and royal family prepare to escape—Farewell to Naples—A perilous voyage—Arrival at Palermo.

THE peace between France and Naples had never given promise of long duration. Both the King and Queen knew perfectly well that Napoleon was only biding his time to attack them; consequently they occupied themselves with plans of defence, which on the 22nd of May, 1804, were confided to Nelson by Ferdinando in the following letter:

"To you, my dear Lord Nelson, I recommend myself again, whatever may occur in case of the renewal of the war. The ship which you leave me becomes more and more necessary in this bay. My wife, son, and I shall divide ourselves. She will take upon herself the defence of Naples, my son of Calabria, and I shall go to Sicily, while the rest of the family will remove to Gaeta."

That Ferdinando had at any rate returned to his old habit of trusting to his wife and placing the heaviest burdens and most weighty affairs upon her shoulders appears evident from this proposal to retire himself to Sicily, leaving the defence of the capital, the most important post and the most immediate danger, to the Queen.

Maria Carolina was quite ready and willing. She was meanwhile occupied by a secret correspondence with several European governments concerning a new combination against France.

England, Austria, Russia, and Sweden were entering into a secret alliance, which was eagerly joined by Naples; and Maria Carolina, sanguine as ever in spite of all the reverses she had met with, again began to feel her hopes and spirits revive.

Outwardly the court of Naples, in spite of want of money, threatening calamities, and secret intrigues, was occupied with amusements and interests of an intellectual and artistic order. The music of Paisello was just then the rage; Cimarosa had died not long after the intervention of the Emperor to save him from the consequences of his political folly.[1]

The excavations at Pompeii and Herculaneum were a perpetual interest; many beautiful works of art were unearthed, besides coins, frescoes, and antiquities of all kinds. Discoveries were being made besides in Sicily, at Pæstum, and in various places. The Queen, her children, and the many foreigners who just then flocked to Naples, took the keenest interest in all this, and were continually

---

[1] Cimarosa composed a hymn for the Parthenopeian Republic. When the royalists regained Naples he was attacked by the mob, his piano thrown out of the window, and he himself arrested, but released at the intercession of the Emperor Paul.

at Pompeii and Herculaneum, watching the progress of the work and listening to the explanations and theories of the professors and learned men who lectured and disputed over the ruins.

Other and less intellectual amusements of course were plentiful: the theatres, *tableaux vivants*, which Lady Hamilton had brought into fashion, balls without end. The King occasionally gave a great ball at the Favorita; every week smaller dances were given by the Queen, the invitations to which were issued in the name of the young Prince of Salerno, and thus being regarded as informal, all ceremony was dispensed with, and the Queen was not obliged to invite persons whose presence she did not desire. She was feeling ill and anxious at this time, was suffering from fever and cramp, and was under the hands of her doctor; but desiring that her children should have all the enjoyment and advantages possible, she encouraged and took part in the festivities and entertainments, which were now a penance rather than a pleasure to her.

The aspect of affairs was too threatening to allow much peace or tranquillity of mind to any except quite young people or else those who, like the King, thought and cared only for the amusements of the moment.

The presence of the French troops in the kingdom was like a perpetual blister, and there was a powerful fleet at Toulon which was a continual menace.

To her daughter the Empress, Maria Carolina wrote sadly that the *fêtes* of the Carnival were without real gaiety, that there was a feeling of suspense in the air, and everybody was inclined to be in low spirits.

Napoleon, whose spies had revealed to him the correspondence going on between the Powers, and who saw that all attempts to flatter and cajole the Queen of Naples were useless, was once more furious against the woman whom, perhaps with truth, he regarded as his most determined enemy.

On January 15, 1815, the French Ambassador asked for an audience, and the King being as usual amusing himself at one of his country palaces, Alquier was received by the Queen with the mutual courtesy which was now customary between their Neapolitan Majesties and the more polished representatives employed by France since the accession of Napoleon to supreme power.

He presented a letter which he said he had been commissioned to give to the King, and which fortunately the Queen did not open until he had left her.

After bitter reproaches for the intrigues discovered, it contained these words: "The moment war breaks out you and your family will have ceased to reign, and your children will wander all over Europe asking for help for their parents. . . ." He observed that she might consider it a compliment to hear such plain warnings from him, "for only to a person of so masculine a character, and who rises so far above the ordinary measure, would I take the trouble to write with such undisguised clearness."

The Queen, however, was very far from seeing anything either complimentary or endurable in this missive. She tore it to pieces, threw it on the ground, walked up and down the room in a transport of rage and excitement, and finally retired to bed with an attack of fever which kept her there for twenty-four hours.

Then she got up and set off to Belvedere to find the King, whom she brought back to Naples; another audience took place, and affairs were patched up for a little longer.

The 13th of June being the anniversary of the recovery of the kingdom of Naples, the royal family went to a service in celebration of that event at the church of Sant' Antonio. The day before, the Prince of Salerno, now fifteen years old, had been confirmed. "He has been in retreat for a week, three days of which of great strictness," writes the Queen to her eldest daughter. "He has been very devout and earnest about his duties. Our brave Cardinal Ruffo was his godfather."

Notwithstanding the Queen's preference for the country, especially during the hot weather, the almost continual absence of the King compelled her to be in Naples much more than she liked. As usual the business of the State was laid upon her shoulders, while Ferdinando was hunting or fishing or farming. Even if obliged to attend to some indispensable matter, he was only impatient to get it over and go back to Belvedere, or whatever palace was the scene of his amusement. The Prince Royal, who much resembled his father in tastes and habits, was of no assistance to his mother in the transaction of business, but was always at his country house at Caserta.

It was the 26th of July, the hottest month of the

burning Italian summer, for the shortening days of August bring relief, and after the violent thunderstorms which generally come towards the end of that month the heat is seldom so overpowering.

During the whole of the day everyone felt an extraordinary lassitude and depression. The heat had been more oppressive than usual; in the afternoon the sky became overcast, the clouds flying rapidly past as if driven by a hurricane, whereas not a breath of air was stirring below, this ominous condition of things being followed after sunset by a furious gale of north wind.

Night came on with no change for the better. The Queen and her children had retired to their apartments in the *Palazzo reale*, when suddenly a fearful shock of earthquake, accompanied by a terrible rumbling noise, shook the city.

The sofa upon which the Queen was sitting was overturned, throwing her on to the ground. Prince Leopold, without shoes or stockings, rushed into his mother's room, and was shortly followed by his sisters, who had gone to bed and had been awakened out of their sleep by the noise and the fearful movement. Springing out of their beds, they had both taken refuge under the archway of a door, where they waited during the first three shocks, watching with fear and trembling the walls, which bowed towards them and seemed about to fall upon them. After the third shock the earth seemed to become steadier, and, hastily putting on some clothes, they hurried to their mother's room, and, escaping as quickly as possible into the open air, they spent the rest of the night in a carriage outside the palace.

The King at Portici and the Prince and Princess Royal at Caserta had the same experience, and, like everyone else, spent the night out of doors.

For six hundred square miles the ground was convulsed, thousands of people were killed, and fifty-nine cities or towns destroyed. The calamity was greatest near the Apennines, where the ground cracked in many places and flames burst forth, Monte Frosolone shone like a fiery meteor, and the air was filled with a suffocating smell of sulphur.

The casualties in Naples itself were not nearly so severe; few persons were either killed or injured, though a good many houses were damaged and some destroyed.

The Princesses were all the more frightened as not long before their apartment in the palace at Portici had been struck by lightning, which had destroyed an embroidery frame in the Princess Amélie's room. They were at church with their mother when it happened. The Princess Amélie was always very much afraid of earthquakes and thunderstorms during the rest of her life.

Shocks of earthquake kept occurring for a considerable time, and after three weeks Vesuvius began to pour forth streams of lava and show various signs of unquietness.

Another treaty between France and Naples was concluded in September and signed on October 9th, but it was to be of short duration. Some writers assert that at the same time another, a secret treaty, was signed at Vienna, by which Naples entered the league of Austria, Russia, and England against France.

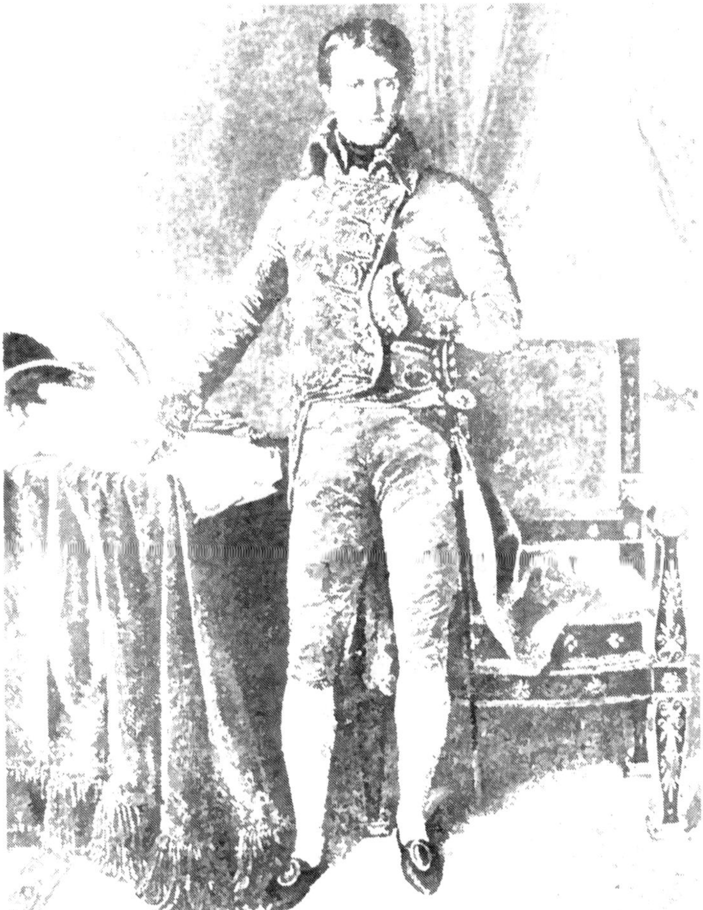

Other historians declare that no such treaty existed,[1] but whether it did or not, there was no possible concealment of the direction in which the sympathies of the greatest part of the Neapolitan people lay.

When he was crowned at Milan, Napoleon had vented his rage against the Queen of Naples in public threats to the Neapolitan Ambassador, declaring that her sons would curse her, and that they should seek in vain for a place for their tombs.

Ten years afterwards, in answer to Napoleon's complaints to his stepdaughter during the Hundred Days, that his first wife, Joséphine, had asked for assistance from the allied powers, Hortense replied:

"My mother had no one to support her but herself in the struggle, when she was involved in the vengeance you had provoked. Was she then not *even to ask to secure a tomb in the place where, after possessing two thrones, she was reduced to fear not to have a refuge where she might die in peace.*"

The tidings of the French victory at Elchingen under Ney, Soult, Marmont, and Murat, with the surrender at Ulm of Mack and his whole army, was at first not known and then not believed at Naples. It was no wonder, for seldom has been experienced by any state a disaster so crushing and so disgraceful. A German army of a hundred thousand men

---

[1] "Ce prétendu traité n'exista jamais. . . . (Il) n'a d'autre fondement qui le bruit populaire et le fait postérieur du débarquement des coalisés. . . C'était un dessein vague, une simple eventualité."—Ulloa.

"Königin Karolina von Neape lund Sicilien im Kampfe gegen die Französische Weltherrschaft" (Helfert).

was hopelessly beaten; sixty thousand prisoners, amongst whom were the Commander-in-chief, twenty-nine generals, and two thousand officers, had fallen into the hands of the conquerors. Those who remember Sedan and Metz will know something of what it meant to the vanquished.

The Archduke Ferdinand, resolved not to be taken, had left the place secretly, and with four squadrons of horse, riding by deserted roads, he endeavoured to elude or surprise the French posts, and succeeded by rapid marches and bold rencounters in effecting his escape with a few followers into Bohemia.[1]

Gradually this crushing blow began to be realised and believed in Naples, but Austria was not their only ally. Still remained the great armies of Russia and the mighty fleet of England, and quickly came the news of a great victory at Trafalgar.

Both the French and Spanish fleets were utterly destroyed, but Nelson was dead.

In England itself the mingled triumph and grief were scarcely more intense than in Naples. The King and Queen were in despair at the death of the great Admiral, their friend and protector, and their sorrow and tears were shared by all the loyal and national party, who began to grumble at the Prime Minister, Medici, allude to the old accusations against him, which were probably unfounded, declare he was half a Jacobin, which was quite untrue, and wish they had Acton back again.

Meanwhile all kinds of reports of French victories

[1] Coletta. Storia del Regno di N.

and alarming events were circulating in the city. No one knew what to believe.

On the 17th of November the King wrote from Belvedere to the Empress of Germany: "I assure you, my dear daughter, that I am in the greatest agitation and perplexity, no news being attainable except what the French wish to be believed, which, in consequence, is entirely in their favour and to their advantage, and would be overwhelming if it were true."[1] The most impatient of the anti-French party began to call upon the government to declare itself decidedly, and to murmur that they would wait until the French appeared and no preparations had been made to resist them.

The crisis, however, arrived when, on the 17th of November, a fleet appeared in the bay of Naples with English and Russian troops on board.

Alquier had already addressed a sharp remonstrance to the government, which had lately allowed a thousand horses for remounts to be sold to the English. He had on the 17th threatened to depart, and the following day sought in vain for an audience with the King and Queen. He now removed the arms of France from the embassy and demanded his passports.

There was dissension in the council; several of the ministers, supported by the Prince Royal, and some said by the King himself, were opposed to

---

[1] "Ti assicuro, figlia cara, che la mia agitazione e angustia è estrema, qui non pervenendo altre notizie che quelle che si vogliono far capitare i Francesi, ed in conseguenza tutte quelle a loro vantaggive e favoreroli, quali se fossero vero sarebbero desolanti" (Helfert).

this undoubted breach of neutrality and of the treaty still in existence with France.

But the opinions of the Queen and her party prevailed; twenty thousand English, Russian, and Montenegrin troops[1] landed, and the French ambassador left Naples.

Everyone crowded to the shore to see the landing of the troops, who were received with all honour by Ferdinando. The Queen was at Portici, the life and soul of the eager consultations held there with the generals; but the scarcity of French news still misled them, and prevented their seeing the pressing danger of the situation.

The King, not knowing what to decide, took refuge, as usual, in hunting; the Prince Royal, who had from the first disapproved of the breach with France, gave free course to his forebodings of evil and regrets that his advice had not been taken.

The Queen, now uneasy and filled with misgivings, moved into Naples to be more in the centre of things, and kept writing to the Emperor and Empress begging them not to forsake them.

"Nous sommes entièrement exposé a la haine de Buonaparte par le debarquement des Anglo-Russes chez nous et dont certainement il cherchera à se venger," she wrote on December 1st, not knowing that they were powerless to protect her, having fled from Vienna, which the French army had entered in triumph.

Soon came the news of Austerlitz, and early in January that of the approach of Massena with a

[1] Six thousand English, two thousand Montenegrin, the rest Russian. (See I., p. 1.)

powerful army. It was the beginning of the end.

Naples was in fact helpless. Even if her fleet had not been destroyed and her army miserably reduced, how could she, without allies, resist the immense armies and victorious generals, with the greatest commander in the world at their head?

For the peace of Presburg with Austria and Russia put an end to any hostile action of those powers against France; the handful of English then at Naples would have been of no use to oppose Masséna and his army, and were therefore of course withdrawn, in spite of the entreaties of the Queen, who was anxious to defend the city to the last, and, dressed in deep mourning, went with her children in procession to the chapel of Sta. Anna on the Chiaja, hoping to excite the warlike and patriotic feelings of the populace.

It was of no use. Ferdinando had already fled to Sicily, the French army was drawing nearer every day, they must escape while there was yet time.

To most people it must appear strange that the Queen, who was so ready for flight in 1798, should have been so anxious on this occasion to remain and defend the capital and kingdom.

For on the former occasion it would have been much more possible to do so, although Nelson himself was of opinion that the royal family should for the time retire from turbulent Naples to loyal Sicily.

But things were not then in such a desperate condition as now. They had still the splendid fleet, so ruthlessly destroyed to save it from the hands of the enemy, the army was in a far better state, and the Parthenopean Republic, which disappeared in a few months, was, even when supported by the troops of the French Jacobins, a very different foe from the mighty conqueror with his array of trained, well-tried generals, and his vast armies of apparently invincible soldiers, whose powerful hands held not only the sceptre of France but the destinies of Europe.

Neither was it exactly with the same feelings that she could have regarded this later and far more powerful enemy. For the Jacobins, the murderers of her sister, her nephew, and her brother-in-law, the ruffians whose deeds were the horror of the Christian and civilised world, she could never have any sentiment but that of execration. But Napoleon had nothing to do with the Jacobins. On the contrary he hated them, if possible, as much as she did. The murder of the King and Queen was abhorrent to him; the very mention of the attack of the mob upon the Tuileries enraged him, and he would often regret that he had not then the power to take the command and turn the guns upon that *canaille*. He had swept away the Jacobins, their institutions and principles, and rejoiced, as he boasted, in "doing away with all their inventions."

But Maria Carolina was never calm or prudent; and it is true that the mean, cowardly subservience of the King of Spain did not save his country from one of the most frightful, devastating wars of modern times. In any case it was too late to avoid the consequences of what had been done;

the only thing now was to make preparations for departure.

Both the Queen and her daughters felt convinced that they were leaving Naples for ever, and their tears could not be restrained as they occupied themselves during the last days with the packing of their possessions. Only the Princess Royal showed no feeling or concern in the disastrous state of affairs.

She had just recovered from a slight illness, and went about as coolly and indifferently as if they had all been preparing for a journey of pleasure, much to the annoyance of the Queen.

"I am writing on the good Mimi's *fête*-day," she says in one of her letters to the Empress. "We spend the days in all the horrors of packing and in tears. I am prepared for anything, but shall endeavour to die without remorse. My daughter-in-law . . . sees all the packing going on and everyone crying, and she is just like a log, understanding and feeling nothing. Her husband is all fire, preparation, honour, and courage, and I pity him. Leopold is also full of enthusiasm, but it can only end in horror."

On the 11th of February, 1806, all was ready, and at four o'clock in the afternoon the Queen, her two daughters, her daughter-in-law, her two granddaughters, and eleven ladies and gentlemen of her court, went on board the Neapolitan frigate *Archimede*, after a heartrending farewell to the Prince Royal and Prince of Salerno, who embarked on the *Minerva*, which was to take them to Calabria to join the army there. They were, as before, escorted by a number of other ships laden with fugitives and property; in fact, the sea was dotted over with sails, as there was a general stampede from Naples, either to follow the Queen to Palermo or to escape elsewhere.

It was with a sorrowful heart that Maria Carolina prepared finally to leave the beautiful capital over which she had reigned ever since she was sixteen years old. When she was on board ship, before giving the signal to sail, she wrote to her eldest daughter her last letter from Naples:

"I am going to a poor country, a country without resources, the air of which does not agree with me. . . . The sacrifice is accomplished; we are on board, and I fear we shall never see Naples again. This thought overwhelms me, it is a dreadful misfortune, a crying injustice, for which I hope God will give us compensation."

The presentiment that they were leaving for ever added tenfold to the bitterness of their farewell. For the last time they went to the chapel of the palace to receive the benediction. "There,' says the Princess Amélie in her journal, "we made a short and sorrowful prayer. Mamma addressed all the court in words full of emotion, there were nothing but tears and sobs. I felt my heart breaking."

As during their former flight, they were overtaken by a violent tempest, owing to which it took them five days to get to Palermo, and it was much worse than the last time, as, although the *Archimede* arrived at last in safety, many of the other ships were scattered and wrecked or driven on shore. The Queen wrote to the Empress

"This weather has made us lose twenty-six vessels of transport which the sea drove on shore at Baja, Naples, and Castellamare; a frigate and corvette of our own, all the artillery and furniture, the entire luggage of nearly all our unfortunate people; the archives of the Foreign Office, all the correspondence, have fallen into the hands of the French."

They were, besides, very short of money. In all the danger and excitement the Princess Royal, who was expecting her confinement in a month, was just as unconcerned and in as good spirits as if nothing was the matter; but on this occasion the Queen regarded her with approval, almost with envy, remarking that she had a tranquil, happy disposition, and that if it had been her own case it would probably have killed her.

CHAPTER XXIII

Palermo again — Discomforts and hardships — Acton — The Princess of the Asturias—Terrible tragedy—Suspicions of poison—The war in Calabria—Fra Diavolo—Agostino Mosca, the brigand—Conspiracies at Naples—An infernal machine—Admiral Collingwood—The Sicilian farm of the Prince Royal—The Princess Royal—Domestic life of the Queen and her children.

AGAIN the Queen and her daughters entered the royal palace of Palermo and with heavy hearts took possession of the rooms so long disused, in which at first they were extremely uncomfortable.

On their former arrival after the disastrous voyage they had been escorted and protected by their powerful English allies, had been welcomed with transports of loyalty in Sicily, and had brought with them riches and luxuries enough to transform any palace, however dilapidated, into an abode of comfort and splendour.

Now, it was very different. A great deal of furniture and necessaries of all kinds had been lost in the wrecked ships; they were obliged, out of what was left, to help their unfortunate attendants, many of whom had lost all or nearly all their things, and they were so short of money that they were forced to dismiss most of their servants because they had not enough to pay their wages.

So diminished was the royal household at first that when the two little princesses, daughters of the Prince Royal, were taken out to walk, their aunts, the Princesses Christine and Amélie, were obliged to stay at home, or else there would not have been people enough left in the apartments in the palace.

In spite of its enchanting scenery, delicious climate, and general picturesqueness, the Queen had never liked Sicily. It was a poor country, she said, in which traces of poverty and misery met you everywhere; the people were in rags, there was nothing to be bought, or if the necessaries and decencies of life were to be got, the prices charged for them were exorbitant. After Naples it seemed sad and gloomy.

The season was an unusually bad one; there was snow in March, and to make matters worse the Queen had something wrong with her eyes which interfered seriously with reading and writing. She shut herself up either in the palace at Palermo or in a royal villa in the country close by, and seldom went out except to church. The Princesses attended the offices of the churches, visited the convents, especially that of the *Cappuccinelle*, made friends with the nuns, did what they could to help the poor, and consoled their mother.

The only members of the royal family who were perfectly happy and comfortable were the Princess Royal, who never troubled herself about anything or anybody, and the King, who thought no more than usual about the affairs of his kingdom, seemed perfectly resigned to the loss of Naples—at any rate for the present—and thoroughly enjoyed the country life and sport in Sicily, which he found entirely to his taste.

He had villas on the shore for his fishing, ancient picturesque castles in the forest where he went for hunting and shooting, and his country house, Colli, near Palermo, where he planted, farmed, gardened, and amused himself to his heart's content.

"Votre cher père se porte bien et sort à chaque peu de beau temps ; vos pauvres sœurs font ma seule compagnie mêlant leurs larmes aux miens et notre douleur ensemble," wrote the Queen soon after their arrival.

Her eyes appear to have recovered after a time, for she wrote as usual to her absent children, especially to the Empress of Germany, to whom she poured out all her anxieties, fears and troubles.

"We have now irretrievably lost the kingdom of Naples, and are in great danger of losing that of Sicily also"; and she went on to say that in that case they would have nowhere to go : Leopold might enter some foreign service, Franz and Isabel could go with their children to Spain, and Theresia must get her sisters, with what jewels and money were left to them, into some noble order (Damenstift). Very likely the King would go to England. As for herself, she would wish to end her days in a cloister. And who would "Buonaparte" place on the throne of Naples ? A Spanish Infant, or "our son," or a "Buonaparte" ?

For more than a month after their arrival in Sicily they had no news whatever from Naples. Not a paper, not a letter; the severity of the French police regulations allowed nothing to pass. Joseph Buonaparte entered Naples, where he was received with glacial submission and secret hatred by the people, but many of the friends loved, trusted, and loaded with kindness by the King and Queen mingled with the courtiers and flatterers of the usurper, amongst others the ever-treacherous Marchesa di San Marco.[1]

If the King and Queen were poorer and less powerful than during their former residence in Sicily, neither were they so popular. They had lost prestige, their government was criticised, and their return to Sicily, instead of bringing trade, employment, money, and prosperity, brought the expense and burden of a war; a crowd of needy Neapolitan officials, courtiers, and people of all sorts, who had to be assisted and have posts found for them, still further impoverishing the island, which was poor enough before, and exciting the jealousy of the Sicilians by the favour and affection shown them by the King and Queen.

And as matters in the royal households became a little more comfortable and decent, Ferdinando and Carolina also became again more extravagant and careless.

The danger of an attack upon Sicily by Buonaparte was of course ever present. But England, resolved that, in her own interests still more than in those of the King and Queen of that country, the great island should not fall into the hands of France, prepared to defend it, and a large body of troops quartered there increased the expenses which;

[1] Or Sammarco.

though unavoidable, fell heavily upon the poverty-stricken inhabitants.

General Craig was occupying Messina, the landing place to be defended in case Calabria should fall; but the island could only be protected by means of a fleet, which was commanded by Admiral Collingwood.

The Queen had tried to persuade him to defend Naples, and in the last extremity had even written to ask for quarter from Napoleon, who had taken no notice of her letter.

Directly the King landed he wrote to Collingwood begging him to come with a powerful fleet to defend Sicily and help to reconquer Naples. Acton also, who had regained all his influence over Ferdinando, was strongly in sympathy with England. The Queen, however, had taken a dislike to Acton, once her friend, minister, and chief supporter : her disagreement with him was now so marked that Kaunitz, in a letter to Vienna, says : " La Reine repugne à se trouver avec Acton." [1]

Months passed away, the Princes were in Calabria with Cardinal Ruffo and the army, the war going on with all the horrors and cruelty of that of 1798.

The unfortunate marriage of her youngest daughter, the Princess of the Asturias, was an additional sorrow to the Queen and the Princesses.

The Princess Amélie especially, who was devoted to her youngest sister, was very unhappy about her, and relates in her journal that one night she saw in a dream the figure of a man wearing the dark robe of a penitent, who approached and

[1] Helfert.

asked for alms in exchange for the prayers about to be offered by the confraternity for the repose of the soul of her sister Antoinette.

The Princess awoke in tears and trembling with fear, and a few days later wrote in her journal: "J'ai failli tomber la face contre terre en lisant dans le *Moniteur de Naples* la mort de ma sœur chérie, de ma bonne amie, de ma tendre compagne, de la moitié de moi-même, de ma chère et bien-aimée Toto" (June, 1806).

They had had no letter from Antoinette herself since the middle of January, which caused them the greatest anxiety, and of which the Queen wrote uneasily to the Empress in April. They had received from time to time letters from Madrid saying that the Princess of the Asturias was ill, and the accounts of her health grew gradually more alarming. In May reports that she had been poisoned had already reached Palermo, and the Queen, beside herself with terror and suspense, did not know what to believe. "I tremble every time I open a newspaper," she wrote to Vienna, "lest I should see a calamity; it is a sorrowful life that I lead." When she read the terrible news in the *Moniteur* she was in her robes of state, about to open Parliament.

"It *cannot* be true!" she exclaimed; "there has been no messenger to announce it from Madrid; or would they have the infamy not to write to me? I am beside myself. I do not live; I am as in a death struggle. The cruel, dreadful uncertainty is worse than anything."

Days, even weeks, passed before the Queen

could be certain of the truth of this catastrophe, of which she was finally convinced by hearing that the Spanish troops and ships in central Italy were in mourning. Even then, such was the enmity of the Spanish court that no announcement was sent to the parents of the Princess of the Asturias, and when six weeks later a Neapolitan *diplomate* came from Spain he brought only a pearl necklace for the Princess Royal, and a box of jewels bearing the names of the other members of the family, but neither letter nor message; the reason given for this unheard-of conduct being that the King and government of Spain did not know by what title to address them!

It was generally believed that the Princess of the Asturias was poisoned at the instigation of the Queen and her infamous favourite, Manuel Godoi, and there would seem to be more probability of the truth of the supposition than can be usually attached to rumours of this kind.

The atrocious character of the Queen and Godoi, and their hatred of the Prince and Princess of the Asturias, of the Neapolitan and Austrian families, made it likely enough. The Duchess d'Abrantès, who was at Madrid at the time, certainly believed it. She speaks in her "Memoires" of the sufferings of the Princess, of the despair of her husband, who never left her night or day, of the impossibility she herself found of getting permission to see her, living or dead; and she goes on to say "Strange rumours were circulated about the illness of the Princess of the Asturias; it was only spoken of with trembling, but in private conversations the terrible word 'poison' was pronounced even by persons most attached to the Queen. . . . At any rate it was the general opinion. Since the accession of Ferdinand VII. I have heard that the apothecary who gave the poison came forward and accused himself; but I was not then in Spain and cannot affirm it. All I can certify is the universal concurrence which prevailed in this opinion." [1]

The Prince of the Asturias was, the Duchesse d'Abrantès says, half mad with grief and despair; but one might have supposed that in that case he would have had the common decency to write to the father and mother of his wife, who were also his uncle and aunt, to inform them of the death of their daughter. The Spanish royal family then existing were the most contemptible of beings.

The war in Calabria meanwhile was carried on with the wildest fury and the most ferocious atrocities. Those writers on the radical and republican side, whether French, English, Italian, or German, while eager to publish, describe, and exaggerate the severities and cruelties of the punishments dealt out with such rigour to the rebels and Jacobins, and to ignore or excuse the crimes they had committed and the untold suffering they had caused, almost invariably draw a veil over the at least equal horrors perpetrated by their own party when they in their turn got the upper hand.

[1] "Mémoires de la Duchesse d'Abrantès."

To any one who reads with attention the history of those transactions of a hundred years ago, in the pages of the writers of different politics and nationalities, the conclusion to be arrived at would appear to be that the only difference between the contending parties was that the royalists, who were supported by the mass of the people, were fighting for their King, their religion, and their native country, while their opponents were supporting a political party obnoxious to most of their compatriots and striving to place their country under a foreign yoke.

But whichever of these aims may appear to one the most worthy, there was no difference in the manner in which they were carried out. In rapacity, unscrupulousness, cruelty, and horrors of all kinds, one side was just as bad as the other. The deeds ordered, authorised, and connived at by the French commanders and their officers would have disgraced a horde of savages. General Colletta, who himself fought for the Jacobins, does not venture to deny the atrocities that went on; in fact, he confesses that he had himself seen a man impaled by order of a French colonel. Old men, women, and children were murdered by the republicans for the crime of having given food or shelter to a father, a son, or a husband; one woman was put to death for having saved a baby of a few days old belonging to a friend, because its father was a brigand. Towns were given over to fire and slaughter; prisoners of war, whose only crime was fidelity to their King and country, were murdered in cold blood.

In July, 1806, the brilliant victory of Maida, gained by Sir Robert Stuart and the English troops over General Reynier with a much larger force, had filled Palermo with exultation. With Calabria loyal and supported by such allies, success would yet attend their arms. But it was a shortlived hope. Great Britain, though resolved to support the King in the possession of Sicily, was not prepared to undertake the conquest of Naples; therefore Sir Robert Stuart, having beaten the Jacobins, thrown garrisons into the chief fortresses, and done his best to encourage the peasantry to fight for the King, was obliged to return with his army to Sicily, and the French regained the ground they had lost.[1]

It was a bitter grief to Maria Carolina, aggravated tenfold by the knowledge that Austria had acknowledged Joseph Buonaparte and sent an ambassador to Naples.

The people, as a rule, hated the French and were loyal to the King, but many of the middle classes and of the nobles had hastened to transfer their allegiance to Joseph Buonaparte, and it was maddening to the Queen to hear of one after another of those who had professed friendship and loyalty and who hastened to desert them.

The Marchesi di San Teodoro and San Gallo,

---

[1] "Storia d' Italia " (Botta); " Maria Karolina, Königin von Neapel und Sicilien, u. s w." (Von Helfert); "Storia del Reame di Napoli" (Colletta); " Queen of Naples and Lord Nelson " (Jeaffreson); "Marie Caroline, Reine des Deux Siciles" (A. Bonnefonds).

ambassadors of Ferdinando to France and Spain, became the ambassadors and ministers of Joseph Buonaparte; many other nobles followed their example, whilst their wives vied in their eagerness to cringe and obtain places in the household of his wife, Julie Clary, daughter of a silk merchant at Marseille, a kind, excellent, very plain woman, hating court life, for which she was absolutely unsuited.

Notwithstanding her failing health and many sorrows, the Queen threw all her energies into the prosecution of the war, and was no more particular than her opponents in the choice of the instruments she made use of.

She sent Fra Diavolo with three hundred convicts released from the galleys to join the army in Calabria, the scene of his birth and early career,[1] and she had also at her disposal other brigand chiefs, to whom remorse and scruples were unknown, ready to avenge her wrongs and recover the inheritance of her children.

Agostino Mosca was one of these, and he lay in wait, fully armed, among the mountains of Gragnano, with the intention of attacking and killing Joseph Buonaparte, who was travelling that way. The plan, however, failed, and Mosca was captured, condemned, and executed. He had a gold bracelet sent him by the Queen, which he wore on his left arm; and a letter from her in his possession, if it did not absolutely prove that she was aware of his intention, looked very like it, more especially as another letter which

[1] Fra Diavolo was at last captured and executed.

he had received from one of her ladies more openly urged him to the commission of the deed.[1]

The anxieties, dangers, and sorrows of late years had told upon the brave, high-spirited, generous, affectionate, but haughty, violent, rash, and imperious nature of Maria Carolina. Restless and unhappy, she clung to the hope of regaining Naples, and her passionate longing to accomplish this grew into a frenzy which shrank from no means by which it could be attained.

Plots and counter-plots went on in Naples and Sicily. The Buonapartist police agents and spies lured the Bourbonists by forged letters and every sort of infamy to take part in pretended conspiracies, and then betrayed them to imprisonment and execution. Death, prison, or confiscation was the lot of all who refused to acknowledge the usurper at Naples, and plots against his life and those of the most cruel and oppressive of his satellites were rife at Palermo.

Early in 1807 the palace of Serracapriola, which was now inhabited by Salicetti, Minister of Police, a bloodstained miscreant, steeped in the worst crimes and cruelties of the Jacobins at Paris and very nearly executed in his own country, was partly blown up by an infernal machine. He, however, escaped without any mortal injuries. Some of the conspirators fled to Sicily and elsewhere, some were taken and executed, among them the son of Viscardi, an old man of seventy-six, who saved his life by betraying his companions, his own son amongst them.

[1] Colletta, Jeaffreson, &c.

Various plots were at the same time discovered, and correspondences with the Queen of Sicily. The plot against Saliceth had been organised at Palermo by certain persons patronised by the Prince of Canosa; whether he actually knew what was intended, or how far the Queen was cognisant of the various plots and conspiracies carried on by her party, it is impossible to say; but even if these schemes, as foolish as they were wicked, had succeeded, they could have done no good. The death of the weak, incapable, but by no means evilly-disposed Joseph Buonaparte could have been of no possible use to the Bourbon cause as long as Napoleon was able to place another of his puppets on the throne of Naples; plenty of ministers equally cruel and equally capable were ready to replace Saliceti; the only person it would have been the least use to kill was Napoleon himself, who, however, always, by the vigilance of his police spies or by a lucky accident, escaped the various attempts projected or made upon his life.

"I suppose you have heard from General Fox," wrote Collingwood to General Sir Henry Dalrymple, "that the court of Sicily is exceedingly impatient to undertake the conquest of Naples. The general, who is wary, and looks at every circumstance with the eye of an experienced soldier, does not approve it, and will not move the troops; in consequence of which . . . they are to conquer Naples . . . without our help."

The Queen's untiring energy and over-sanguine rashness pressed on the policy opposed by Acton, the King, and the Prince Royal, when he returned to Sicily.

A short time previously Kaunitz wrote :

" Le crédit de la Reine remporte presque tous les jours quelques petites victoires sur celui du Général Acton. Cette Princesse combat la dissimulation de ce vieux Politique avec toutes les armes que Son esprit et la droiture de Ses intentions Lui donnent."

Collingwood, on the other hand, says :

"The Queen's party, I understand, now prevails, many of whom are French ; and Sir John Acton, who was considered as the Minister who preserved the King from being led away by the caprices of the Queen and her adherents; and advised him for the true interests of his country, is dismissed from the Ministry."

Thus the exiled court was torn with disputes and hampered with debts and want of money. Collingwood declared that this was a great deal owing to mismanagement, and that if Mount Etna were made of gold they would still be poor. The English Government allowed them £300,000 a year, which was afterwards increased to £400,000, to maintain the court and army ; besides which, in spite of the destitution and hardships of their first arrival, a large amount of specie had been safely transported from Naples to Sicily.

But besides the Queen's incapacity for any methodical or economical management, she spent immense sums on her spies, plots, and secret service ; the expenses of the war were enormous, and so were the sums required to help and often to support the numbers of loyal refugees who had ruined themselves to follow them to Sicily, and whom the Queen—always generous and true to her friends—would not forsake. As usual, she was sometimes imposed upon, but most of them were honest and deserving persons, upon whom she spent far more than upon herself.

The Princes soon returned from Calabria, where they were of no use; and the Prince Royal, Duke of Calabria, established himself and his family in a farm, where he lived contentedly, amusing himself with sport and farming. Both he and his father sold butter and game to any one who wanted it, receiving the money themselves.

"Franz is a thoroughly good man," says the Queen to the Empress; "he bears with resignation what is laid upon us. . . . Isabel spends eight or ten hours a day on horseback, nurses her baby in the day when she is in the humour to do so, but never at night; she lets it cry for ten hours, but it goes on all right. Franz alone looks after the children, for his wife does not love them, but often says she hates children. Is not that rather unnatural in a mother? . . . Franz has a little house near Palermo. . . . I am in the town, where it is very hot. Your good sisters are my only companions; they look after me, stay by my side, and try to comfort me in all the trouble which weighs upon me. God bless and reward them! . . . Leopold is as tall as I am; he has a happy nature: he is very good and studies steadily. . . . He is now almost a man. He is quick, impetuous, but without violence or self-will; he has an excellent heart.

"In this way we live all together; we generally walk or drive in the evenings, and sit round a table to read, work, or write. We have one single theatre, but do not care to go there; I have only been twice in the last three months.

"The environs of the city are pretty. One day we went for a walk which very much reminded me of the road to Maria Zell. I thought you would have liked it."

The monotony of this simple life was now and then broken by a visit from the King in the intervals of wild boar hunting and tunny-fishing, or when the Queen insisted on his coming for some matter of business.

The *fêtes de famille* were always kept, either amongst themselves or now and then in society; as, for instance, on the Queen's birthday, August 13, 1806, a grand *fête* was given by the Prince of Trabbia in the garden of his palace, which amused the young Prince of Salerno and his sisters, but which the Queen could not enjoy, filled as she was with anxiety and care.

The Prince of Salerno was extremely fond of his sisters, and especially devoted to Amélie; these three and their mother clung all the closer together in their fallen fortunes. The King, though on friendly terms with them, still led his usual half wild life by the sea or in the woods, with a mistress and his sport and farming to amuse him and fill up his life. As long as he could do this he was perfectly happy, always said he would some day recover Naples, and meanwhile lived contentedly, his island kingdom protected by the English troops and ships.

His eldest son and daughter-in-law followed his example, and it was a pity that a little of their coolness and philosophy could not have been shared by the Queen, who, with far greater talents and superior qualities, was much more unhappy. But this is usually the case; the people who go through life most happily and comfortably are generally those to whom has not been given the capacity fully and acutely to enjoy, suffer, love, and hate. Could they decide upon their own fate and gifts, few young people would choose these negative qualifications; but after half a century's experience of life they might possibly change their opinion.

CHAPTER XXIV

The Princess Christine and the Duke of Genoa—Their marriage—Death of the Empress of Germany—Despair of the Queen—Sicily threatened—The Queen's letters—The son of Égalité—The love-affairs of Princess Amélie—The King refuses consent—The Princess threatens to take the veil—Her marriage to the Duke of Orléans.

CARLO FELICE, Duke of Genoa, brother of the King of Sardinia, had long been sincerely attached to the Princess Christine, who returned his affection, but was a gentle, submissive sort of character, supposed to have no will but that of her parents; which circumstance is evidently recorded as a compliment by the historian who mentions it. Perhaps the Duke of Genoa may not have regarded it with such satisfaction, but might have preferred that she should have shown a little more of the spirit and resolution which her aunt, the Archduchess Christine, displayed in her love for Albrecht of Saxe-Teschen.

Carlo Felice had not been altogether refused by the King and Queen when they were at Naples, but only told that he was not "at present" a sufficiently good *parti* for the Princess. But as years passed his fortunes improved; he was heir-presumptive to the throne of Sardinia, and was still as devoted as ever to the Princess, whose position was less desirable and more precarious in Sicily than at Naples.

He now renewed his offer, and obtained the consent of the King and Queen to the marriage, which was celebrated at Palermo in the cathedral with all due ceremonial and rejoicings that lasted three days, during which a hundred and ten poor girls were married, also at the cathedral, their dresses and dowries being given them by the Queen. They were afterwards entertained at a dinner in the palace, at which the royal family appeared. The festivities concluded with a drive round the city in carriages lent by the court.

But scarcely were they over when the Queen received what was perhaps the heaviest blow and deepest sorrow of her life. The Empress Theresia died in consequence of a confinement from which she had not fully recovered.

The Queen was broken-hearted, for this, her favourite daughter, had always been her stay and pride; more than all the rest she was bound up with her beloved Austria and the ties and affections of her childhood and of her own race; much older than her remaining daughters, she had for many years been her friend and confidant, and to her powerful protection she looked as a refuge for herself and her remaining children.

Amélie and Leopold removed with her to a house in the country with a garden, in which they spent their days, doing all they could to console her. Christine and her husband, who were living near, came every day to dine with them, and their constant affection helped her to bear her sorrow.

"God has chosen to take from me her upon whom I depended to take my place with my dear children," she wrote to the Emperor. "His holy will be done; but I count with confidence upon your goodness and friendship after my death to give your kindness and protection to my dear children." She goes on to beg for a prayer-book, a crucifix, *anything* that Theresia had used during the last days of her illness.

But either the "kindness" or "protection" of the Emperor Franz was a broken reed to lean upon. He was another of those persons of shallow feeling and obtuse nature upon whom nothing could make a deep impression. As long as the Empress lived he had been happy with her and fond of her; when she was dead he soon forget her, and before many months the news of his engagement to the young and beautiful Ludovica of Modena was a fresh wound to the Queen, who was indignant that her Theresia should be so soon forgotten.

Her letters to the Emperor no longer begin "My dear son and nephew," or "My very dear Son."

Once she writes: "My very dear Son,—Pardon me if for the last time I make use of a name which was so dear to my heart." In future her letters began "Your Majesty," and ended "Your much attached aunt and servant," instead of "Mother" or "Mother-in-law." With apologies she begged for his kindness and care for her grandchildren, hinting that his young wife would have children of her own and would not trouble herself about the first family. However, these fears were unfounded, as Ludovica never had any children.

The Duke and Duchess of Genoa left Palermo at the end of September, 1807, to live at the court of Sardinia.

The Princess Amélie, thus separated from the last remaining of her sisters, had felt an unconquerable depression and dread of being left with only Isabel, who was no use as a companion.

But she used afterwards to say that she found so much consolation in the affection and tenderness of her mother, now that they were thrown entirely upon each other for comfort and sympathy, that the months they passed together at the Queen's country house, Tamastra, were amongst her dearest recollections.

And now also began a time of anxiety and excitement which left no leisure for brooding upon past troubles.

An attack upon Sicily was expected, as Joseph Buonaparte, having successfully defeated the King's armies in Calabria, was now preparing an expedition for the conquest of the island kingdom, which was, in consequence, a scene of commotion and warlike activity.

Reinforcements were sent from Malta to Sir John Stuart, who lay encamped at Melazzo; troops were raised as fast as possible; everywhere they were being armed and drilled. The Prince of Salerno was placed in command of the volunteers, amongst whom were many strangers who had come over to offer their services. Amongst these the Princess Amélie's attention was attracted to a young Hungarian noble, the Baron de Geramb, whose strange and picturesque costume made him conspicuous amongst his comrades. Twenty years afterwards she saw him again in France, where he was *procureur-général* of the order of La Trappe, and had changed his gay, fantastic dress for the austere woollen robe of the Trappists.

The defence of the coast at Palermo was chiefly directed by the Marquis de St.-Clair, a French *emigré* who had long been in the service of the King. The Queen had placed him at the head of the household of the Prince of Salerno at Naples, appointed him his governor, and showed him considerable favour and friendship; which was very natural, as, besides being an *emigré*, he was a capable and excellent man and a faithful friend.

General Colletta, who was not likely to be prejudiced in his favour, says of him:

"Lieutenant-General St. Clair, a Frenchman, who had been an *emigré* in his boyhood, flying from the civil commotions in his country. He had served in the Neapolitan armies, was a favourite at court, and beloved by Queen Carolina of Austria, to whom he was a prudent friend in prosperity and constant in adversity. He was humane, honest, and benevolent, and died beloved and lamented."[1]

But it would have been impossible for Maria Carolina, unless she had led the life of a nun in a convent, to escape from the calumnies invented and circulated by her enemies, from revenge, from political reasons, or from both reasons; and one of the most preposterous accusations brought against her was that of a *liaison* with M. de St.-Clair.

That there was not the slightest shadow of proof

[1] "Storia del Reame di Napoli" (Colletta).

of anything of the kind is needless to say. There never was any sort of proof of any love intrigue whatever with any one of the persons with whom the Queen's name was so slanderously connected; but as the government of the kingdoms was in her hands, it was impossible that she should not be continually associated with ministers, state officials, officers in the army and navy, foreign envoys, &c., and what was easier for those who were anxious to injure her than to say, and to make other people believe, that they were her lovers?

Of her enormous family of children, none were ever supposed to have belonged to any one but the King; but that was because they were all so like him that it would have been no use saying to the contrary. The Bourbon nose, though it may not have been ornamental, may in this case have been useful.

The only reasons advanced in support of the accusations of immorality against the Queen were, in the first place, that she did not love her husband, and, in the second, that she was fond of pleasure and admiration.

But it is by no means true that Maria Carolina did not care for her husband. That she had not for Ferdinando the romantic love of her sister Christine for Albrecht von Saxe-Teschen is unquestionable; and considering that Ferdinando, however much he was in love with her in his way, was habitually unfaithful to her, it would not have been possible. But for all that, and in spite of his infidelity, to which she soon became resigned, she certainly did regard him with affection and consideration. There is apparently only one occasion on which she speaks of a quarrel between them, and that was about Lady Hamilton. In her other letters she writes of him with nothing but affection and consideration. If he was ill, she nursed him with care and anxiety; as far as she could she shared in his pursuits and amusements; the domestic life of the royal family was spoken of with admiration by persons of all nations by whom they were visited.

As to the second reason, if because women are fond of amusement and admiration they are to be supposed to be guilty of immorality and crime, Heaven help them!

To the suggestion of a radical writer who has heard that there were letters and journals of an objectionable kind of Queen Maria Carolina's in the archives of Naples, which were suppressed out of regard to the feelings of the Austrian royal family, one can only say that an assertion which can neither be proved nor disproved is not worthy of being considered evidence. But considering that Maria Carolina had a perfect mania for correspondence, and that an immense amount of letters to and from her still exist, in not one of which there can be found, according to the expression of one of her bitterest enemies, a line that could not be read to a young girl, but all of which, on the contrary, express the most religious, domestic, and moral sentiments, is it credible that those, and those only, which happened to be in the archives of Naples should be absolutely and in all respects the opposite?

If the Queen had been given to writing improprieties they would be found in some of her numerous letters, and would certainly have been eagerly produced and quoted by her enemies.

The slanderous gossip about Acton and Guarini, when the Queen was a young woman in the height of her beauty, however unjust, was not surprising. But the accusations brought against her relations with St.-Clair and with Captain Afflitto, an officer who took the place of the former during a short absence, can only be called monstrous, when one considers that she was then nearly sixty years old, broken in health and spirits, bowed down with grief for the loss of her children, especially suffering from the fearful shocks caused by the death of the Princess of the Asturias and the Empress of Germany, tormented with the wearing pain of neuralgia, injured by the strong doses of opium she took to relieve it, fretting after the loss of Naples, her whole mind and thoughts concentrated upon the means of regaining it and the necessity of protecting Sicily and her remaining children. She had also now lost all trace of beauty, and appeared even older than her age. Her hair was perfectly white, her face lined and worn with care, anxiety, and ill-health, her strength exhausted by the constant strain of her life.

The immediate danger of a French invasion of Sicily passed away in an unexpected manner. The subservience of the Spanish court to France had not availed to preserve the country from the ever-increasing ambition of Napoleon, who was now resolved to place his brother Joseph on the throne of Spain, replacing him at Naples by Murat, the husband of his youngest sister, Caroline. His attention therefore being directed to the conquest of Spain, Sicily was for the present left alone.

The only daughter for whom the Queen still had to provide was the Princess Amélie, and in the following year (1808) a possible and suitable husband for her appeared in the person of Louis Philippe, Duc d'Orléans, who came with some Sardinian officers to Sicily.

In her journal the Princess thus records the first day of their meeting:

"*22nd June.*—Mamma sent for Isabel and me, and presented the Duke of Orléans to us. He is of the ordinary height, rather inclined to be stout, in appearance neither handsome nor ugly. He has the features of the house of Bourbon, and is very polite and well-educated."

It was not an enthusiastic description, but the Sicilian royal family were rather surprised and pleased to find him so unobjectionable, having naturally the strongest prejudice against him.

The Queen especially had the greatest horror of meeting him, and afterwards owned to him that the very sound of his name made her shudder. It was no wonder, for he was the son of the regicide and traitor to his own blood, the bitter and cruel enemy of Marie Antoinette, the infamous "Égalité."

But years had passed since Égalité had met the reward of his crimes upon the scaffold to which he had helped to bring his victims; his son had always regarded with horror the crimes by which his father had disgraced the name of Orléans, and in his long years of exile had abjured the irreligious and republican opinions instilled into his mind in early youth. He was most anxious to be reinstated and forgiven by his relations and connections, and to blot out the remembrance of Égalité and the Jacobins, which still clung to and separated him from the princes of every royal house.

For this purpose nothing could be more effectual than to marry a daughter of the King and Queen of Naples, the bitterest enemies of the Jacobins, the most ardent champions of the *ancien régime*. The Princess Amélie, besides being Bourbon, Habsburg, and the niece of Marie Antoinette, was very sympathetic to him; the King and Queen approved; all went smoothly.

After a few weeks came an interruption to the progress of his love affairs.

The King of Spain had abdicated, and with his son been conveyed by Napoleon to France. The people, rising in insurrection against the French, and having now no princes of their own to lead them, the King of Naples, as nearest of kin, declared himself Regent of Spain, and sent his son—the Prince of Salerno—to Cadiz to represent him.

The Duke of Orléans offered to accompany and look after Leopold, who was only eighteen, and not in the least fitted to conduct so difficult and doubtful an enterprise.

The King and Queen gladly accepted the proposal, and before they went on board the *Thunderer*, which was to take them to Spain, the Duke of Orléans declared his love to the Princess Amélie, who accepted it, and commended her brother to his care.

LOUIS PHILIPPE, DUC D'ORLÉANS,
KING OF FRANCE.
After the painting by Gérard.

The project of the regency was not consented to by the British Government, and the expedition came to nothing. The Duke of Orléans went to England to try to influence the ministers in its favour, but without success. In April, 1809, he returned to Sicily, and found that the King had been prejudiced against him by some of the *emigrés* at the court of Palermo, and would not allow the marriage.

After some difficulty his objections were so far overcome that the Duke of Orléans went to find his mother and obtain her consent, and returned by Malta, bringing with him his sister, Mdlle. d'Orléans, the favourite pupil of the celebrated Mme. de Genlis. The Princess Amélie found in Adélaïde d'Orléans a sister in place of those she had lost—a great additional happiness after the many sorrows of her life.

But still the King tried to put off the marriage, pretending that the treasury was too exhausted to allow of the immediate payment of the dowry of the Princess.

The Duke of Orléans, however, declared that he would not claim it, and the Princess Amélie, who had not the absolute submissiveness of her sister Christine, declared that if the marriage were prevented she would take the veil in the Capucin convent.

When the King heard this he sent for the Princess, and putting his arms round her, asked her with anxious affection whether she really wished so much for this marriage. On hearing that she had set her heart upon it, he withdrew his opposition, and in

October the Duchess of Orléans, her future mother-in-law, arrived at Palermo.

The marriage was celebrated on the 25th of November in the room of the King, who had fallen down the staircase of the palace and hurt his leg. The wedding-party then descended to the chapel of the palace for the *Te Deum* and benediction, after which the Duke and Duchess of Orléans showed themselves to the crowds assembled in their honour.

The King gave them a large and ancient villa named Santa Teresa, which was afterwards known as the *Palazzo d'Orléans*, where, when it was ready for them, they took up their abode, and where in the following year their son, the Duc de Chartres, was born.

The following letters of the Queen of Naples were written about this time. They are in the collection of MSS. of Mr. A. F. Broadley:

"Recevez ma chere Barone dans cette lettre ce que je ne puis jamais assez bien exprimer de vive ce que sont mes Sentimens bien sincères de Recconoissance pour le temps que vous avez passé avec nous et le plaisir avec lequel je vous reverrois toujours je vous souhaite de cœur un heureux et propre voyage, tant de mere que de Terre, et que vous retrouviez vos Enfans couvert de joie et humeur, pour que vous ne nous oubliez, point je vous prie d'accepter nos portraits a nous tous avec les assurances de nos Cœurs Recconoissants une de nous n'est plus dans ce Monde, mais elle priera Dieu pour vous.

Ne m'oubliez point mes vœux et ma pensee vous accompagnera dans ma si chere et bien aimé patrie rapellez moi au Souvenir de ceux qui veulent encore penser a qui leur est si attachee L'honeur et gloire dont le Couvrent mes Braves et chers Compatriotes me Comble de Consolation dites leur bien que unique fille de L'imortelle Marie Therese je partage leurs Sentimens et Gloire ne m'oubliez point et croyez moi jusqu'au tombeau votre recconoissante
"CHARLOTTE."

"Je profite de l'occasion du départ de ma bonne amie la Duchesse de Vienne pour m'informer avec un bien vif et sincère intérêt de votre Santé, comment vous vous Sentez, et coment vous étes content, dépuis votre départ de notre triste file. je n'ai reçus, qu'une seule fois de vos nouvelles, et en ai été penetrés de la plus profonde Recconoissance. L'aimable Duchesse si elle arrivera bien portante, et come je fais bien des vœux pour elle vous pourra doner de mes nouvelles, ma santé est entierement détruite, et je n'ai jamais encore été si afligée que je le suis actuellement : les dernières inconcévables vilanies de ma ci Devant famille et de qui m'appartiens de si près m'a tellement afectée que je ne puis m'en remettre j'ai au moins la satisfaction que malgré les liens si etroits qui nous unissent on rend assez de justice à ma façon de penser, pour n'avoir pas osé m'en écrire un mot ; et mes dernières lettres D'Allemagne sont du 16 Janvier, ainsi fine sais toutes ces infamies, et basses, que par les *Gazettes* ; elles m'ont tellement afectée que j'en suis toute malade, la bonne Duchesse vous pourra parler de ma Santé, qui est très mal réduite de notre position, qui est infiniment triste et de tout ce qui me concerne, Le Roi a été huit mois enfermé, s'etant fait male à un Genoux, actuellement il Comence à marelier, mais avec paine. jugez combien cella l'a ennuyé. Toute ma famille a été incomodé ; ma belle fille est accouchée d'un fils. très à propos, le jour de la naissance du Roi ; Cet Evénement, qui d'autre fois aurait animé L'Entousiasme publique, étant L'héritier du Throne n'a produit aucun effet. Ma fille Amélie est mariée avec le Duc D'Orleans ; est très Contente nous vivons en famille très tristement, attendant encore quel sera notre triste Sort ; vous sentez, que à qui reflechit, *conait tout* cella ne fait pas bon Sang, mais tel est notre triste sort, j'ai le malheur d'être méconus de nos amis, persécuté de nos féroces enemis, et extrémément malheureuses ; ne m'oubliez pas entièrement un souvenir d'un homme de mérite, et de Bien, comme vous. Console quand on est aussi malheureux, come je le suis. adieu ; donez moi de vos nouvelles quand vous le pouvez, sans vous compromettre ; defendez moi vous ne ferez, que rendre justice à une qui prise plus l'honeur que la vie, et qui ne vacillera jamais dans Ses principes. Je suis mère de famille, j'ai les droits de mon mari et Enfans à Soutenir, et c'est un devoir sacrée pour moi, mais quand on pense ainsi ou peut compter sur de pareils caractères, qui ne se deshonoreront jamais, et on doit leur rendre justice voila ce que j'osé dire à un ami comme vous. Adieu, ne m'oubliez point et envoyez moi de loin, ou de près heureuse ou malheureuse, votre sincère Récconoissante

" CHARLOTTE."

" le 24 Avril, 1810.

"Je vous prie de faire bien mes Complimens et me rapeller au Souvenir de la bonne Md. Drummond et de Lapinet de mon bien récconoissant souvenir."

CHAPTER XXV

"My grandmother the Queen of Sicily"—Obstinacy of Maria Carolina—The Duke and Duchess of Orléans—Illness of the Queen—Troubles and difficulties—Lord William Bentinck—Renewed troubles—The Queen leaves Palermo—The King agrees to the regency of the Prince Royal and retires to the country—A last attempt—Return of the King—Failure—Farewell to Sicily.

THE marriage of the Queen's eldest granddaughter, the Archduchess Marie Louise of Austria, with her arch-enemy Napoleon, in 1810, whatever might be the shock it was likely to cause the Queen, was in fact an advantage to her.

The Emperor Napoleon, in spite of the exalted position to which he had raised himself and the vast power and riches he had won by his sword and his genius, had never been satisfied until he allied himself with those ancient families amongst whose members he had found so many of his puppets and victims.

Transported with delight that his children would now be the grandchildren, nephews, nieces, and cousins of most of the sovereigns and royalties in Europe, and that he himself could now talk, as he loved to do, of his "poor uncle, Louis XVI.," and his "aunt, the Queen, Marie Antoinette," he was enchanted with the young Archduchess to whom he owed this crowning satisfaction, and eager to please and indulge her. And when she begged him not to allow her grandmother to be any further molested, his inclination to grant a request which was inspired, not by political reasons, for which she cared nothing, but by family affection, may not have been uninfluenced by the fact that his arch-enemy was now his "grandmother, the Queen of Sicily."[1] At any rate he would not allow Murat to invade that island, much to his displeasure.

It is a melancholy reflection that if only the Queen would have taken care of her health, lived quietly at Palermo for a very few years longer, and so far yielded to the necessities of the circumstances and the requirements of the times in which she lived as to agree to the constitution desired by the Sicilians, she would have regained all she had lost and returned in triumph to Naples. But she would do nothing of the kind. The very name of a constitution was abhorrent to her; the slightest and most reasonable concession to liberal ideas was a weakness and a danger, if not a disgrace.

The detestation and contempt she had always felt for the feebleness and vacillation of Louis XVI. had led her into the opposite extreme; the reasonable reforms called for by the Sicilians and supported by the English, who had been her constant friends and protectors, were as obnoxious and impossible

---

[1] In a letter to Savary, July 2, 1813, Napoleon: "I told you to have everything published in the *Moniteur* which appeared in the English papers about their proceedings in Sicily . . . amongst others of their violence against Queen Caroline, whom they have sent to Constantinople" (Helfert).

to her as if they had been the frantic demands of the Jacobins.

The ancient laws of Sicily gave her parliament control over the taxes, and when that body assembled, the Princes di Cassera and Belmonte-Vintimiglia were deputed to represent to the sovereigns two perfectly legitimate grievances; one being that all the important posts in Sicily were bestowed upon Neapolitans, to the great hardship and discontent of the natives of the island, the other that the taxes laid upon them were so heavy and so exorbitant that they were impossible to be borne by so poor a country.

The Queen not only turned a deaf ear to these remonstrances, but, indignant at meeting with opposition, resolved to get the money without the assistance of parliament, and in order to do so levied a tax of one per cent. upon all sales, and put a number of ecclesiastical benefices into the lottery; and when the barons protested against these illegal measures, arrested the Prince of Belmonte and four other leaders of the party of the barons.

The Duke of Orléans, to her great indignation, took the side of the barons; and the Duchess of Orléans, in a painful position between her mother and her husband, agreeing with the latter and deploring the despotic government and violence of the former, tried to mediate between them, at first with so little success that it was rumoured that the Duke was to be arrested also.

Prince Belmonte was a deadly enemy of the Prime Minister, Medici, and a great friend of the Duke of Orléans, who, when this quarrel arose, was commanded by the King to discontinue any intercourse with him. Lord Amherst, the English Ambassador, expostulated with the Queen, pointing out the impossibility that England could permit a country protected by their arms and supported by their money to be plunged into the disorders of a revolution.

Self-willed and unable to comprehend the uselessness of resistance, the impossibility of her plans, and the folly of quarrelling with her sole and powerful allies, Maria Carolina fell into a frenzy of rage and despair which lasted for several days, during which she either gave vent to denunciations and wild lamentations, or, exhausted by the violence of her emotions, sank into an apathetic gloom and misery which terrified everyone, especially her daughter, the Duchess of Orléans. Their alarm was necessarily heightened by the ever-increasing effect of the opium which she had for some time taken to relieve neuralgia, and in July, 1811, the news spread through Palermo that the Queen was lying between life and death, prostrated by a fit of apoplexy. After being unconscious for twenty-four hours she slowly recovered, and if she had been a woman in any other rank she would henceforth have been considered, if not an invalid, a person whose health was the first consideration, and for whom rest, quiet, and a peaceful life, with freedom from anxiety and care, were of the first necessity. Maria Carolina, on the contrary, was no sooner in some measure restored to health than she resumed her usual occupations, and plunged again into the vortex of strife, turmoil, and confusion of Sicilian affairs.

The visit of her daughter Christine, who, with her husband, the Duke of Genoa, came to Palermo to see her, was one of the few peaceful enjoyments left to her.

Even amongst her children the differences of opinion, although they did not destroy their affection, disturbed its harmony and peace. Christine was, of course, not concerned in the political affairs of her parents' kingdom, but the Prince Royal and the Duke of Orléans sided with the barons and the English. Amélie agreed with them, though she tried not to oppose her parents more than she could help. Leopold entirely took the part of his father and mother.

The expense of the army of spies maintained by the Queen was enormous; her incapacity for economy, and, it must also be said, her charity and generosity, were just the same as ever.

At her wits' end to find money, she entered into a secret arrangement with a certain Castroni, who was her chief commissioner for spies, and owner of a fleet of thirty privateers, with which he harassed the mercantile marine of France, of Murat, and of the other foes of the King and Queen of Sicily, that part of the profits of every prize taken should be received by herself.

It happened, however, that, amongst others, one of these privateers seized an English ship, and made considerable difficulties when required to give her up. It was declared not to be the first time this had happened. There was a great commotion; the Queen's interest in the enterprise was discovered, and a quarrel between her and

Lord Amherst was followed by his recall to England.

It was asserted that Maria Carolina, in her anger and desperation, having not only lost all hope of reconquering Naples by the aid of the English but found that they were bent on interfering in the government of Sicily itself, began a secret correspondence with the Emperor Napoleon, offering to help him to gain possession of Sicily if he could reinstate her husband at Naples.[1]

Affairs in Sicily went from bad to worse. Another parliament had been summoned, and was equally resolved to refuse the supplies demanded. The Queen, on the other hand, was equally determined to have her own way; the King was, in all political matters, guided by her. The troops were clamouring for their arrears and on the brink of mutiny, for there was no money to pay them.

In this state was Sicily found by Lord Valentia, who was sent out from England to report on the condition of affairs. The necessity for immediate reform was evident, and so were the obstinate folly of the Queen and the impracticability of her plans, but he believed and repeated as facts all the atrocious lies and cruel slanders first invented and circulated against her for their own purposes by the Jacobins, then by Napoleon, and now by the party of the barons, who also saw in her their arch-enemy, and strove to blacken her character and enlist the sympathy of the English against her.

They succeeded perfectly, and some of the most

[1] This, however, was disbelieved by Lord William Bentinck, and denied absolutely by the Queen herself.

shocking and absurd statements published against her were believed on his authority, of which the most outrageous were not only morally but physically impossible in a woman bowed down with sorrow, broken in health, and still suffering from the effects of paralysis, of the terrible neuralgic pain, and of the opium she took daily to mitigate it.

She was, in fact, a prematurely old and shattered woman, who, from the causes just mentioned, was often scarcely responsible for her actions, especially for the bursts of ungovernable fury which were the unavoidable consequences; but that such a person should be the object of a love intrigue would be a supposition too ridiculous to be entertained, even supposing there had been any proof of immorality in her earlier life.

Temperate as she had ever been in food, taking scarcely any wine, but daily doses of opium, Maria Carolina, whose health had been failing for the last five years, was now pale, emaciated, and melancholy, only roused by the proud, restless, indomitable spirit which neither sorrow nor illness could subdue, and which still defied the barons and held the King under her sway.

When it was known that Lord William Bentinck was appointed English Ambassador to Naples, the Queen, alarmed at what she had heard of his despotic character and unbending resolution, exclaimed in consternation:

"They are sending us a viceroy, not an ambassador!" to which Ferdinando replied with a laugh: "What difference does it make to me and my subjects ? We shall only have a master instead of a mistress to manage us."

Of Ferdinando, in spite of his cruelties at Naples, the open, outrageous immorality and selfishness of his life, and his utter neglect of his government, his people, and in fact of everything but his amusements, Lord Valentia and others speak with liking and praise. His faults were laid upon the Queen, the good she did was attributed to him—such is human justice.

Respecting the new English ambassador the worst misgivings of the Queen were realised. He went out to Colli to see the King, who was there, as usual, perfectly happy with his mistress, his farm, and his sport, and with whom he got on very well.

He had an interview with the Queen, in which he informed her that he had been sent out to support the cause of the barons and demand the immediate release of those imprisoned and the repeal of the illegal edicts levying taxes.

It is not surprising that the Queen asked, with astonished indignation, what he meant by speaking as if he were King of Sicily.

Lord William Bentinck replied that he was certainly exceeding his instructions, but that, as it was a choice between a more liberal constitution and a revolution, he would return to England for larger powers to enforce what, in his opinion, was absolutely necessary in the situation; after which he took his leave and sailed from Sicily.

The King was resolved not to quarrel with England, but Maria Carolina, exasperated and unconvinced, was irritated at the attitude of the Duke of Orléans, whose melancholy reserve expressed his opinion in a manner which made her exclaim to her daughter, "Since I committed the folly of taking him for my son-in-law, I must put up with him as your husband and the father of your child. But he ought to realise that legitimate authority is always successful, and that to it one must remain attached."

She shed indignant tears as she related to her daughter the particulars of her interview with Lord William Bentinck, and growing more and more excited when she heard that he had sailed, she broke into imprecations against the English, declaring that sooner than yield to their demands she would seek the protection of Napoleon or throw herself into the power of Murat, even if it cost her life.[1]

In three months Bentinck came back again, armed with full authority to act as he thought best, and the course he chose to take was one intolerable to the Queen, and also to the King, who supported her. Even then Maria Carolina might have saved the situation by recognising the inevitable and accepting the new constitution, the reforms of which were most necessary, and which contained nothing derogatory to the dignity of the Sovereign, but was only modelled after that of England. And even if it had been objectionable, she had no power to resist, and her doing so could only make matters worse.

However, she did refuse to listen to reason, upon which the ambassador proceeded to threats,

[1] "Vie de Marie Amélie, Reine des Français" (Auguste Trognon).

FERDINANDO IV., KING OF THE TWO SICILIES.
From an original water-colour given by Queen Maria Carolina to Sir Thomas Hardy, and now in the possession of Mr. Hardy Manfield.

which, unlike her own, he had power to carry out.

If it became expedient he would send the King and Queen to England, and place the little son of the Prince Royal, then two years old, upon the throne, under the regency of the Duke of Orléans and Prince Belmonte.

The Queen replied that she would resist by force of arms, to which he answered that he had the power to suspend the British subsidy of four hundred thousand pounds.

There was no more to be said. The Queen left Palermo and retired to one of her country houses in the neighbourhood, leaving the King to make what terms he could.

The following deed of appointment was the result:

"Ferdinando IV. of Naples and Sicily to his son Francesco, Hereditary Prince.

"My most esteemed son Francis, Hereditary Prince of the Two Sicilies,—Being obliged through indisposition and from the advice of the Physicians to breathe the air of the country and to withdraw myself from all serious application . . . I constitute and appoint you my Vicar-General in this my Kingdom of Sicily in the same way as you have been already twice Vicar-General in my Kingdom of Naples; and I yield and transfer to you with the ample title of 'Alter Ego' the exercise of all the rights, prerogatives, pre-eminences and powers which could be exercised by myself. . . .

"Given at Palermo this 16th day of January, 1812."

It was privately understood between Ferdinando and Bentinck that this indisposition should continue as long as it was supposed to be for the English and Sicilian interest; and as the Prince Royal was not in the least under the influence of his mother, her power would be at an end.

Everything was now in the hands of Lord William Bentinck, who proceeded to arrange the affairs of Sicily in imitation of England. It was endowed with a House of Lords, a House of Commons, responsible ministers, independent judges, and a constitution as like the English one as could be framed for the occasion. All sorts of necessary reforms were made, and Ferdinando remained quite happily in the country amusing himself; while Maria Carolina fretted and raved in her enforced retreat, brooding over her wrongs and troubles, and waiting for an opportunity to escape from her present intolerable position.

How far the new English constitution was popular in Sicily, how long it gave promise of lasting, how long the Sicilians would have borne the yoke of England, are not questions to be entered into in a book of this kind; neither are the quarrels and intrigues of the barons, for the prosecution of which they made use of the various transactions and commotions in the revolution going on. How Belmonte hated Medici and cajoled, flattered, and laughed at Bentinck—in fact, the whole tangled mass of plots, quarrels, reforms, misrepresentations, public professions, and private interests of this period, would be far too long and too tedious to relate.

The Prince of Salerno, in opposition to the

English party, his brother and brother-in-law, remained either with his father or his mother, and the Queen was secretly exercising her still powerful influence over the King to counteract the proceedings of their enemies.

The English constitution was not popular with the Sicilians, who hated foreigners and declared that the state of famine prevailing in the island was caused by them. The overbearing manners of Bentinck made him disliked.

One day the King suddenly re-appeared in Palermo, announced that his indisposition was cured, ordered a *Te Deum* to be sung, and prepared to reassume the government. But it was useless: the English troops were in possession. Bentinck sent the Duke of Orléans to the King with remonstrances and threats; Ferdinando yielded, countermanded the *Te Deum*, and returned to his hunting at La Favorita, five miles from Palermo.

The Queen took refuge in a castle in the mountains, where she prepared to defend herself with a guard of eight hundred peasants, providing for the subsistence of her garrison by pawning her jewels. But this, of course, could not last long. Besieged in her rocky fortress by the English troops with cannon, she surrendered, and retired to a palace, where, virtually a prisoner, though treated with all outward forms of respect and ceremony, she passed the last months of her Sicilian life.

However one may recognise the faults, follies, and errors of the Queen, and deplore the infatuated obstinacy with which she refused all advice or concession, persisted in following her own way, quarrelled with or alienated her friends and ruined her life, one cannot but see that her lot was an unusually hard one.

Sicily was now in the hands of the English, as Naples had been in those of the French; and although they were neither guilty of cruelty or bloodshed, did not attempt to exclude the royal family from the throne or deprive them of their property, or in any way oppress the people, still the fact remained that it was Lord William Bentinck, not King Ferdinando or Queen Maria Carolina, who was now the ruler of Sicily, and after her last rash and futile attempt at resistance had failed, her sentence of exile from her own kingdom was passed by the foreigner, representing the allied and friendly power to whom she had hitherto looked for protection.

Even now her power over the king would prevail, and as long as she remained in the island the new government and policy would never be safe; and Bentinck, in constant fear of her influence and hostility, insisted on her retirement to Austria. To this, however, Ferdinando would not consent, and for a long time he persisted in his refusal, which was only extorted at last by threats. At length he was induced reluctantly to sign the order for her departure—"*Come amico te lo consiglio, come marito te lo demando, come Re te lo commando.*"

On the 15th of June, 1813, Maria Carolina, accompanied by her youngest and dearest son, sailed from the shores of that lovely island which had been the scene of so many sorrows, and turned her steps towards her native land.

CHAPTER XXVI

Departure from Palermo—The Queen's journey with Prince Leopold—The Marchesa Solari—Sad recollections—Arrival in Austria—The castle of Hetzenberg—Fall of the Emperor Napoleon—Arrival of the Empress Marie Louise—Her affection for her grandmother, the Queen of Naples—The King of Rome—The Queen's love for him—King Ferdinando orders the *Minerva* to fetch back the Queen and Prince Leopold—Death of the Queen.

IN spite of the curious terms on which the King and Queen of Naples had of late been living, Ferdinando did not wish Maria Carolina to go. He had refused his consent to her departure until it had been forced from him, and when he could not help himself he wrote to the Emperor Franz, begging him to receive his wife and son, "for reasons very displeasing [to me], my most dear wife being obliged to leave this kingdom . . . to avoid greater misfortunes to us both."[1]

The Duchess of Orléans also wrote commending to the Emperor's care the mother "whose departure plunges me into the deepest affliction."[2]

[1] "Per ragioni ben dispiacevoli essendo costretta l' amatissima mia moglie ad allontanarsi da questo Regno . . . per evitare ad entrambi maggiori dispiaceri. . . ."
[2] "Dont le départ me plonge dans la plus vive et la plus juste affliction."

Many of the people who disliked the English complained loudly and vehemently of the departure of the Queen, who was exceedingly charitable and kind to them; in fact, directly she was gone there was a riot.

Maria Carolina and her son slowly and leisurely pursued their journey, taking precautions to avoid meeting the ships of the enemy, and stopping at one place after another on their route.

They spent some time in Sardinia with the young newly-married Ferdinand and Marie Beatrix of Este, and then sailed to Zante, where they also stayed.

While she was in that lovely island the Queen received a visit from the Marchesa Solari, the faithful and devoted servant and friend of Marie Antoinette. Eighteen years had passed since the Marchesa had come to her at Naples to bring her the last news of her murdered sister.

Then, although bowed down with grief and horror at that fearful tragedy, she was in her immediate surroundings powerful and prosperous, still beautiful, honoured, and flattered, with her children around her in her brilliant capital, ruling over her husband, her court, and her two kingdoms. Now, a wandering, broken-hearted exile, separated from her husband and all her remaining children but one, with no trace of her former beauty, her spirits and health shattered, she would not allow the Marchesa to kneel and kiss her hand.

"No!" she exclaimed; "it would now be a mockery and an insult to my present condition. The daughter of Maria Theresa, a wanderer and an outcast, must no longer receive the mark of distinction which were the right of the Queen of Naples. You see me now in a very different position from that in which you found me when you brought me the letters of my dear murdered sister."

When the Marchesa expressed the hope that her Majesty would return after a time to her husband and children in Sicily, she answered:

"Never! never! I shall be one of the few Queens who end their days in the place which gave them birth. I pardon Lord William, as I do all my enemies. Not only England but all Europe will one day do me justice."

During the course of their long conversation she had, however, spoken with bitter indignation of Lord William Bentinck and the treatment she had experienced from him.

"I have been deprived of the government of my own country, of the dignity of my character, of the affection of my husband and children! But *he* has never been a father—*he* has never been a sovereign, and cannot therefore have the feelings of insulted majesty. And then I am accused of treason because I wish to recover my just rights as a sovereign, a wife, and a mother."

She would talk often of her past life, and once remarked sadly:

"For a long time I have believed that I knew how to govern, and I have only found out my mistake when it was too late. In order to rule men wisely one should study and understand them; this I did not do. If ever God should restore me to the throne, I will begin a new life."

She always took with her and kept in her room the family portraits she loved, amongst them those of Marie Antoinette and her husband. The fan she used had on it pictures of Naples and Palermo.

After leaving Zante, the royal travellers were delayed by various reasons—by storms, by the obstacles to the entrance of the Sicilian ships into the Bosphorus, and by the plague at Constantinople, where they remained for a considerable time.

It was not until nearly Christmas, in all the rigour of wintry weather, that they arrived at Vienna, where they were received with due honour, and where the royal castle of Ofen had been prepared for their residence.

As the Queen wished to be nearer to her grandchildren, this castle was exchanged for that of Hetzenberg.

The castle of Hetzenberg was a pleasant, stately home, the most peaceful refuge that could have been found under the circumstances for the sad and weary woman who had fled to the shelter of the beloved scenes of her childhood. Prince Leopold, who had always loved his mother with devoted affection, was now her chief support and comfort. To him the Austrian castle was home as long as it was inhabited by her, and the society of her grandchildren was also a pleasure and interest to her. She seldom went into Vienna, but remained nearly always in her country house, which was not far from Schönbrunn.

To her daughter Christine, afterwards Queen of Sardinia, she wrote in a melancholy vein:

VIENNA.

"Rien ne me touche plus sur la terre; mon sort a été jugé et decidé le jour où j'ai été chassée comme une femme de théatre, et jetée hors de la Sicile. . . . Ma vie est terminée en ce monde. . . . Je ne suis plus un objet d'intérêt que pour quelques vieilles femmes qui ne sortent jamais de chez elles, et qui sortent pour voir le dernier des enfants de la grande Marie Thérèse. . . . Le Prater est dans son beau vert, tout en fleurs, mais il n'y a plus rien de beau pour moi."[1]

A new and unexpected interest was, however, even now to arise for her, and to give a certain amount of comfort and occupation to her thoughts in these last days.

The events of the early part of 1814 had been watched from her Austrian refuge by the exiled Queen, who must have often reflected with bitter regret that the combination of allied powers, had it been as successful more than twenty years ago, would have saved her sister from death and herself from ruin.

The victories of the allies, the fall of the Empire, and the captivity of Napoleon followed in rapid succession; and now Marie Louise, the wife of her arch-enemy but the child of her favourite daughter, came, like herself, to take refuge in the home of her childhood and at the court of her father.

And far better than father, brothers, sisters, or friends the banished Empress loved the grandmother whose warm heart, high spirit, and strong

[1] Journal manuscrit de la reine Marie Caroline, adressé à sa fille la Duchesse de Genevois, plus tard Reine de Sardaigne.—"Vie de Marie Amélie, &c." (Trognon).

affections formed the most complete contrast to her own cold, apathetic nature.

It often happens that opposite dispositions attract each other; and Marie Louise turned from all her family to the grandmother who, while she loved her and saw in her only her own granddaughter and her Teresa's child, did not hesitate to say what she thought, and to express in no doubtful terms her disapproval of the conduct of the young Empress during the late and present circumstances.

To Maria Carolina, who, in spite of all his faults and infidelities, had stood bravely and faithfully by Ferdinando to the utmost of her power, it was inconceivable that Marie Louise should not have followed her husband into exile; and she indignantly declared that, rather than consent to the separation, the Empress should, if there were no other means of escape, have tied her bed-curtains together and let herself down from her window to join him. "At least, that is what I should have done in her place, for when one is married it is for life."

Of Napoleon she spoke with the generosity of a brave nature to a fallen enemy.

"I had much to complain of from the Emperor in former years," she said one day to a French gentleman of her granddaughter's household. "He persecuted me and wounded me in my most sacred feelings. I was ten years younger then, but now that he is in adversity all that shall be forgotten."

She reproached her granddaughter also that she shrank from mentioning her husband's name to her father, or from having his portrait in her rooms; in consequence of which Marie Louise, with whom her grandmother had more influence than any one else, got out the portrait of Napoleon and put it upon her writing-table.

The little child, lately King of Rome, afterwards Duke de Reichstadt, she adored. He was her only great-grandchild, and from the first he was devoted to her, and she never tired of caressing and indulging him, regarding him with mingled compassion and foreboding, which his melancholy life and early death amply fulfilled.

For the Queen there seemed now better hopes for a brighter future. There had been a talk of the Duke and Duchess of Orléans coming to Vienna, where, the Duchess wrote, she hoped to see her dear mother and brother; and as the Emperor wished to see the Princess Carolina, daughter of the Prince Royal of Naples by his first wife, the Archduchess Clementine, she was to come also.

The Congress was sitting at Vienna; Ferdinando was again supreme in Sicily, and already the *Minerva* was to sail for Trieste to bring back the Queen and the Prince of Salerno.

But it was too late.

On the 7th of September, 1814, the Queen had retired to bed apparently in no worse health than usual: on the morning of the 8th her women, going into her room, found her lying dead with her hand stretched out as if to ring the bell, having again been struck by apoplexy.

It was by some attributed to her grief on learning, the evening before, that the allies proposed to allow

Murat to remain in possession of Naples; but this is uncertain.

A little longer and she would have lived to see the death of Murat and to enter Naples with her husband and sons, but it was not to be; the brilliant, changeful, stormy life was over, and the wearied, restless spirit had passed away. Shortly after her death Ferdinando married his mistress, Lucia Migliaccio, widow of the Prince of Partanna.

To those who unjustly attribute the cruelties of Ferdinando to the influence of Maria Carolina, it may be pointed out that it was when she was away from him that all his worst cruelties were perpetrated.

It was during her absence in Sicily and in Austria that the horrors of the trials and executions were committed in Naples; and when, after the death of the Queen, the Two Sicilies were restored to Ferdinando, he was a far worse man and a more cruel and tyrannical ruler than he had ever been during the life and influence of the sister of Marie Antoinette, the last remaining daughter of the great Empress.

INDEX

Acton, Sir John, Prime Minister of Ferdinando IV., King of Naples and Sicily, 101–104, 117, 144, 160, 161, 163–165, 168, 176, 185, 209, 223, 225, 311, 338, 343, 346, 357, 391

Albrecht, Duke of Saxe-Teschen, son of Augustus the Strong, King of Poland, 21, 40, 43, 99, 107, 137, 327

Amalie, Archduchess of Austria, Duchess of Parma, 10, 28, 57; betrothal and marriage to Duke of Parma, 60–62; visit of Emperor Joseph, 79, 80; unhappy married life, 85, 86; Mme. Le Brun, 119

Amélie, Princess of Naples, afterwards Queen of France, wife of Louis Philippe, daughter of Ferdinando IV.: birth and early years, 115, 116, 197; studies and superior talents, 198; affection for her father, 200, impression caused by the murder of her aunt, Marie Antoinette, 202; her governess, 202, 233; flight to Sicily, 257; life at Palermo, 264; to Vienna, 314; life at Vienna, 325–331; the Archduke Anton, 332; horror of a Spanish marriage, 333; Naples, 336; grief at the marriage of Princess Antoinette, 338; her sister-in-law, 341; projects of marriage, 341; earthquake, 366–368; second escape to Sicily, 376–377; hardships, 378–381; alarm about the Princess of the Asturias, 383; life near Palermo, 392–393; domestic sorrows, 376–378; the Duke of Orléans, 403; her engagement to him, 404–405; marriage, 406; difficult position, 412; sorrow at her mother's departure, 421

Antoinette (Marie Antoinette), Archduchess of Austria, wife of Louis XVI., 10, 28, 54, 56,

67, 86, 103; project of marrying the first Dauphin to Princess Amélie of Naples, 114; Marie Antoinette proud of her superior position to those of her sisters, 116, 117; eve of the Revolution, 118; failure of opportunities of escape, 129-131; imprudence of Marie Antoinette, 132; the *nécessaire de voyage*, 133, 134; Varennes, 135, 136; attempt to save Marie Antoinette, 171; her death, 200

Artois, Charles, Comte d', afterwards Charles X, King of France, 128, 137

Asturias, Antoinette, Princess of Naples, wife of Fernando, Prince of the Asturias, 115, 314; betrothal to the Prince of the Asturias, 332; marriage, 337-339; unhappy life, 340-352, 383-385; death of the Princess of the Asturias, 385

Baccini &c., conspiracy of, 272-275, 305

Caracciolo, Prince, 255-258, 269-269

Carl, Archduke of Austria, son of Emperor François and Empress Maria Theresa, 16; favourite son of Emperor and Empress, 18, 19, 23; betrothed to Ludovica of Spain, 29; his death, 30, 31

Carl VI, Emperor of Germany, 2-5, 8

Carlos III, King of Spain, 59, 60, 73, 74, 99, 111, 112, 117

Carlos IV, King of Spain, 112-114, 339, 343, 353

Caserta, 71, 82, 90-91, 99, 115

Christine, Archduchess of Austria, Governess of the Netherlands, wife of Albrecht, Duke of Saxe-Teschen, 10; favourite daughter of the Emperor and Empress, François and Maria Theresa, 18, 19; romantic love for Albrecht von Saxe-Teschen, 21, 22; friendship with Isabella of Parma, 32-36; Governess of Hungary, 43-44, 137; visits her sister at Naples, 107-108, 228; her death, 264

Christine, Princess of Naples, afterwards Queen of Sardinia, wife of Carlo Felice, Duke of Genoa, King of Sardinia, 107, 108, 264; the Duc de Berri wishes to marry her, 314; sails for Livorno, 315; Vienna, 314-325; Naples, 330; projects of marriage — the Duke of Genoa, the Grand duke Ferdinand, 353, 354, 367, 375-379; marries the Duke of Genoa, 395-396; sails for Sardinia, 398, 412

Elisabeth of Würtemberg, wife of Emperor Carl VI, 5, 10, 28

INDEX

Elisabeth, Archduchess of Austria, Abbess of Innsbruck: beauty and liveliness, 22; dislike to being Abbess, 23, 40; failure of marriages proposed, 41; her beauty destroyed by small-pox, 45, 122, 325

Elisabeth, Madame, sister of Louis XVI., 128–131; Varennes, 135, 136, 171

FERDINAND, Archduke of Austria, Duke of Modena, 10, 28, 32, 41

Ferdinand, Grand-duke of Tuscany, second son of the Emperor Leopold, 317, 328, 353, 370

Ferdinando IV., King of Naples and Sicily: betrothed to Archduchess Johanna, 29; to Archduchess Josepha, 41; to Archduchess Maria Carolina, 57–60; marriage, 71, 72; early life and habits, 73, 75; the *lazzaroni*, 76; love for the Queen, 77; reply to the Grand-duke of Tuscany, 80; love for his children, 87; popularity, 88; *liaisons*, 90; story of an old peasant woman, 91; intrigues and love-affairs of Ferdinando, 95, 96; his eldest daughter, 99; jealousy of Acton, 104; splendour of court, 106–107; goes to Vienna for marriages of his children and coronation of Emperor Leopold, 121, 124, 127; Rome, 127; Lady Hamilton, 153; death of Louis XVI., 160; refuses to receive French Ambassador, 161; French Admiral threatens Naples, 165; Ferdinando and Charles I. of England, 167; neglect of business, 173; the King and his children, 198; his love for the Princess Amélie, 199; acknowledges Louis XVIII., 227; strange diversions of Ferdinando, 230, 231; domestic affection, 233; delight at the Battle of the Nile, 245; enters Rome, 247; defeated, 248; escapes to Sicily, 257; estrangement from the Queen, 267, 268; gives his father's sword to Nelson and makes him Duke of Bronte, 275; contented life at Palermo, 287; re-enters Naples, 292; Order of S. Ferdinando, 295; cruel severity, 301–307; return to Palermo, 308; Naples, 313; autograph letter, 313; takes leave of the Queen and his children on board ship, 314; anxiety for their safety, 322; renewed confidence in the Queen, 319; receives the Queen at Naples, 356; marriage of Princess Antoinette to the Prince of Asturias, 338; the new Princess Royal, 341; country life, 349, 350; letter to Nelson, 363; society at court, 364, at Portici during the earthquake, 368, alarming prospects, 371, council of war, 372, Ferdinando escapes to Sicily, 373, unfortunate position, 381, lives happily in the country in Sicily, 393, Ferdinando and Maria Carolina, 400, marriage of Princess Amelie, 405-406, interference of England, 414, Ferdinando resolves not to quarrel with England, 415, resigns government to Prince Royal, 417-418, influenced by Queen suddenly resumes power, 419, resigns again 419, refuses and at last consents to the Queen's departure, 420, 421 victories of, dies, 425, Ferdinando again supreme in Sicily, 427, orders a warship to bring back the Queen and Prince Leopold, 427, death of the Queen, 427, Ferdinando marries Lucia Mighaccio 428

Fra Diavolo, 270, 388

Francesco, Prince Royal of Naples, afterwards Francesco I, 98, 112, 114, 124, 127, 238, 337, 338, 340, 341, 355, 366, 371, 372, 375, 379, 392, 412, 417

François, Duke of Lorraine Grand duke of Tuscany Emperor of Germany, Franz I, betrothed to Maria Theresa,
2, 4, marriage, 5, elected Emperor 9, adventure in vineyard 13, splendour of court at Vienna, 14, engagements of the Emperor and pursuits of the Empress 15, their favourite son and daughter, 19, difficult position of the Emperor, 22-25, liaisons of the Emperor 25, 26, Princess von Auersperg, 26, death of Prince Carl 31, death of the Emperor François de Lorraine, 38

Franz II, Emperor of Germany, afterwards of Austria, 121-124, 324, 327, 397, 427

Frederick the Great, King of Prussia 5, 8

HAMILTON, Sir William, 147, marries Emma Hart, 151, 155, 194, 203, 244, 256, 257, 259, refuses to acknowledge treaty of surrender, 288-291, 293, 309, receives portrait of King, 310, recalled, 312, leaves Palermo 314, leaves Vienna, 324, his death, 341

Hamilton Lady Emma Hart was Amy Lyon, arrives at Naples, 153, proceedings there, 154, 155, mistress of Sir William Hamilton—left Naples and returned with him as his wife, 156, friendship with the Queen, 194, 196, 203, 205, 209, 219, 233, the ships of Nelson, 242, 243,

INDEX

alarms, 251; voyage to Sicily, 256, 293–294; helps to save prisoners, 298, 305, 309; receives magnificent presents from the Queen, 310; *liaison* with Nelson, 314; returns to England, 325; extravagance and rapacity of Lady Hamilton, 359–360; her ingratitude to the Queen, 361

ISABEL of Spain, wife of Francesco, Prince Royal of Naples, 337, 340, 341, 356–357, 375, 377, 392

Isabella of Parma, betrothed to the Crown Prince of Austria, 29; their marriage, 32; strange history of Isabella, 33–36; her death, 37

JOHANNA, Archduchess of Austria, daughter of Emperor and Empress François de Lorraine and Maria Theresia, 10; betrothed to King of Naples, 29; her death, 36

Joseph II., Emperor of Germany, King of Hungary, Bohemia, &c., 10, 18, 19, 23, 24; betrothal to Isabella of Parma, 29; his love for her, 30; marriage, 32; devotion to Isabella, 33–36; despair at her death, 37; marries Josepha of Bavaria against his wishes, 37–38; succeeds his father as Emperor, 39; love for his sister Josepha, 41; grief at her death, 48; despair at the death of his daughter Theresia, 49, 50; visits his sisters at Naples and Parma, 78, 79; second visit to Naples, 111; his death, 119

Josepha, Archduchess of Austria, daughter of François de Lorraine and Maria Theresia, 10; favourite sister of Emperor Joseph, 41; betrothed to King of Naples, 41, 42; preparations for wedding, 46; dies of small-pox, 48

Josepha of Bavaria, second wife of Emperor Joseph II.: unhappy married life, 37, 38; dies of small-pox, 45

KAUNITZ, Wenceslaus Anton, Prinz von, Prime Minister of Maria Theresia, 16, 17, 58, 60

LE BRUN, Mme. Vigée, 118, 145, 148

Leopold, Prince of Salerno, son of Ferdinando IV., King of Naples and Sicily, 113, 275, 314, 331, 336, 375, 392, 393, 396, 404; takes part with his parents against the Sicilians and English, 419; accompanies his mother to Austria, 420; lives with her at Hetzenberg, 424

Leopold II., Emperor of Germany, King of Hungary and

Bohemia, Grand-duke of Tuscany, &c., 10, 18, 19, 30; Grand-duke of Tuscany, 32; marries Ludovica of Spain, 38; accompanies Maria Carolina to Naples, 67; his affection for her, 67-71; leaves Naples, 78, 80, 85, 101, 113, 114; succeeds to the throne, 119; weddings and coronation, 122, 123; popularity of Leopold, 124; projects of Leopold and Carolina to rescue Marie Antoinette, 125; the Grand-duchy of Tuscany, 138-140; death of Leopold, 158

Louis XVI., King of France, 118, 128-131, Varennes 135, 136, 144, 161, 167

Louis XVII, King of France, 115, 133, 217, 218, 225, 227

Louis XVIII., King of France, 129, 130, 137, 220-229

Louis Philippe, King of France, Duc d'Orléans 405-407, 410, 412

Ludovica, Princess of Naples, Grand-duchess of Tuscany, daughter of Ferdinando IV., King of Naples and Sicily 120, 122, 313, 326, 336

MARIA CAROLINA CHARLOTTE Archduchess of Austria, Queen of Naples and Sicily, birth 2, 10-28, letters of the Empress to her, 54; betrothed to King of Naples, 53-65; her marriage 66, journey to Naples, 66, 71; letters to her governess 72, 73; becomes reconciled to her life, 73; influence over Ferdinando 77; rules the kingdom, 80-82; affection of Carolina for her mother, 87; birth of her daughters, 87, of the heir to the throne, 87; disputes between King and Queen, 98; birth of Francesco, 98; death of Carlo, Prince Royal, 99; government of the Queen, 100; the fleet, 101, 102. Acton, 101-103; gossip at court, 103; jealousy of Ferdinando, 104; society at Naples, 105, 106; Neapolitan convents, 107-109; a voyage of pleasure, 111; death of two sons of Carolina 112, 113; projects of marriage for her children, 114, 115; interference of Carlos III. 117, 118; journey to Vienna, 120; return to Vienna 121 marriage of the eldest daughter with Crown Prince of Germany and Grand-duke of Tuscany, and betrothal of Prince Royal to Archduchess Clementine, 122-124; visit to Rome, 127, 128; eve of the French Revolution, 129; terrors and anxiety, 130, 131; return to Naples, 138; awakening 139, 142, change of system, 142, 145; first sees Lady Hamilton, 153; splendour of the career of Queen Maria Carolina, 156, 157; success of allied troops, 162; their defeat, 162; approaching dangers, 162; Ambassadors of France, 162, 163; threatened bombardment of Naples, 164, 165; outrageous conduct of French Ambassador, 168; declining popularity of the Queen, 173; her reforms and good government, 174-178; slanders circulated by her enemies, 179-183; her secret police, 186; the plots of the Jacobins, 187-189; her friendship with Lady Hamilton, 195, 196; the Queen and her children, 197-199; murder of Marie Antoinette, 200; solemn requiem, 200; vows of vengeance, 201, 204; courage and energy of Maria Carolina, 206; her warlike preparations, 207, 208; court and society, 210; eruption of Vesuvius, 211; plots and spies, 215, 221; Jacobin conspirators and secret arrests, 222, 223; Prince Caramanico, 224, 225; the Queen shares the amusements of the King, 229-231; nurses him in illness, 233; arrests and trials, 234-236; alarm at approach of French t, 239; rejoicing at victory of Nile, 247; disturbances at Naples and flight to Sicily, 251-265; the court at Palermo, 265-266; estrangement of the King and Queen, 266; letter to the Empress of Germany, 286; to Lady Hamilton, 297; remains at Palermo, 301; charity and generosity of Maria Carolina, 309-311; she becomes ill and depressed, 311, 312; resolves to go to Austria, 314; sails from Palermo, 315; Marengo, 316; journey to Vienna, 317-322; life at Vienna, 322-336; return to Naples, 337; grief at the death of Clementine, Princess Royal, 335; dislike to Isabel of Spain, second wife of Prince Royal, 341; gratitude to Nelson and England, 342; her renewed influence over the King, 344; correspondence with Napoleon, 345, 346; anxiety for the Princess of the Asturias, 346-348; domestic life of the Queen and her children, 354-358; threatening letter from Napoleon, 365; fearful earthquake, 366-368; landing of allied troops, 373; Austerlitz, 372; second flight of Queen and royal family to Palermo, 374-377; hardships of their arrival, 377-381; English allies, 384; news of the death of the Princess of the Asturias, 383–385; war in Calabria, 385–388; Fra Diavolo, 388; attempts to reconquer Naples, 389; rashness and obstinacy of the Queen, 391; extravagance and mismanagement, 391; country life of the royal family in Sicily, 392–394; marriage of Christine to the Duke of Genoa, 396; death of the Empress of Germany, 397; threatened attack upon Sicily, 398; more slanders against the Queen, 399, 402; marriage of Amélie to the Duc d'Orléans, 406; disputes with Sicilian Parliament, 410; the Queen struck with apoplexy, 411; resumes her political affairs, 411–413; Lord William Bentinck, 416, continued strife, 417, 420; the Queen leaves Palermo with Prince Leopold, 421; retires to Austria, 424; the castle of Hetzenberg, 424; Marie Louise, 426, death of Maria Carolina, 427, 428

Maria Theresia, Empress of Germany, Queen of Hungary and Bohemia, Archduchess of Austria, &c., wife of François de Lorraine: her vast inheritance, 4; her marriage to François de Lorraine, 5; succeeds her father, 8; Empress, 9; her court, government, and family, 10–16; her Prime Minister, 17; her children, 18–23; the Emperor, 24–26; projects for her children's marriages, 29, 30; death of her favourite son, 31; her first daughter-in-law, 32–37; her second daughter-in-law, 38; death of the Emperor François, 38; despair of the Empress, 39; resumes the government, 39; marriages of her daughters, 40–65, 85; her death, 101

Marianne, Archduchess of Austria, Abbess of Prague, eldest daughter of François de Lorraine and Maria Theresia, 10, 18, 20, 122

Marie Louise, Archduchess of Austria, wife of Napoleon, Empress of France, marries Napoleon, 408–409; retires to Vienna, 425; her affection for her grandmother, the Queen of Naples, 426, 427

Marie Thérèse de France, daughter of Louis XVI. (Madame Royale), 225–229

Maximilien, Archduke of Austria, Elector of Cologne, 10, 28, 137, 228

Metternich, Prince, 95

NAPOLEON I., Buonaparte, Emperor of France, 207, 239, 315, 317, 327–329, 337, 345, 365, 369, 374, 404

Nelson, Horatio, Admiral of the English Fleet, 192–193, 196, 197; Battle of the Nile, 241–247, 253–261, 275, 289–296, 300, 310, 317, 322, 324, 341, 342, 359, 362; Trafalgar, 370

SCHÖNBRUNN, 11, 12, 18, 19, 20, 326

TERESA, Princess of Naples, Empress of Germany, eldest daughter of Ferdinando IV., wife of Franz II., 87, 99, 114–116, 120; marries the Crown Prince of Germany, 121–124, 125, 168, 197, 198, 224, 323, 324, 344, 354, 355, 356, 357, 358, 364, 372, 375, 377, 380, 392; her death, 396

THE STORY OF THE NATIONS
A SERIES OF POPULAR HISTORIES.

Each Volume is furnished with Maps, Illustrations, and Index. Large Crown 8vo, fancy cloth, gold lettered, or Library Edition, dark cloth, burnished red top, 5s. each.—Or may be had in half Persian, cloth sides, gilt tops; Price on application.

1. Rome. By ARTHUR GILMAN, M.A.
2. The Jews. By Prof. J. K. HOSMER.
3. Germany. By Rev. S. BARING-GOULD, M.A.
4. Carthage. By Prof. ALFRED J. CHURCH.
5. Alexander's Empire. By Prof. J. P. MAHAFFY.
6. The Moors in Spain. By STANLEY LANE-POOLE.
7. Ancient Egypt. By Prof. GEORGE RAWLINSON.
8. Hungary. By Prof. ARMINIUS VAMBÉRY.
9. The Saracens. By ARTHUR GILMAN, M.A.
10. Ireland. By the Hon. EMILY LAWLESS.
11. Chaldea. By ZÉNAÏDE A. RAGOZIN.
12. The Goths. By HENRY BRADLEY.
13. Assyria. By ZÉNAÏDE A. RAGOZIN.
14. Turkey. By STANLEY LANE-POOLE.
15. Holland. By Prof. J. E. THOROLD ROGERS.
16. Mediæval France. By GUSTAVE MASSON.
17. Persia. By S. G. W. BENJAMIN.
18. Phœnicia. By Prof. G. RAWLINSON.
19. Media. By ZÉNAÏDE A. RAGOZIN.
20. The Hansa Towns. By HELEN ZIMMERN.
21. Early Britain. By Prof. ALFRED J. CHURCH.
22. The Barbary Corsairs. By STANLEY LANE-POOLE.
23. Russia. By W. R. MORFILL, M.A.
24. The Jews under the Romans. By W. D. MORRISON.
25. Scotland. By JOHN MACKINTOSH, LL.D.
26. Switzerland. By Mrs LINA HUG and R. STEAD.
27. Mexico. By SUSAN HALE.
28. Portugal. By H. MORSE STEPHENS.
29. The Normans. By SARAH ORNE JEWETT.
30. The Byzantine Empire. By C. W. C. OMAN.
31. Sicily: Phœnician, Greek and Roman. By the late Prof. E. A. FREEMAN.
32. The Tuscan Republics. By BELLA DUFFY.
33. Poland. By W. R. MORFILL, M.A.
34. Parthia. By Prof. GEORGE RAWLINSON.
35. The Australian Commonwealth. By GREVILLE TREGARTHEN.
36. Spain. By H. E. WATTS.
37. Japan. By DAVID MURRAY, Ph.D.
38. South Africa. By GEORGE M. THEAL.
39. Venice. By ALETHEA WIEL.
40. The Crusades. By T. A. ARCHER and C. L. KINGSFORD.
41. Vedic India. By Z. A. RAGOZIN.
42. The West Indies and the Spanish Main. By JAMES RODWAY.
43. Bohemia. By C. EDMUND MAURICE.
44. The Balkans. By W. MILLER, M.A.
45. Canada. By Sir J. G. BOURINOT, LL.D.
46. British India. By R. W. FRAZER, LL.B.
47. Modern France. By ANDRÉ LE BON.
48. The Franks. By LEWIS SERGEANT.
49. Austria. By SIDNEY WHITMAN.
50. Modern England. Before the Reform Bill. By JUSTIN MCCARTHY.
51. China. By Prof. R. K. DOUGLAS.
52. Modern England. From the Reform Bill to the Present Time. By JUSTIN MCCARTHY.
53. Modern Spain. By MARTIN A. S. HUME.
54. Modern Italy. By PIETRO ORSI.
55. Norway. By H. H. BOYESEN.
56. Wales. By O. M. EDWARDS.
57. Mediæval Rome. By W. MILLER, M.A.
58. The Papal Monarchy. By WILLIAM BARRY, D.D.
59. Mediæval India under Mohammedan Rule. By STANLEY LANE-POOLE.
60. Buddhist India. By Prof. T. W. RHYS-DAVIDS.
61. Parliamentary England. By EDWARD JENKS, M.A.
62. Mediæval England. By MARY BATESON.
63. The Coming of Parliament. By L. CECIL JANE.
64. The Story of Greece. From the Earliest Times to A.D. 14. By E. S. SHUCKBURGH.

In Preparation.
The Story of Greece. From the Roman Occupation to A.D. 1453. By E. S. SHUCKBURGH.
The Story of the Roman Empire (B.C. 29 to A.D. 476). By H. STUART JONES.

T. FISHER UNWIN, Publisher, 1, Adelphi Terrace, London, W.C.

The First Novel Library.

A series devoted to the first novels of such new authors as show exceptional talent.

"It has given us ten stories which have all been distinguished by something fresh and uncommon."—*Times*, 5th May 1905.

Each Volume Crown 8vo, Cloth, 6s.

Vol. I.—Wistons A Story in Three Parts. By MILES AMBER.
"A piece of very fine workmanship."—*Speaker*.

Vol. II —The Searchers. A Story in Four Books. By MARGARETTA BYRDE
"A novel that deserves, and will command attention."—*Pilot*.

Vol. III.—From behind the Arras. By MRS PHILIP CHAMPION DE CRESPIGNY.
"Mrs de Crespigny's first novel is in no way inferior even to the best work of Mr Stanley Weyman "—*St James's Gazette*

Vol. IV —A Lady's Honour A Chronicle of Events in the time of Marlborough. By BASS BLAKE.
"Decidedly a success "—*Spectator*

Vol. V.—The Flame and the Flood. By ROSAMOND LANGBRIDGE.
"We wholeheartedly like this first effort, and shall look eagerly for a second."—*Manchester Guardian*

Vol VI.—A Drama of Sunshine played in Homburg. By Mrs AUBREY RICHARDSON.
"The novel has the unusual merit for a 'first' of giving the whole strength and point of a situation without a needless word."—*Graphic*

Vol VII.—Rosemonde. By BEATRICE STOTT.
"There is exceptional talent in the picture of the insanely jealous Stafford "—*Pilot*

Vol. VIII.—The Cardinal's Pawn. By K. L. MONTGOMERY.
"A volume, the wealth of which is almost confusing in its lavish abundance, in its poetry and suggestion."—*Times*.

Vol. IX.—Tussock Land —By ARTHUR H. ADAMS.
"One of the most promising that the 'First Novel Library' series has included '—*Bookman*

Vol. X —The Kingdom of Twilight. By FORREST REID.
"It will strongly interest thoughtful readers."—*Manchester Guardian*.

Vol. XI.—A Pagan's Love. By CONSTANCE CLYDE.

Vol. XII.—Saints in Society. By MARGARET BAILLIE-SAUNDERS.

T. FISHER UNWIN, PUBLISHER,
1, ADELPHI TERRACE, LONDON, W.C.

A SELECTION FROM THE

GREEN CLOTH LIBRARY.

In uniform Green Cloth. Large Crown 8vo. 6s. each.

By Beach and Bogland.
By JANE BARLOW, Author of "Irish Idylls," etc.

Through Sorrow's Gates: A Tale of the Wintry Heath.
By HALLIWELL SUTCLIFFE.

"A study full of power and originality."—*Westminster Gazette.*
"As an example of a well-knit story, utterly free from loose ends, it would be difficult to mention anything in recent fiction to rival this splendidly masculine work of a writer who is comparable with even Mr Thomas Hardy in his deep knowledge of, and true sympathy with, the people of the soil."—*Daily Mail.*

Mistress Barbara Cunliffe.
By HALLIWELL SUTCLIFFE.

"The novel is indeed a fine one, with characters whom it is good to know, and situations well developed "—*Spectator.*

Ricroft of Withens.
By HALLIWELL SUTCLIFFE.

"It is impossible to speak except in terms of unqualified eulogy of this remarkable novel, a novel that will assuredly give its author a place in the front rank of romancists. —*Aberdeen Free Press.*

A Bachelor in Arcady.
By HALLIWELL SUTCLIFFE.

"To our mind Mr Halliwell Sutcliffe has previously done nothing so good as his latest 'rough notes,' as he modestly calls them, of that West Riding he knows and loves."
—*Pall Mall Gazette.*

Evelyn Innes.
By GEORGE MOORE.

"A great achievement "—*Athenæum.*
"The sanest, most solid, and most accomplished book that Mr Moore has written. . . . Mr George Moore has written nothing hitherto that was so masterly."—*Saturday Review*

Sister Teresa.
A Sequel to "Evelyn Innes."
By GEORGE MOORE.

"Like 'Esther Waters,' Mr Moore's later study in feminism has a stimulating effect. It helps us to see more and to understand better. Prophecy is a thankless task, but we should not be surprised at any one's prophesying that these books will live; they certainly stand far above the fiction of the day in sincerity and power."—*Times.*

T. FISHER UNWIN, PUBLISHER,
1, ADELPHI TERRACE, LONDON, W.C.

Six Standard Works.

COMPLETE POPULAR EDITIONS. ILLUSTRATED.
Large Crown 8vo, Cloth.   Price **2/6** net.

The Life of Richard Cobden.
By John Morley.

"One of the most important and interesting works of its class in the English language."—*Daily Chronicle.*

The Life and Times of Savonarola.
By Professor Pasquale Villari.

"The most interesting religious biography that we know of in modern times. It is difficult to speak of its merits without seeming exaggeration."—*Spectator.*

The Life and Times of Machiavelli.
By Professor Pasquale Villari.

"Machiavelli is represented for all time in the pages of Villari."—*Guardian.*

The Lives of Robert and Mary Moffat.
By John Smith Moffat.

"A loving record of a noble life, which has left the world a lesson for all time of the power of earnest labour and simple faith."—*Daily Chronicle.*

The History of Florence.
By Professor Pasquale Villari.

"This volume is indeed worthy of the reputation of its author. . . . We feel very grateful to him for having given us the most concise, and at the same time perhaps the most complete constitutional history that has yet appeared of the first two centuries of the Florentine Republic."—*Speaker.*

English Wayfaring Life in the Middle Ages (XIVth Century).
By J. J. Jusserand, French Ambassador at Washington

"One of those enchanting volumes which only Frenchmen have the gift of writing. Buy it if you are wise, and keep it as a joy for ever."—Dr Augustus Jessopp in the *Nineteenth Century.*

T. FISHER UNWIN, Publisher,
1, Adelphi Terrace, London, W.C.

Standard Works.

COMPLETE POPULAR EDITIONS. ILLUSTRATED.
Large Crown 8vo, Cloth. Price 2/6 net.

Lord Beaconsfield: A Biography.
By T. P. O'Connor.

"Clever and brilliant. . . . Worth reading by everybody who either admires or hates his subject."—*Guardian*

"A slashing and vastly interesting book."—*Pall Mall Gazette.*

Rome and Pompeii. Archæological Rambles.
By Gaston Boissier.

"M. Gaston Boissier is one of the few living archæologists who can make the dead bones of the past live again. While his researches show the accuracy and thoroughness which we associate with German scholarship, he has a gift of exposition which is wholly French. We can imagine therefore, no better handbook for traveller or archæologist than this one. —*Daily Mail.*

Holyoake: Sixty Years of an Agitator's Life.
By George Jacob Holyoake.

"A valuable contribution to the political, social, intellectual, and even revolutionary history of our time."—*Times.*

"The book is full of interest; it produces a vivid, personal impression, it contains contemporary notes on men and women of the century, it has shrewd and vigorous sentences, and illustrates our own progress in civilising thought."—*Spectator.*

Sir Walter Raleigh.
By Major Martin A. S. Hume.

"An admirable book which ought to be read by every one who takes any interest in things that ought to interest all—the building of the Empire and the men who built it. There is not a dull page in it, and with his skilful telling of it, the story of Raleigh's life and of his times reads like a romance."—*Pall Mall Gazette.*

T. FISHER UNWIN, Publisher,
1 Adelphi Terrace, London, W.C.

By W. Jenkyn Thomas

THE WELSH FAIRY BOOK

Few countries have so rich and so exquisite a treasure of fairy-lore as Wales, yet though this may be found embedded in the transactions of folklore societies, there is no collection suitable for boys and girls and the general reader. It is hoped that this book will remedy the deficiency.

Illustrated by WILLY POGANY.
Cloth,
6s.

T. Fisher Unwin

Lightning Source UK Ltd.
Milton Keynes UK
UKHW020626260519
343334UK00004B/17/P